JAMES
CLAVELL

JAMES CLAVELL

A Critical Companion

Gina Macdonald

CRITICAL COMPANIONS TO POPULAR CONTEMPORARY WRITERS
Kathleen Gregory Klein, Series Editor

Greenwood Press
Westport, Connecticut • London

Library of Congress Cataloging-in-Publication Data

Macdonald, Gina.
 James Clavell : a critical companion / Gina Macdonald.
  p. cm.—(Critical companions to popular contemporary
writers, ISSN 1082–4979)
 Includes bibliographical references and index.
 ISBN 0–313–29494–1 (alk. paper)
 1. Clavell, James—Criticism and interpretation. I. Title.
 II. Series.
 PS3553.L365Z75 1996
 813'.54—dc20   95–43265

British Library Cataloguing in Publication Data is available.

Library of Congress Catalog Card Number: 95–43265
ISBN: 0–313–29494–1
ISSN: 1082–4979

First published in 1996

Greenwood Press, 88 Post Road West, Westport, CT 06881
An imprint of Greenwood Publishing Group, Inc.

Printed in the United States of America

The paper used in this book complies with the
Permanent Paper Standard issued by the National
Information Standards Organization (Z39.48–1984)

10 9 8 7 6 5 4 3 2 1

To the survivors of the
Changi prison camp

Contents

Series Foreword

The authors who appear in the series Critical Companions to Popular Contemporary Writers are all best-selling writers. They do not have only one successful novel, but a string of them. Fans, critics, and specialist readers eagerly anticipate their next book. For some, high cash advances and breakthrough sales figures are automatic; movie deals often follow. Some writers become household names, recognized by almost everyone.

But novels are read one by one. Each reader chooses to start and, more importantly, to finish a book because of what she or he finds there. The real test of a novel is in the satisfaction its readers experience. This series acknowledges the extraordinary involvement of readers and writers in creating a best-seller.

The authors included in this series were chosen by an Advisory Board composed of high school English teachers and high school and public librarians. They ranked a list of best-selling writers according to their popularity among different groups of readers. Writers in the top-ranked group who had not received book-length, academic literary analysis (or none in at least the past ten years) were chosen for the series. Because of this selection method, Critical Companions to Popular Contemporary Writers meets a need that is not addressed elsewhere.

The volumes in the series are written by scholars with particular expertise in analyzing popular fiction. These specialists add an academic focus to the popular success that the best-selling writers already enjoy.

The series is designed to appeal to a wide range of readers. The general reading public will find explanations for the appeal of these well-known writers. Fans will find biographical and fictional questions answered. Students will find literary analysis, discussions of fictional genres, carefully organized introductions to new ways of reading the novels, and bibliographies for additional research. Students will also be able to apply what they have learned from this book to their readings of future novels by these best-selling writers.

Each volume begins with a biographical chapter drawing on published information, autobiographies or memoirs, prior interviews, and, in some cases, interviews given especially for this series. A chapter on literary history and genres describes how the author's work fits into the larger literary context. The following chapters analyze the writer's most important, most popular, and most recent novels in detail. Each chapter focuses on a single novel. This approach, suggested by the Advisory Board as the most useful to student research, allows for an in-depth analysis of the writer's fiction. Close and careful readings with numerous examples show readers exactly how the novels work. These chapters are organized around three central elements: plot development (how the story line moves forward), character development (what the reader knows about the important figures), and theme (the significant ideas of the novel). Chapters may also include sections on generic conventions (how the novel is similar to or different from others in its same category of science fiction, fantasy, thriller, etc.), narrative point of view (who tells the story and how), symbols and literary language, and historical or social context. Each chapter ends with an "alternative reading" of the novel. The volume concludes with a primary and secondary bibliography, including reviews.

The Alternative Readings are a unique feature of this series. By demonstrating a particular way of reading each novel, they provide a clear example of how a specific perspective can reveal important aspects of the book. In each alternative reading section, one contemporary literary theory—such as feminist criticism, Marxism, new historicism, deconstruction, or Jungian psychological critique—is defined in brief, easily comprehensible language. That definition is then applied to the novel to highlight specific features that might go unnoticed or be understood differently in a more general reading of the novel. Each volume defines two or three specific theories, making them part of the reader's understanding of how diverse meanings may be constructed from a single novel.

Taken collectively, the volumes in the Critical Companions to Popular Contemporary Writers series provide a wide-ranging investigation of the complexities of current best-selling fiction. By treating these novels seriously as both literary works and publishing successes, the series demonstrates the potential of popular literature in contemporary culture.

Kathleen Gregory Klein
Southern Connecticut State University

Acknowledgments

I owe a debt of gratitude to a number of people who made this book possible. Andrew Macdonald's careful reading of the text in progress, his positive assurances, loving support, and sound advice have made this book far better than it would have been otherwise. So, too, have the invaluable editorial advice and corrections of my Loyola colleague Raymond McGowan, who assisted with the final version. My thanks also go to series editor Kathleen Gregory Klein for advice about cutting and focus. Yasuko Honda clarified Mr. Clavell's use of Japanese. Yuko Kishida and Ting-Chen Yang also assisted with the vocabulary section, as did my Loyola colleagues Paulina Bazin and Ellen Plaisance. Jeanie Duvall contributed computer expertise and artistic skill to refine and clarify the map and genealogy. I appreciate the insights of Deborah Rosen and of Burt Kwouk, both of whom worked with Clavell and shared with me their perceptions of him.

1

The Life of James Clavell

"The child is father to the man."

William Wordsworth

CHILDHOOD

James du Maresq Clavell, self-described as a "half-Irish Englishman with Scots overtones," was born in Sidney, Australia on October 10, 1924, the son of Richard Charles and Eileen (Collis) Clavell. He attended Portsmouth Grammar School, but after that, his education varied as his family followed his father's military duty stations. Both his father and grandfather were British Royal Navy careerists who regaled young James with stories of the sea and of exotic ports worldwide. Clavell's father, reputedly a descendant of Norman conqueror Walterus de Claville, instilled in him a strong sense of obligation and responsibility to this heritage, reminding him, "Remember, you are blessed by being British" (*Current Biography* 1981: 83). Clavell recounted this sense of heritage and duty in *King Rat*, in Peter Marlowe's descriptions of his family military tradition and his training in proprieties. Often, British colonial settlers—Britishers who settled permanently in English colonial enclaves far from England— were reportedly more English than the English, and this was the case with the Clavells. Naval duties meant that the Clavells were stationed in a number of Commonwealth port cities, including Hong Kong, so young James at an early age experienced firsthand the differences between Chinese and British world views that drive *Tai-Pan*, *Noble House*, and *Gai-Jin*. His linguistic aptitude led him to pick up the foreign words and phrases that later became a natural part of his literary vocabulary, so that, for example, the reader of *Shogun* learns many unforgettable phrases, whose repetition throughout the book and whose meaning acquired through context imitates the natural way in which the young James must have absorbed a smattering of different languages, including Cantonese, Mandarin, Malay, and Japanese. [A glossary of foreign words and phrases Clavell uses throughout his canon appears after chapter 8.]

MILITARY CAREER

Clavell, following family tradition, chose a military career; however, his duty was on land, not sea. After finishing high school in England at age sixteen, Clavell joined the British Royal Artillery. He served from 1940 to 1946 and earned the rank of captain.

After military training, the seventeen-year-old Clavell was sent to the jungles of Malaysia, where he was wounded by machine-gun fire in 1941 and spent several months hiding in a Malay village. The similar experience of Peter Marlowe, the main character in *King Rat*, suggests personal parallels: an affection and respect for the villagers who hid him, an understanding of the danger he was to them, and perhaps even a love affair with a village girl. When Japanese soldiers captured Clavell, he spent the rest of the war in two Japanese prisoner-of-war camps: one was located in Java, and the other was the notoriously barbaric Changi prison near Singapore, where 140,000 out of 150,000 inmates died—that is, only 10,000, or one in every fifteen, survived. Military accounts of Changi emphasize the total absence of any animal or large insect life in the area—there were no birds, no grasshoppers—because all had been consumed by starving men. No birds sang at Changi. Somehow Clavell endured a nightmarish three and a half years of internment. In an interview with Bart Mills for the *Manchester Guardian* (October 4, 1975), Clavell called Changi his "university," "a school for survivors," one that gave him "a strength most people don't have," "an awareness of life others lack." He was puzzled that "those who were supposed to survive didn't" and wondered what made the difference between living and dying. He said that Changi was "the rock" or foundation of his life because as long as he could remember his experiences there, he would know he was "living forty borrowed lifetimes." Having endured to the limit, Clavell asked, "What else can they do to me?" and concluded, "I feel very fortunate to be alive."

Clavell's horrifying Changi experience infuses his first novel, *King Rat*, with chilling power, an unnerving force based on convincing detail and the matter-of-fact recitation of appalling but everyday conditions. Clavell claims to have fictionalized the exploits of a U.S. Army corporal he knew at Changi, but *King Rat* is also very firmly based on the teenage Clavell's personal experience. The eighteen-year-old Peter Marlowe, resilient, adaptable, schooled in British military values, but forced to question those values in the brutal conditions of Changi, is a literary self-portrait. Criticism that Clavell turned human tragedy into a best-seller ignores the biographical nature of Clavell's work and the function of fiction to distance deeply felt emotions. Projecting himself into a fictive Peter Marlowe helped Clavell confront his own guilt and elation at having survived while others did not. At Changi, he tested his father's idealistic code against the unholy realities of a Japanese prison camp and developed a counterconception born of his own terrible wartime experiences. He defended these newly acquired values throughout his life: the value of the individual; loyalty to a small, interdependent group; and the importance of free enterprise and capitalist venture.

SEARCH FOR A CAREER

After the war, a motorcycle accident in England left Clavell lame in one leg and ended his military career. Given a disability discharge in 1946, he entered the University of Birmingham, where he wavered between engineering and law. When he met an aspiring ballerina and actress, April Stride, he fell in love for a lifetime; they married on February 20, 1951. They had two daughters, Michaela and Holly. At one point, because of his wife's profession, and at her urging, they visited a movie set, where Clavell saw his first director and suddenly found a new direction for his life. In an interview with Edwin McDowell (*New York Times Book Review*, May 17, 1981), Clavell facetiously reported asking his wife about "a nasty little man in a chair" who had such great power that "whenever he spoke or got up a hush fell over the set and people rushed to do his bidding." He claims he resolved then and there to become a director, and dedicated his life to that goal. He worked for several years in film distribution and in 1953 immigrated to the United States, where he worked for a short time in television production in New York. He had developed a fondness for Americans at Changi and a distaste for the behavior of many fellow British, so America was a natural choice. Besides, there were greater opportunities in the United States than in Britain for becoming a director.

Still in pursuit of his dream, he next moved his family to Hollywood, California, in search of a screenwriting position. To keep his family fed and sheltered, he worked as a carpenter. He claims his British accent and his cheeky assertion of his own brilliance landed him his first Hollywood job, a collaborative screenwriting of *Far Alert*, which, though never produced, nonetheless began his successful career in the movie industry.

SCREENWRITER

The abortive *Far Alert* also began Clavell's writing career, first as screenwriter and later as novelist. His first screenplay to be produced was the classic science fiction thriller *The Fly* (1958), in which a scientist builds a machine that breaks down human cells for quick travel, and then recombines them on arrival. However, a tiny horsefly in the system leads to bizarre results—a man with the head of a fly, and a fly with the head of a man. Pleading for help, the transformed scientist can only emit a fly-like buzz. Starring Vincent Price and Herbert Marshall, this highly praised, imaginative movie grossed $4 million and spawned two sequels and a 1980s remake starring Jeff Goldblum as the transmutated scientist.

Two memorable films followed, *Watusi* in 1958 and *The Great Escape* in 1960. *Watusi*, starring Michael Caine, stirringly depicted an African uprising against British colonialists, and paid evenhanded tribute to the fearlessness of the Watusi warriors and the bravery of their British opponents, but received limited critical notice. *The Great Escape*, in contrast, with its stellar cast (which included Steve McQueen, James Garner, Richard Attenborough, Charles Bronson, James Coburn, and David McCallum), was a major success. Clavell based his script on a true story, an account by Paul Brickhill of a mass escape from a German POW camp accomplished by digging three underground tunnels. Because of his own experience at Changi, Clavell was able to capture the spirit of endurance and of defiance against impossible odds that enabled the main character, the "Cooler King" (played by McQueen), to endure extended solitary confinement as punishment for daring escape attempts. Changi prisoners developed intricate mental games to help them endure weeks of confinement in dark, dirty pits. To keep his sanity, one prisoner imagined the architectural plans of his dream house, deciding on materials, building the structure, decorating and furnishing its interior, and then imagining eating breakfast in its sunny, spacious dining area and enjoying the running water in its bathroom (Daws 1994: 127). Clavell drew on his personal knowledge of men under such conditions to strengthen his writing, but tempered it with the fantasy Hollywood demanded. *The Great Escape* has thus become a classic, its witty bravado and its jaunty prison humor defining the escape genre. Clavell received a Screen Writers Award for his screenplay.

In 1963, Clavell became an American citizen. The screenplays for *633 Squadron*, a World War II thriller, and *The Satan Bug*, a science-fiction thriller about a deadly virus developed by the military, followed in 1964 and 1965 respectively.

A TRIPLE ROLE: WRITER, PRODUCER, DIRECTOR

Writing screenplays provided Clavell with an opportunity to move toward a new goal: to totally control his story by not only writing but also producing and directing a film. His first try at this three-hatted role was a low-budget, Twentieth Century-Fox production, *Five Gates to Hell* (1959), a film about French medics in Indochina. Although not highly successful, it moved *New York Times* critic Howard Thompson to call Clavell "a man to watch." It also marked the beginning of Clavell's interest in Vietnam.

In 1960, Clavell wrote, produced, and directed *Walk Like a Dragon*, the story of the rivalry between a white gunman and a Chinese immigrant, set in the 1870s. Another movie Clavell wrote, produced, and directed was *To Sir with Love* (1967), an acclaimed classic starring Sidney Poitier and Judy Geeson. According to *Current Biography* (1981: 84), Poitier and Clavell contracted for percentages of the profits instead of salaries. The London-based film cost $625,000 to make, but returned $15 million gross—a huge profit for what Clavell called "a positive story" about a black teacher whose unorthodox methods and treatment of tough slum pupils as adults win him respect, overcome the students' resistance, and open their minds and hearts to learning. This is a story that could easily have degenerated into sentimental cliche, but Clavell's interesting casting, credible dialogue, and confident directing made it work. Clavell's film *Where's Jack?* (1968) realistically depicts the exploits of the legendary eighteenth-century British highwayman Jack Sheppard.

More than a decade after *Five Gates to Hell* Clavell made his most telling commentary on Vietnam: a screenplay written in 1969 and brought to the screen in 1971, *The Last Valley*. Set during the Thirty Years' War in Europe, it is both a bloody action film and a haunting, literate comment on a war without purpose. In it an invading army pillages and destroys an idyllic Swiss village. Its release date and its vivid evocation of a devastating war that destroyed beauty and innocence made critics see in it a personal criticism of America's military devastation of Vietnamese villages.

By the time *The Last Valley* came out, Clavell had already begun to explore questions raised by Vietnam in another medium: the novel. In *Tai-Pan* he had used a father-son disagreement about historical British politics to reflect the Sixties' generational divisions about the American role in Vietnam. Later, *Noble House* would depict Russian spies gathering information on an American carrier destined for Vietnam, and secret, prewar operations, particularly a clandestine CIA airline—in real life, Air America—in action before American soldiers moved into Vietnam in strength. In *Whirlwind*, Vietnam would come up again in the reminiscences of the S-G company's helicopter pilots who, as they begin their exodus from Iran, remember lost comrades and the final exodus from Saigon. In other words, at about the same time that Clavell began producing and directing, he also began a career as a novelist.

NOVELIST

Writing screenplays had given Clavell the skills and confidence he needed to tackle a new kind of writing, and his own private nightmares provided the motivation, for Changi had remained an inescapable touchstone of experience. Clavell had kept the unspeakable horrors of Changi bottled up inside, and they became haunting nightmares. Seeing that he had reached a point where he needed to talk about Changi, his wife, April, urged him to seek an outlet in writing—to project his personal conflicts and dilemmas onto fictional representatives—through which he could explore his struggle to survive and perhaps find meaning in the act. A 1960 Hollywood screenwriters' strike provided the leisure, and April pretended to lock him in his workroom to encourage him to begin.

Once Clavell started, the Changi experiences he had suppressed exploded in a fury of writing; he completed the manuscript of *King Rat* in twelve weeks. Then began a new agony common to anyone with a great deal of emotional investment in what he is writing: revision. Clavell's first editor, Herman Gollub of Little, Brown and Company, attacked the manuscript with blue pencil, calling it "pretentious" and "overwritten" (*Current Biography* 1981: 84). Clavell later confided to *New York Post* interviewer Archey Winsten (May 17, 1971) that Gollub really taught him how to write (Winsten 1971).

Thus Clavell's first novel was a therapeutic working out of past experiences. Clavell told Edwin McDowell, in an interview for the *New York Times Book Review*, that writing *King Rat* was a catharsis, a purifying release of long-pent-up emotions that resulted in spiritual renewal and a lifting of the terrible burden of unshared memories (McDowell 1981). In it, Clavell defends flexibility, adaptability, and rebellion as necessary for survival, in opposition to rigid adherence to duty. The young Clavell must have been deeply torn between the theoretical advice of his father and the practical survival lessons of the American and Australian black marketeers he observed in Changi. Clavell depicts himself as the youthful Marlowe, who values the traditions and heritage of the British service, but who responds to the easygoing camaraderie offered by the pragmatic American corporal, "the King," and sees in his ingenious trades hope for survival. Provost marshal Robin Grey, who is, in part, a projection of Clavell's father's view, but is weakened by being less than noble, in turn, defends the order and discipline of military codes over the chaos and rampant individualism of Darwinian struggles for survival, but views these codes as ultimately for the personal benefit of an elite few. The moral ambiguity of *King Rat* bothers many readers, but the book is a deeply felt, intimate look at the choices that face humans reduced to subhuman conditions by brutal circumstances. Marlowe defends free enterprise as life-giving, arguing that the King's entrepreneurial methods saved thirty Americans and improved the conditions and spirits of many more.

The middle-aged Marlowe of *Noble House* is a survivor who has kept his ideals and has discarded the pretensions and hypocrisies that still drive Grey, who by the 1960s has become a thorough villain. Just as his ambition and rigidity led Grey to do the dirty work of the Japanese camp officials in *King Rat*, so they lead him to join the British Labour Party (an anathema for Clavell), to undermine free enterprise and the potentials of the working man, and to become a secret Russian agent in *Noble*

House. In *King Rat* Grey denounced Marlowe as an "exploiter" for interpreting Japanese and Korean for the King and for living well while others starved. His continued insults—"Marlowe old chap, are you still in
trade?" (*Noble House* 603)—would cut deep for an Englishman proud of
his descent from a long line of officers. However, the Marlowe of *Noble
House*, like Clavell himself, has learned to live with the past. He recognizes in his nemesis a tortured man, filled with self-loathing, incapable
of putting the past behind him, and unable to find loyalty or love or
hope for the future—a man whom Clavell could have become had he
made different choices. Grey's description of his suffering provides insights into Clavell's own. Some twenty years after his release from
Changi, Grey says that the experience is best forgotten, but inside he
wants to shout that he can't forget the tens of thousands dying, the starvation, the lack of hope, the bodies rotting away, the absence of women
and laughter, food, and drink—and that he was only twenty-one and in
despair. Changi remains a never-ending nightmare that surviving and
returning home to England cannot end, and, in fact, the return heightens
the nightmare experience:

> home gone, parents gone, world gone . . . nobody caring and
> oh Christ, the change. Coming back to life after the no-life of
> Changi, all the nightmares and the no sleeping in the night,
> terrified of life, unable to talk about it, weeping and not know-
> ing why . . . , trying to adjust to what fools called normal. Ad-
> justing at length. But at what cost, oh dear sweet Jesus at what
> a cost . . . (*Noble House*: 861–62)

This description of posttraumatic stress disorder (the psychological reactions of traumatized victims of wars and disasters) helps explain why
Clavell waited so long to deal with his Changi experiences.

Clavell depicts Marlowe, like himself, as lucky: a man who has endured, found love, and rediscovered life, and who can move forward
with hope. In *King Rat*, Marlowe was simply the central character, but
in *Noble House*, he is emphatically a projection of Clavell. In *Noble House*,
Marlowe, like Clavell, has authored a controversial book on his Changi
experience and has sold the film rights to Hollywood to support his
family while writing a second book about Hong Kong; he is a freelance
writer and screenwriter, a family man still in the process of coming to
terms with his past, a man who at every turn sees interesting stories and
despairs at the lack of time and space to tell them all. Marlowe describes

his book, *Changi*, like Clavell's *King Rat*, as accurate about incidents and events, for, though not literally historical, "people like them did and said those sort[s] of things and did those deeds" (*Noble House*: 913). In *Noble House*, Marlowe, like Clavell, proves initially reticent about revealing who he is in his book and is sensitive to questions about the costs of survival. He argues that Changi (or Dachau or Buchenwald) cannot be equated with normality, that there were different rules and different patterns, and that most of the soldiers and prisoners of war were teenagers, whose worlds had been turned upside down: "Changi was genesis, everything new, upside down" (*Noble House*: 1218). Clavell records the standard rations—a quarter pound of dry rice a day, some vegetables, one egg a week—and the psychological trauma of two thousand miles of enemy-occupied territory in every direction, malaria, dysentery, and a terrible death rate.

Changi shaped Clavell's self-image, and writing novels helped him deal with a shattering experience that redefined his image of the world and of himself. Changi changed his attitudes about heritage and class, survival and human relationships. Changi lay behind his appreciation of enterprise, ingenuity, individualism, and strength of will, and his distrust of group-think. It helped him appreciate American attitudes enough to make that country his home. It explains his strong, lifelong defense of free enterprise as the hope of Third World nations and his promotion of international ties that he believes one day will bind so tightly that nationalistic differences will be forced to yield to international interests. One might argue that Clavell's defense of capitalist enterprise is a personal defense of himself and of his survival of Changi.

Once he had written the story he had held inside him for so long, Clavell was ready to write novels based on his knowledge of the Far East. *King Rat* was a catharsis that allowed him to create a world view about Asia. Starting with the best-seller *Tai-Pan*, Clavell wrote very long, very carefully researched, intriguing historical Asian tales. His childhood tied him emotionally to Hong Kong and Macao, and his feelings for the Chinese were intensified because they also had suffered tremendously under Japanese oppressors who slaughtered tens of thousands in Shanghai and Nanking during the war. Clavell and his family spent 1963 in Hong Kong so that he could reacquaint himself with the city, research its history, and take in the sights and sounds that make his Hong Kong novels rich in local color. An appreciation of Chinese culture permeates his novels.

However, Clavell wrote not only about Chinese culture, but also about

Japanese culture. Writing about Changi made Clavell rethink the Japanese. He told Edwin McDowell that he started reading about the history and culture of Japan and reinterpreting memories in the light of new knowledge. At Changi, a Japanese officer had offered to lend Clavell not only his personal *hara-kiri* suicide kit, complete with sharpened swords for disemboweling himself, but also an assistant to chop off his head once the disemboweling cut had been made. Clavell did what most Westerners would have done: politely but firmly rejected the kind offer. The Japanese officer was highly offended and contemptuous of Clavell thereafter. At the time, Clavell did not understand why, but his new readings provided an answer: "They [the Japanese] thought we were dishonored, because it's totally wrong in their culture to be captured, while we believe that by surviving we live to fight another day" (McDowell 1981). His decision that their view was not wrong, just different from his, led to one of his finest works, *Shogun* (1975). The book marked a new stage of understanding for Clavell, a reconsideration of the Japanese, and a new appreciation of cultural relativism, the perspective that allows him to show us the Japanese on their own terms.

Whirlwind grew out of Clavell's personal sympathies with expatriate British and Iranian friends whom he visited while the Shah was still in power. Clavell told *Publishers Weekly* interviewer Stella Dong that the heroics necessary for his characters to extract themselves from the midst of revolution makes for a good read. Clavell also says that Iran offered an effective platform for an epic story about ordinary people caught up in "extraordinary circumstances and exposed to danger" (Dong 1986: 55). Though *Whirlwind* focused on Iran rather than Pacific Asia, Clavell found in Iran the same alien, Eastern twists of logic and attitude that defy Western thought in China and Japan.

He titled his six novels "Asian Saga" to suggest an integrated whole. Characters from one book reappear in another; the descendants of characters from one novel continue the conflicts and goals of their ancestors. This Anglo-Asian mix sums up Clavell's vision of human realities:

1. Contact weakens the ethnic and cultural differences that separate; interacting cultural groups learn from each other, and gradually change both psychologically and culturally, until the end product is an amalgam, an intriguing mix of East and West.

2. Maintaining a separate continuous identity and valuing

purity and homogeneity is ultimately dangerous internationally and leads to barbaric treatment of outsiders.

3. A total rejection of the West by the East is highly injurious to both sides.

4. The human picture cannot be measured in a year or even a decade, but only long-term, over several generations.

5. Heritage provides a sense of self and place and human continuity, but ultimately each individual must achieve for himself in order to be worthy of that heritage.

6. Sexual differences are inescapable, but an understanding of the interlocking nature of yang and yin can help both males and females lead fuller, more satisfying lives.

7. Women may have different skills and different social functions, but they deserve equal rights, equal education, and equal treatment.

8. By valuing the group over the individual and by theoretically reducing all to the same low-level common denominator, Communism denies the value of human differences and restricts human potential, while capitalism, in turn, though subject to the excesses of greed and human selfishness, ultimately encourages individualism and differences and, through free enterprise, allows class differences to be negated and the entire society to prosper.

9. Survival of the fittest means survival of the most flexible, adaptable, and resilient (often within the context of a small group loyally taking care of its own).

FILM VERSIONS OF HIS NOVELS

The popularity of Clavell's novels led naturally to film versions. Columbia Pictures bought the screen rights to *King Rat* and paid Clavell $25,000 a year for five years. The movie version, which came out in 1965 and was produced by James Woolf and adapted and directed by Bryan Forbes, starred Tom Courtenay as Marlowe, James Fox as Grey, and George Segal as the King. The film has been called "powerful," "tense," "unvarnished," and "provocative." Though nominated for Academy Awards for its black-and-white cinematography, its art direction, and its set decorations, it was released at a time when American audiences were thinking positively of war and were not ready to deal with a realistic treatment of nonheroic suffering.

Clavell sold the movie rights to *Tai-Pan* to Metro-Goldwyn-Mayer, and the film, produced on location in Hong Kong, came out in 1986. Clavell had nothing to do with the screenplay or the filming. It was directed by Daryl Duke and starred Bryan Brown, Joan Chen, and John Staton. Despite heavy cuts to Clavell's plot and numerous changes in characters and situation, it nonetheless captures the nasty rivalries, free-wheeling trade, and exotic atmosphere of the novel.

Clavell was the executive producer of the two television miniseries versions of his books, *Shogun* (in 1980), starring Richard Chamberlain, and *Noble House* (in 1986), starring Pierce Brosnan. *Shogun*, made by Shogun Productions, was a five-part, twelve-hour television adaptation, shot in Japan at a cost of $22 million. It was viewed by an estimated audience of 130 million. Orson Welles narrated the series, Jerry London directed it, and Eric Bercovici collaborated with Clavell on the screenplay and produced it. Clavell acted as executive producer, for a million dollar fee. In 1981, a highly compressed version of *Shogun*, filmed in conjunction with the miniseries, was released as a two-and-a-half-hour movie. Clavell worked on most aspects of the production, from choosing the film crew and casting the actors (fifteen European actors and twenty-eight Japanese), to developing a script and approving footage. He worked closely with Bercovici to make sure the film version contained the cultural and psychological nuances of the book. Clavell courageously insisted that, for the sake of authenticity, the Japanese speak in their native language, with no subtitles provided. As a result, this is one of the first films in which extended multilingual exchanges occur and the viewer, as in real life, must guess meaning from context, from individual reactions and facial expressions, or from listening to rephrasing by English-speaking characters. The Japanese actors dominate the film, as they do the book, and Toshiro Mifune convincingly captures the essence of Toranaga: full of life and spirit, inscrutable, highly competent, powerful, and all-knowing, a true puppetmaster. As a consequence of this commitment to accuracy of theme and setting, the *Shogun* miniseries comes as close as the film medium can come to the complexity of the novel, though of course it can never equal its subtlety.

The *Noble House* miniseries is less successful at bringing novel to screen. Although it captures the fascination of Hong Kong and portrays rampant capitalism at work (fragile businesses broken by unscrupulous trading, rapid fluctuations in the stockmarket, double-dealing in the board room, and under-the-table negotiations), the series fails to capture the essential virtues and vices of the Chinese in the subtle and humanized way *Shogun* does for the Japanese. Partly, the difficulty is that the central characters, whether of British or of Chinese descent, are very clearly Western, and the Chinese psychology that dominates key figures like Ian Dunross in the book appears only superficially in the film. The heavy-handed comic sections, based mainly on stereotyped figures, fall flat, but John Rhys-Davies humanizes Quillan Gornt in a way that Clavell does not, and the performances of Pierce Brosnan (Ian Dunross) and Deborah Raffin (Casey Tcholok), among others, are very much in the spirit of Clavell's novel. Brosnan is convincing as a wise and wary Hong Kong player, willing to gamble huge sums to save the family business but knowledgeable enough to use circumstances and back-room deals to hedge his bets, while Raffin steals the show as a competent, humane American who tempers business acumen and skill with common sense and a commitment to honest dealings. Whereas the book is dominated by Hong Kong and Red Chinese business practices, underhanded double-dealing, espionage, and cultural interaction, with romance present but secondary, business and romance together dominate the miniseries.

These miniseries also increased the audience for all Clavell's novels, so that millions worldwide learned about the history and flavor of Japan, China, Macao, Hong Kong, and finally Iran. Clavell had hoped to do a miniseries on *Whirlwind*, but died before he could.

OTHER DIRECTIONS

In addition to his screenplays and novels, Clavell wrote a play called *Countdown at Armageddon*, some poetry, and two children's books. *The Children's Story* is a controversial fable about the brainwashing of young people, and, in a totally different vein, *Thrump-O-Moto* is a Japanese-style children's fantasy.

The Children's Story, which originally appeared as a short story in the *Ladies' Home Journal* in 1980, elicited an angry barrage of letters from American readers who failed to understand its satiric nature and democratic intent. In his introduction to the book Clavell himself called it "a gift to my adopted land," and, after dinner at the White House, presented President and Mrs. Ronald Reagan with first copies of the Delacorte Press edition of the novelette. The story had grown out of a conversation Clavell had with his daughter Michaela, who, at age six, was asked to recite the Pledge of Allegiance at school. Her father, helping her practice for her recitation, discovered that she did not understand the meaning of what she was memorizing. Twenty years later, the story he began in reaction to her lack of understanding was published. It is a short, didactic protest against what Clavell feared could be a school system's manipulation of the vulnerable minds of children for political ends. Set in an America conquered by a dictatorial enemy, this novelette describes how an attractive, well-trained teacher endears herself to her elementary school students and then, having won their trust, reshapes their views about country, religion, and parents. Her final act is to persuade them to rip apart an American flag. It is this act that *Ladies' Home Journal* readers misunderstood, and that Delacorte was careful to explain as satiric in a publicity campaign. Clavell's premise is that parents should assume responsibility for the intellectual development of their children and that failure to do so could mean leaving children as pawns in the hands of unscrupulous educators who pass on values and perceptions that should be questioned. His goal was to outrage parents and to motivate them to be better parents and better Americans by taking a personal interest in what their children are taught. Instead, he enraged the John Birch Society. In *Whirlwind*, Clavell attacks a similar type of brainwashing in his depiction of the rise to power of the Khomeini regime in Iran and the forced manipulation of attitudes and values, not simply of children, but of easily swayed, semiliterate adults. In both cases, undeveloped minds prove vulnerable to psychological persuasion that translates into political action.

The children's book *Thrump-O-Moto* is in a much lighter vein, its goal a lesson in cross-cultural awareness. A tiny Japanese apprentice wizard with fantastic powers transports a crippled young Australian girl to Japan, reduces her to his size, and teaches her Japanese customs of courtesy and of the tea ceremony before helping her face an ordeal that could change her life. This ordeal involves traveling through an enchanted forest, battling and defeating a scary ghoul, and appeasing magical forest beings. This experience of trial and conflict in a fantasy land helps the young heroine overcome the curse that has debilitated her, so that at the end of the story, thanks to Japanese magic, she can walk again.

WRITING PATTERNS AND PERSONALITY

Clavell's Delacorte editor, Jean Bernkopf, describes Clavell's writing as steady and purposeful: he wrote between ten and fifteen pages daily on a word processor and stuck to five-year plans. Bernkopf calls him "a dream to work with," and various interviewers and colleagues have commented on his warmth and friendliness, his gentle voice, his kindly, deferential manner, his knowledgeability, and the smile that lit up his face. They emphasize his concern for the quality and psychological and cultural accuracy of his materials. A producer with whom Clavell clashed over a directing decision described him as "cold, hard, ruthless and ready to kill" (Dong 1986: 54), but this reaction reflected Clavell's strong desire to control the artistic image he was creating, whether in film or literature, rather than his basic nature. Burt Kwouk, who starred as Phillip Chen in the miniseries *Noble House*, found Clavell "quiet," "gentle," and "well-mannered," but also "a shrewd businessman who exercised considerable control over how his work was used by others." Kwouk describes Clavell as "the completely objective observer who hardly ever participated in the milieu in which he found himself"; this description is in keeping with the qualities Clavell ascribes to his ship-wrecked English pilot Blackthorne, who at times seems to stand outside himself, observing, but distanced. These are qualities shared by survivors who have faced death, as Clavell did at Changi, and who can never again shake off the distance that experience creates between their vision of the world that was and the world that is. It is also a quality sometimes shared by military personnel who have spent a great deal of time abroad and no longer belong to one place. Like his *tai-pan* heroes, Clavell was an imposing man: he was over six feet tall and solidly built, with broad shoulders, a strong Scottish chin, and a ruddy complexion. His thick eyebrows set off soft brown eyes that were tolerant, accepting, yet some-how strong.

As a writer, Clavell began with what he knew or had learned and then projected and speculated based on personal instinct and a sensitivity to intercultural interaction. For example, Clavell and his wife's interest in flying and in helicopters, in particular, resulted in descriptions of a helicopter service in Iran that are well informed and that capture the joy of flying ("the nearest thing to becoming a bird" says Clavell). Clavell makes clear the expertise required (Clavell's pilots practice instrument checks, landings, and other necessary maneuvers blindfolded to test their training), the uniqueness and versatility of helicopter flight (close to the ground or waves, below radar, with sudden shifts upward or downward), and the conflicting Muslim attitudes toward such technology. When asked about his amazing knowledgeability about Asian cultures, a knowledgeability that has astounded Hong Kong Chinese and Japanese historians, Clavell explained that he read widely, conversed with people from the cultures he was interested in, and then used his imagination to build a picture. He told interviewer Stella Dong that his experience with film made him think in visual terms, so that, while writing, his imagination would oscillate from picture to picture, image to image, and, at night, dream to dream (Dong 1986: 54).

During his moviemaking and writing career, Clavell traveled a great deal. As the son of a naval officer, he was used to suddenly packing up and moving on. This pattern of his youth became a lifetime pattern, as it does for many children of military families. Clavell and his family resided in a number of places, including England, California, British Columbia, the south of France, and Switzerland. At one point, in 1981, because of increased prices and taxes when the Mitterrand government came to power, they left France for Switzerland. On the recommendation of the actor David Niven, who lived there himself, they settled in Gstaad, a wealthy mountain resort, with their German shepherd Rebel. There they found pleasant people who respected their privacy (Dong 1986: 55). The actor Roger Moore was a neighbor, and a close friendship developed between the two expatriates. Clavell kept up a FAX correspondence with fellow conservative William Buckley as well.

DEATH

Clavell died in Vevey, Switzerland, on September 6, 1994, at age sixty-nine, from cancer and then a stroke. He was survived by his wife of forty years, April Clavell, and two married daughters. A friend and one of his editors, Eric Major of Hodder and Stoughton, a London publishing house, said, "he was one of the great epic storytellers of our age—a man who was deeply imbued in tradition, and also enormous fun to work with." This statement is a fitting epitaph for a writer who both teaches and entertains, who opens up new worlds and new cultures while reaffirming the historical foundations of the old.

2

James Clavell's
Literary Heritage

Oh, East is East, and West is West, and never the twain shall meet,
Till Earth and Sky stand presently at God's great Judgment Seat.
But there is neither East nor West, Border, nor Breed, nor Birth,
When two strong men stand face to face, though they come from the ends
of the earth!

Rudyard Kipling, "The Ballad of East and West"

Novelist, scriptwriter, director, poet, and dramatist, James Clavell drew on the literary traditions of both his heritages, British and American, as well as on the traditions of the cultures he depicts: Chinese, Japanese, and Iranian.

LITERARY PRECURSORS

Clavell's immediate precursors were eighteenth- and nineteenth-century British adventure novelists and the real-life records of the explorers, adventurers, and seamen on whose adventures the novelists based their works. Typical of these writers are Daniel Defoe (the first English novelist), in *Robinson Crusoe* (1719) and *Captain Singleton* (1720); Richard Dana, in *Two Years before the Mast* (1840); Robert Louis Stevenson, in *Treasure Island* (1883) and *Kidnapped* (1886); James Morier, in *Hajji*

Baba of Isphahan (1824), *Hajji Baba in London* (1828), and *Journey through Persia* (1816); Sir Henry Rider Haggard, in *King Solomon's Mines* (1886); C. S. Forester, in *Captain Horatio Hornblower* (1937); and Rudyard Kipling, in *Kim* (1901) and in his short stories about cross-cultural encounters and adventurers in far-off lands, like "The Man Who Would Be King." British writers such as these combined an exciting adventure story with vivid images of English travelers encountering exotic people and places, strange customs, and peculiar habits.

Daniel Defoe's *Robinson Crusoe*, for example, praises the ingenuity that allows an ordinary English sailor to survive Turkish pirates, shipwreck, and twenty-four years on an isolated island. The literary convention is one of the Englishman abroad who, though totally isolated from civilized people, uses English inventiveness to persevere under adversity and to avoid degenerating into a subhuman. In *Captain Singleton*, Defoe's account of his fictive hero also begins as a sea voyage story, but is half devoted to a trip across central Africa and half devoted to pirate adventures. Captain Singleton was raised by gypsies, captured by Turks and then Portuguese, and dumped on an island near Mozambique, where, assuming leadership of a motley crew of mutineers, he hunted and foraged his way westward across the continent, crossing deserts to reach the Atlantic. There he pirated a ship and sailed in search of gold and booty, trading off the coast of China and provisioning in Java, before retiring to a quiet life of respectability in England. Singleton was very much the type of character Clavell had in mind when writing about his China traders, Dirk Struan and Tyler Brock, in *Tai-Pan*: they were versatile, resilient, adventuresome, and ruthless. Furthermore, Defoe drew on real-life accounts of voyages, travelers' tales, maps, and geographies to give romanticized accounts the illusion of complete authenticity, and there were historical counterparts to the fictive Crusoe and Singleton. That Clavell followed the same strategy is obvious from reviewer guessing games linking his characters to historical figures.

Another example of the tradition in which Clavell works is Richard Dana's *Two Years before the Mast*, set, like Clavell's *Tai-Pan*, in the nineteenth century. *Two Years before the Mast* is a realistic account of the hardships and injustices endured by the common sailor; it, and later books like C. S. Forester's Hornblower series, depicting early nineteenth-century seamen aboard ships of the line during the Napoleonic Wars, were exactly the type of books the son of a British naval officer might read as a youth. Dana's book depicts experiences such as those Clavell's Dirk Struan endured as an apprentice sailor (bad food, cruel officers, rough seas, and hard labor), while Forester's Hornblower series captures the romance, excitement, and heroism of naval battles like those the youthful Phillip Tyrer in *Gai-Jin* imagines. Robert Louis Stevenson's *Treasure Island*, in turn, is a colorful evocation of pirates on the Spanish Main who dream of buried treasure, while Sir Henry Rider Haggard's *King Solomon's Mines* tells the tale of English explorer Allen Quatermain, who braves hostile natives to search for lost treasure. Clavell's heroes are not as piratical as Stevenson's Black Dog and Long John Silver (though his villains are), but they dream of the treasure that will make their fortune, and must beware of Chinese pirates who block the coastal passageways. In *Tai-Pan*, Struan's ship, a Chinese junk loaded with gold bullion, barely escapes a pirate attack, and an English pirate serving aboard a Chinese vessel is slowly tortured to death for betraying a Chinese pirate chieftain. In *Shogun*, the English ship's captain has braved unknown waters to find the treasures of Japan, and the Portuguese captain, Rodrigues, is a hearty, daring rogue whose prototype is a Robert Louis Stevenson hero.

Other examples of the Englishman-abroad and culture-clash tradition in which Clavell works are James Morier's *Hajji Baba of Isphahan* and *Hajji Baba in London*, and Rudyard Kipling's *Kim* and the "The Man Who Would Be King." Morier was an explorer, linguist, and diplomat who was as fascinated with the Near and Middle East as Clavell was with the Far East. He used his intimate knowledge of Persian life, religion, and manners to provide Westerners sympathetic insights into an alien culture. Rudyard Kipling did the same for India. *Kim*, for instance, vividly depicts the complexities of the Indian Raj, and sets native shrewdness and cunning off against British authority. Clavell's British undercover soldier "Johnny Brighteyes" Ross in *Whirlwind* is very much a Kipling-type British hero, one who has learned the secret of languages and disguises, who can fit in with local peoples, fight like a tiger, and earn the respect of any man.

HISTORICAL MODELS

In addition to these literary models of adventure, historical romance, seamanship, and travel in foreign lands, Clavell also had genuine explorers to provide images of the Englishman abroad, enduring the physical trials of alien lands and confronting alien peoples and philosophies. The most notable of these include the nineteenth-century travelers Sir

Samuel Baker, John Speke, Charles Doughty, and Sir Richard Burton. Sir Samuel Baker explored the Nile's tributaries in Ethiopia, discovered Lake Albert Nyanza, and later became governor of the Lake Albert region, south of Ethiopia. Baker's antislavery stance might well have influenced Clavell's depiction of Dirk Struan's views on slavery, and Baker's purchase of his beloved wife in an Istanbul slave market is echoed in Struan's purchase of May-may. Speke was the first European to reach the source of the White Nile, Lake Victoria, and he and Burton were the first white men to view Lake Tanganyika. Lafcadio Hearne's 19th century immersion in Japanese culture provided Clavell a model of the European experience in the Orient.

Burton is the explorer of the period who made the strongest impression on Clavell—for good reason. Burton was a complete Renaissance man: anthropologist, archaeologist, author, convert to all of the world's great religions, diplomat, explorer, inventor, linguist, lover, philosopher, poet, scholar, soldier, and world traveler. As his biographer Byron Farwell asserts, Burton was, above all, an adventurer, a man who deliberately turned his back on European civilization and willingly endured incredible hardships and risked life and health "simply to go and see unknown lands" and "to tell others what he has seen" (Farwell 1963: 1). In *Gai-Jin*, Burton's explorations excite Clavell's Englishmen, who enthusiastically keep track of his travels in month-old newspaper stories, and *Shogun* reflects Burton's lessons on swordsmanship and falconry. Burton translated the *Tales of the Arabian Nights*, the *Kama Sutra*, and a number of Eastern erotic manuals into English, and he described in a total of twenty-one books his adventures traveling in Africa, India, and Arabia. His frankness about sexuality and unusual sexual practices offended many Victorians, but would have endeared him to Clavell. More importantly, his books provided insights into "new" peoples and cultures.

Burton was daring in his exploits and, like Clavell, honest in capturing the sensibilities of people on whom his fellow British looked with disdain. Burton tells of contriving disguises so clever that soldiers from his own division kicked him, thinking he was a native. He stained his skin with henna, grew his hair long, adopted the name "Abdullah," and posed as a street vendor so he could gossip and gather information without arousing suspicion. Much later, as a civilian, he visited the Muslim holy cities of Mecca and Medina, and disguised as a Pathan, the forbidden City of Harar in eastern Ethiopia; his linguistic skills and knowledge of local gestures and manners made his disguises convincing. Burton studied Islam and Sufism, wrote intricate love poetry in a Persian style to lovely foreign ladies, and immersed himself in the philosophies and cultures of the areas he visited. His books note the dichotomy between Sunni and Shiite and record the contempt most Moslems have for the Persian sect, a contempt expressed in both verbal and physical abuse.

Burton's translation of the *Tales of the Arabian Nights* captures the lust, greed, perversion, bravery, and treachery of medieval Persians, and his portrait of Sharazad and life in a Persian household contains patterns Clavell employed in *Whirlwind*. One of Clavell's main female figures in *Whirlwind* is named Sharazad and is described as "the kind of Persian beauty Omar Khayyam had immortalized" (*Whirlwind*: 132) and later as "an apparition, something out of a *Thousand and One Nights*" (190). A confrontation between the village chieftain, Nitchak Khan, and Sharazad's husband, Tom Lockhart, involves an exchange of elegant lines from the *Rubaiyat* about resignation to fate and the turning wheel of heaven (605). Throughout *Whirlwind*, Clavell dramatizes Burton's observations on Persian sexuality: the homosexual proclivities of the males, the incestuous family yearnings, the casual sexual encounters between females in the same household, the male division of all women as either slave-wives or prostitutes. Clavell's Western heroes share Burton's liberal sexual attitudes and immerse themselves in alien cultures as Burton did. Burton's Englishman abroad learning to value alien perspectives is important to understanding Clavell's characters.

Like Burton, Charles Doughty provided Clavell an historical model of travel stories on which to create his fiction. Doughty's *Travels in Arabia Deserta* (1888), one of the greatest travel books in the English language, was based on his two years with nomadic tribes in northwestern Arabia. In it, Doughty recorded a way of life totally strange to Europeans, but did so with understanding. In contrast to the Oriental fantasy stories of harems and romance, Doughty's book captures the hardness of the life, the tyranny of the males, the servitude of the women, the fierce intensity of the people's religious commitment, and their fanatical embracement of fated martyrdom. To convey the linguistic formality and ritualistic conventions of the Arab nomad, Doughty used stilted diction, a technique Clavell uses to convey the intricately formal conventions of the Farsi and the Malay languages. Clavell's observations about Iranians almost a hundred years later suggest that the dichotomy between Westerner and Middle Easterner described by Doughty had not greatly changed.

Doughty influenced T. E. Lawrence, whose *Seven Pillars of Wisdom*

(1926) is one of the great stories of an Englishman in the Middle East. Lawrence was a British intelligence officer during World War I, and then military advisor to Faisal I, who was later king of Iraq. Dressed as an Arab and riding a camel, Lawrence led an Arab guerrilla army that pushed the Turks out of western Arabia and Syria. The Englishman gone native is another of the traditions in which Clavell writes.

Lafcadio Hearn, an Irish-Greek American who fled Western materialism in search of beauty, tranquility, and lasting values, is another traveler who found in a distant culture insights into his own. In 1890, he settled in Japan, took the name Yakumo Koizumi, and became a confirmed Japanophile who interpreted the West for Japanese and the Japanese for the West. He studied and wrote about Japanese life and customs, religion, and legends. *Glimpses of Unfamiliar Japan* (1894) and *Japan: An Attempt at Interpretation* (1904) are his most famous books. Unlike Hearn, Clavell did not reject the West, but he did see himself in a similar role, interpreting Easterners to Westerners and vice versa.

The underlying concept of all Clavell's literary precursors—defining self by seeing an opposite and discovering in the "other" the value and limits of one's self—is of major import. A Japanese student, when asked why he was studying in America, replied, "To learn to appreciate Americans, but more importantly, to learn to appreciate my own culture." This statement sums up, in part, what Clavell draws on from the tradition of his precursors: a fascination for foreign lands and peoples and an appreciation of what we can learn from them and what they can learn from us.

FOREIGN SOURCES

In his novels, Clavell quotes the Persian *Rubaiyat of Omar Khayyam* and ancient Japanese and Chinese poems, and builds plots around historical figures from the nations whose stories he tells. However, the book to which he refers most often is Sun Tzu's *The Art of War*, written in China in 500 B.C. In 1986, Clavell edited an English translation of *The Art of War*, whose careful study he recommended to all military officers as a means of preventing war and avoiding disastrous confrontations. In his foreword, he calls the book "vital to our survival" and to being able "to watch our children grow in peace and thrive" (Foreword to Sun Tzu's *The Art of War*: 7).

The strategies set forth in Sun Tzu's book guide the Russian and *tai-*

pan strategies in *Noble House*, though, ironically, Clavell's Red Chinese quote Buddha instead. Ian Dunross, the *tai-pan* of the Noble House, recommends Sun Tzu's *The Art of War* to the American businessman Linc Bartlett, who calls it "the best book on war I've ever read" (*Noble House*: 131). The two men exchange information about the book (which was published in French in 1782 and possibly read by Napoleon, was popular in Russia, and was a favorite of Mao Tse-tung, who always carried around a dog-eared copy), compare Sun Tzu to the famous sixteenth-century Italian political strategist Machiavelli, and praise his lessons about survival and about handling large groups. Throughout *Noble House*, various characters apply Sun Tzu to modern situations. For example, Dunross uses the statement "Supreme excellence of generalship consists in breaking the enemy's resistance without fighting" to explain his elimination of Alastair Struan from the playing field (132). Later, he plots a strategy for saving Noble House based on Sun Tzu, particularly his perception that confidence and daring sometimes carry more weight than the number of troops and weapons. Dunross also quotes Sun Tzu to the Japanese tycoon Hiro Toda to emphasize anticipating opponent strategy to avoid capture or injury. Toda is impressed since Sun Tzu also guides his business strategy.

Ironically, Clavell's Communists share the same enthusiasm for Sun Tzu that Toda and Dunross, representatives of the driving force of capitalistic enterprise, have. The Russian master spy Suslev, for instance, reflects on Sun Tzu's lessons about spies: the five classes of spies (local, inward, converted, doomed, and surviving), their extreme importance to army maneuvers, and the rules for managing them. Different classes of spies must work in concert to secure the state; the state must reward them all quite liberally, but should assassinate them if they divulge information too soon. Clavell wrote that reading Sun Tzu was the duty of all Soviet officers and that the book was so important to the Soviet elite "that many knew the slim volume by heart" (*Noble House*: 644). In fact, a number of the Russian strategies discussed in *Noble House* are clearly attributed to *The Art of War*. Two Russian spies describe a KGB scam as "classic Sun Tzu: using the enemy's strength against himself" (1088).

In addition to direct statements about or quotations from Sun Tzu, Clavell lends Ian Dunross strength by having his strategy for survival follow the advice of Sun Tzu. Dunross acts with confidence, anticipates the strategies of his opponents, and forms contingency plans. He employs spies and rewards them liberally, and is loyal to employees but demands strict allegiance. He is willing to risk all, but he hedges his bets against risk. He uses his enemies' strengths as well as their weaknesses against them. In other words, Clavell finds in Sun Tzu a pattern for behavior and survival that shapes his heroes and determines their actions.

MODERN PARALLELS

Critics often compare Clavell's novels to James Michener's because of their Eastern settings, their focus on dynasties, their exemplary story-telling, and their sheer length. Both writers depict treachery, intrigue, sex, and violence in unique foreign settings. Like Michener's works, Clavell's historical adventures are notable for their energy and scope; they provide a sweeping panorama, sometimes with as many as thirteen crisscrossing plots, involving a truly international mix and encompassing all strata of society. However, as a writer, Clavell is both more thrilling and more serious than Michener. Partly this is because Michener tries to cover so large a time period—for instance, 12,000 years of the history of Palestine or the story of Hawaii from geological creation to statehood. In contrast, Clavell focuses on a key period, a defining moment. Where Michener opts for a sweeping overview of personalities, Clavell hones in on a pivotal figure and the qualities of personality that transform history. Where Michener gives a kindly, humane view of the world with the optimistic hope of defeating common prejudices and promoting harmonious human relations, Clavell faces harsh truths of barbarism, greed, vulgarity, prejudice, and oppression.

Michener's novels are slow paced; Clavell's novels are action-packed adventures, with riveting descriptions of chases, fights, flight, and confrontation. Clavell dramatizes the way survival instincts change people, values, and deeds, the characteristics and world views that separate cultures, and human adaptability and acculturation. Clavell is sensitive to Far Eastern and Middle Eastern worlds: the commercialism and fatalism of Hong Kong; the political intrigue, barbarism, and high level of civilization of seventeenth-century Japan; the Japanese contempt for *gai-jin* as lacking honor and therefore being unworthy of humane treatment in World War II prison camps; the fanaticism and contradictions of modern Iran. His adventure novels portray Western and Eastern minds in conflict over money, power, and politics, and his central characters wheel and deal on an international scale with international consequences. These qualities raise Clavell's works above being simple travelogues of foreign lands.

Clavell's novels combine a number of literary types: histories, chronicles of manners, sea adventures, romances, Horatio Alger financial fantasies, dynasty sagas, *Bildungsromans* (maturation stories), disaster stories, medical stories, prison camp chronicles, and even spy stories and horse racing scams. As historical novels, they provide a sense of beginnings or foundings (the founding of Hong Kong, the European foothold in Yokohama) and of endings (the ousting of the Shah of Iran, the end of the Chinese-British Hong Kong lease, the freeing of prisoners at the end of World War II). *Tai-Pan*, *Shogun*, and *Gai-Jin* are swashbuckling histories of bygone days, very much in the tradition of the historical novels of Sir Walter Scott, Robert Louis Stevenson, Thomas Costain, and Louis L'Amour. They chronicle the early European contact with Japan and China: the samurai, the Portuguese Black Ships, the opium trade, the China traders, the pirates; then, later, the clipper ships and the exploits of the British Navy; and always the drive for trade. There are slave ships and sea chases, swaggering sea captains, fistfights, sword fights, and huge treasure. The novels provide a sense of the power of the British Navy, and of the drive of the merchant captains who searched for trade around the globe. They also provide contrasting studies of manners, values, and lifestyles, particularly between Easterners and Westerners, but also between subgroups within each category. As such they are novels of manners, explorations of how people behave and why. *Shogun*, the best example of this, provides insights into seventeenth-century Japanese and English culture, philosophy, and social interaction.

Clavell's novels are also *Madame Butterfly*–style love stories recording the cross-cultural romances of their adventuresome heroes: the love story of Dirk Struan and May-may in *Tai-Pan*; the *Romeo and Juliet* romance between Culum Struan and Tess Brock in *Tai-Pan*; the love between the English sea captain John Blackthorne and his interpreter Lady Mariko in *Shogun*; the doomed love affair of Angelique Richaud and Malcolm Struan in *Noble House*; the love of the Finnish Erikki for the Azerbaijani Azadeh and of the American Tom Lockhart for the Persian Sharazad in *Whirlwind*. At the same time, the novels have a feminist orientation, protesting Eastern treatment of women as servants, slaves, and concubines, and prompting readers to think about the difficulties for even supposedly more liberated European women under a system in which women were at best provided limited education and lacked the right to vote, to divorce, or to determine their own fate by choosing their own husbands.

Noble House, especially, raises feminist issues and provides a model of a competent woman outwitting men in the world of high finance.

Clavell's Noble House series, which includes *Tai-Pan*, *Noble House*, and *Gai-Jin*, are dynasty sagas and Horatio Alger financial fantasies. Tyler Brock and Dirk Struan of *Tai-Pan*, Paul Choy and Casey Tcholok of *Noble House*, and Edward Gornt, Angelique Richaud, and Jamie McFay of *Gai-Jin* all start with little and through hard work, an eye for an opportunity, daring, expertise, and luck, build their fortunes. We see most of these financial climbers in the midst of their progression, but are also given details of their harder days. For example, the life of Paul Choy, who was born on a Hong Kong junk and, as the middle son of a pirate and drug runner, had little hope of becoming anything else himself, is a rags-to-riches story. Paul studied hard, learned his lessons about finance well, and earned a fortune on the stock market. Ultimately, he founds the Chinese stock market, serves on the board of the Noble House, and manipulates its internal politics to suit his needs. His is only one of the many success stories Clavell paints.

Clavell's most successful entrepreneurs found dynasties and pass on a tradition of wealth and obligation to later generations, so that the descendants of Dirk Struan and Tyler Brock appear in key roles in later centuries—in *Gai-Jin* and *Noble House*. The House of Toranaga in *Shogun* is also a family dynasty that endures from the seventeenth to the nineteenth century, and it reappears through the Toda Corporation in *Whirlwind*. The diagram of family relationships (see p. 52) clarifies the extent of these dynasties. Related to this pattern of family saga is the pattern of the *Bildungsroman* (maturation story): many of Clavell's novels trace the early development or spiritual education of the main character. *King Rat* comes closest to this model: experiences in Japanese prison camps transform the adolescent Marlowe into a man who questions the values of his childhood and develops a personal philosophy. In *Tai-Pan*, young Culum Struan finds the new British colony of Hong Kong a lesson in contrasting cultures and, if he is to survive, must come to terms with his heritage and his obligations. The novel traces his coming of age as he masters the lessons of both the Struans and the Brocks, and, with the help of a kindly advisor, finds his own way. Although Blackthorne of *Shogun* is older, he too goes through a cultural and spiritual metamorphosis through his contact with Japanese culture.

Clavell's strong visual sense serves him well in recording disaster stories in the tradition of novels like John D. MacDonald's *Condominium* and Ross Macdonald's *The Underground Man* and movies like the *Airport* film series and *Earthquake*, all made during Clavell's days in Hollywood. Clavell captures the power and arbitrariness of elemental forces of nature that undo human schemes. In *Tai-Pan*, the destructive fury of a typhoon decimates the original Hong Kong colony and kills the novel's main characters; in *Shogun*, a typhoon sweeps away a village and an earthquake swallows up many; and in *Noble House*, monstrous Hong Kong mudslides bury the cardboard shacks of the poor and topple twenty-story luxury apartment buildings. Clavell's disasters also include fires. In *Noble House*, a kitchen fire destroys a Hong Kong floating restaurant, and many die in panic at the one exit. In *Gai-Jin* a fire sweeps rapidly through the paper houses of the red light district of Yokohama and spreads to more substantial buildings; and in *Shogun*, a fire resulting from an earthquake destroys sections of Osaka and damages the castle. Clavell also uses medical stories, stories of the pox, the plague, malaria, beriberi, multiple sclerosis, and the toll they take not only on the human body but also on the human psyche. Clavell conveys outrage at diseases that can be controlled but are not, and a sense of impotence in the face of incurable diseases.

Because of his experiences at Changi, it is no surprise that Clavell writes prison camp chronicles. These occur not only in *King Rat*, in which the entire story takes place in a prison camp, but also in *Noble House*, in the stories told about Changi and about the imprisonment of Brian Kwok, who is tortured so that he will divulge the names of traitors and an account of Red Chinese activities in Hong Kong. The description of the imprisonment of Blackthorne and his men in *Shogun* is particularly gruesome: first, they are held in a deep pit in which they languish and rot, beset by disease, covered in filth, and crowded claustrophobically in darkness, and later, in a Japanese prison whose entranceway features the crucified bodies of the condemned and whose interior contains lost souls waiting in a limbo of despair, never knowing when they will die.

Clavell's books are also spy stories. In *King Rat*, a traitor tells the Japanese about the hidden radios. In *Tai-Pan*, the *tai-pan*'s concubine, May-may, and his son Gordon Chen spy for Jin-Qua. In *Gai-Jin* there are spies from competing Japanese political camps, including the lovely Koiko, who spies on the man she loves. In *Whirlwind*, British spies and Russian spies compete for behind-the-scenes control. But *Noble House* contains Clavell's most fully developed spy story, with Chinese and Russian spies, the American Central Intelligence Agency, the British MI-5 and MI-6, and the Hong Kong Criminal Investigation Division.

Always there are exciting action scenes. A minor sequence in *Noble*

House describes Quillan Gornt hurtling down the side of a mountain in a runaway car, the brakes of which have been tampered with. Another scene, a fixed horse race, is in the tradition of a Dick Francis mystery.

Clavell thus combines a series of literary genres and traditions to create a new form: rather than work in a single form, he creates a "blockbuster" of many genres combined, an amalgam that gives breadth and depth to his novels. This multiplicity of genres allows Clavell to explore far more than the story of one man or even one family: he records complex cultural encounters. However, each book is dominated by one pattern more than another, the prison camp pattern taking precedence in *King Rat*, the family and dynasty saga in *Tai-Pan*, the business crisis in *Noble House*, the novel of manners in *Shogun*, the feminist issues in *Gai-Jin*, and revolution and intrigue in *Whirlwind*. By itself, each single pattern would result in a page turner, but to the basic tapestry of each, Clavell adds the threads of many other patterns that weave a subtle, complex, inviting whole: a unique, special blend of East and West.

Clavell is trying to write serious novels in the Burton "culture-clash" mode. His books are all Englishman-abroad stories which also investigate who we Westerners are and what makes our culture unique and valuable. They are also lessons in humility; readers from a youthful culture are invited to share in the wisdom of very ancient cultures, whose citizens have evolved their philosophies and insights over thousands of years. Clavell's novels are not simply histories or romances; instead, they are novels of ideas in which exciting adventure tales invite the readers to share the author's questions about multicultural values, philosophies, and points of view, about the obligations of government, and about what makes for human progress. Behind the multiple genre patterns is a broad overriding political purpose: an assertion that the individual is more important than the family or group, that Western freedoms provide a better life than Eastern restrictions, and that free trade and capitalistic venture better the human condition in ways that socialism and Communism never can.

A FORERUNNER OF MODERN MULTICULTURALISM

Clavell builds on a firm literary tradition, but adds to it two key ideas: first, intercultural contact changes perceptions, and second, these changes have costs.

In his depiction of crossroad encounters between cultures, Clavell paved the way for modern multicultural studies, with their focus on understanding different attitudes toward family, home, and heritage, on tribal conformity versus individualism, on the fences cultures build to define themselves and to separate themselves from others, and on varied attitudes toward the alien, the Other, both within one's own society and in foreign lands. His novels introduce Western readers to the virtues, vices, values, and vantage points of Asians, and vice versa. In doing so, Clavell assumes that experiencing the point of view of other human beings provides valuable insights that affect one's own perceptions. A feature of Clavell's novels at their best is an intentional psychological and perceptual shift that occurs in narrative voice so that readers who have understood the reality of his novels from one perspective find themselves suddenly observing the same reality from a very different perspective. This occurs in *King Rat*, in which the view of the prisoners dominates until a shift at the end which shows them through the eyes of outsiders. It occurs in *Shogun* with a shift from the limited view of Blackthorne to the more informed, complex, and subtle view of Toranaga. Clavell intends readers to undergo similar shifts of perception about other cultures.

However, Clavell's second key point is that everything has a cost. If Asian cultures emphasize family and tribal loyalties, then they take away from individual initiative. If Asians become more individualistic, they loosen the tight family bonds. One can't have both. Paul Choy cannot be both an obedient Chinese son, who grovels before his illiterate father, and a Harvard-educated financial wizard. Seventeenth- and nineteenth-century Japan and twentieth-century Iran can't choose Western technology and, at the same time, shut out the Western philosophical and scientific attitudes that produced that technology. This is the dilemma multiculturalists face, but Clavell's answer is that individual Easterners and Westerners must choose, that in the clash of cultures, ideas and lifestyles battle it out until one takes precedence over the other—for good or for bad. For every gain there is a loss.

Clavell was proud of the achievements of Western technology and Western law, but he also saw advantages in Eastern cultures. He believed deeply in democratic principles and in man's right to peacefully challenge his government and to change laws to keep pace with human intellectual progress, but he understood the pull of a strong leader. He suggests that even the failures of free enterprise are worth the gain in human progress and development. His heroes are doers: entrepreneurs, strong men and women of action, who bear heavy responsibilities but who are not afraid to act. At the same time that he defends with pride the virtues and achievements of the West, he criticizes the ignorance and hypocrisy that have interfered with and limited human achievement. His depictions of China and Japan are equally balanced. He finds in both much to praise, and much that the West could learn from. However, he also finds much that disturbs him in the East: the brutality, the cruelty, the chauvinism, and the arrogant sense of superiority that sometimes afflicts that part of the world in times of crisis. Ultimately, Clavell concludes that contact benefits East and West.

3

King Rat
(1962)

"You said Changi was genesis. What did you mean?"

He sighed, "Changi changed everyone, changed values permanently . . .
it gave you a dullness about death—we saw too much of it to have the same
sort of meaning to outsiders, to normal people. . . . I suppose anyone who
goes to war, any war, sees life with different eyes if they end up in one
piece. . . . What frightens you, doesn't frighten me, what frightens me, you'd
laugh at."

James Clavell, Noble House

Clavell's first novel, *King Rat*, set in 1945, is based on the three years he
spent in the Japanese POW camp at Changi, at the tip of Malaysia, near
Singapore, a haunting experience which shaped his life and philosophy
but which took Clavell over fifteen years to finally speak about. *King Rat*
is a disturbingly realistic portrait of subhuman living conditions, of rats,
cholera, lice, and filth. It grew out of unforgettable personal memories,
events, and character, reshaped into effective fiction.

Overall critical response was enthusiastic. No one could deny the
power of so moving an ordeal. Martin Levin in the *New York Times Book
Review* of 12 August 1962 summed up the general reaction when he said
that Clavell renders "with stunning authority . . . the impersonal, soul-
disintegrating evil of Changi itself."

Figure 3.1
Clavell's Asia

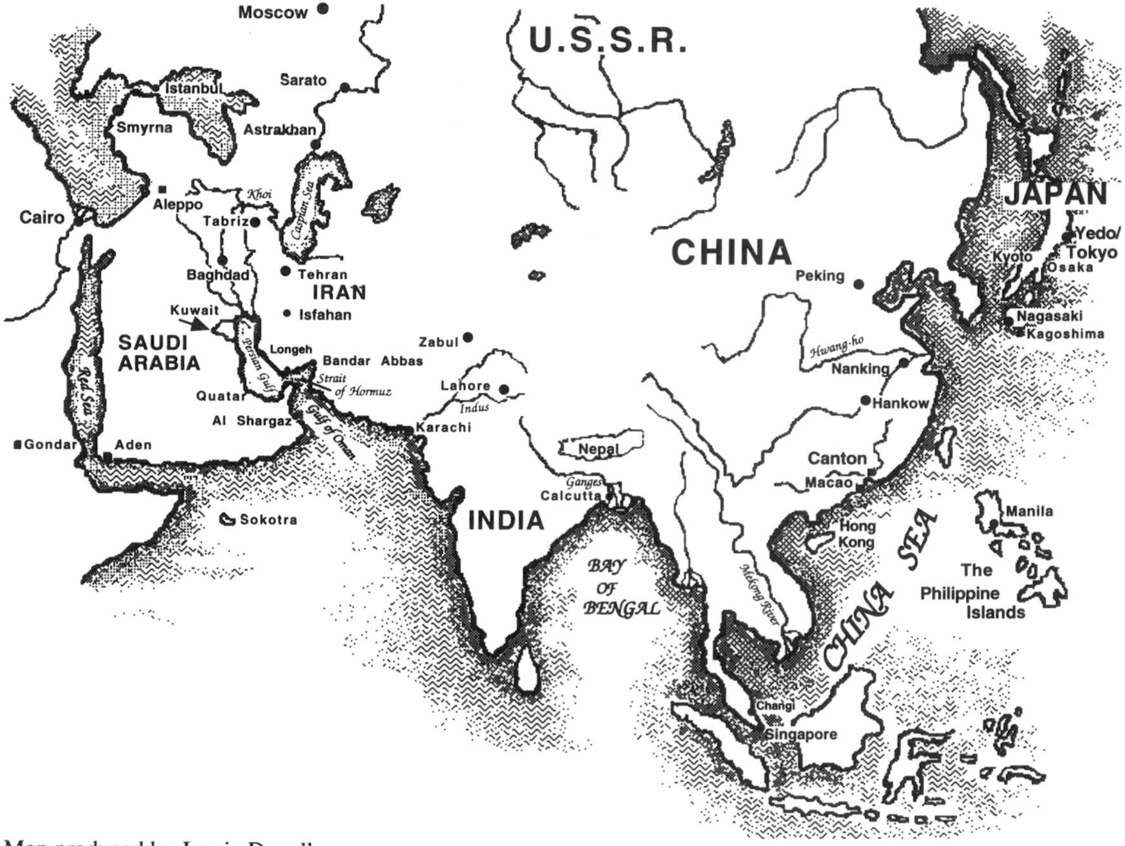

U.S.S.R.

Moscow

Sarato

Astrakhan

Istanbul

Smyrna

Aleppo

Cairo

Gondar

Red Sea

Khoi

Tabriz

Baghdad

Caspian Sea

Tehran

IRAN

Isfahan

Longeh

Bandar Abbas

Strait of Hormuz

Persian Gulf

Gulf of Oman

Kuwait

SAUDI ARABIA

Quatar

Al Shargaz

Aden

Sokotra

Zabul

Lahore

Indus

Karachi

Nepal

Ganges

Calcutta

INDIA

BAY OF BENGAL

CHINA

Peking

Huang ho

Nanking

Hankow

Canton

Macao

Hong Kong

Mekong River

Chungi

Singapore

CHINA SEA

JAPAN

Yedo/Tokyo

Kyoto

Osaka

Nagasaki

Kagoshima

Manila

The Philippine Islands

Map produced by Jeanie Duvall.

PLOT DEVELOPMENT

The story of *King Rat* is simple: the daily routine of a Japanese prisoner-of-war camp, a routine of boredom, disease, gradual starvation, and
death. The third-person omniscient narrative voice notes:

> V-E Day came and the men of Changi were elated. But it was
> just another today and did not actually touch them. The food
> was the same, the sky the same, the heat the same, the sick-
> ness the same, the flies the same, the wasting away the same.
> (*King Rat*: 211)

The prisoners are Americans, Australians, and English, and a few Malaysians and Javanese, all captured in the World War II Pacific theater.
A few are local civilian residents, but most are military personnel, many
young soldiers recently out of basic training. Doctors, clergymen, plan-
tation workers, officers, and enlisted men all live in dehumanizing conditions. The officers' housing is a little better, but even they must adapt
to the brutality of sadistic jailers or die. Basically, the Japanese running
the camp consider the prisoners subhuman because by Japanese codes
of military behavior, they have failed to act with honor: the prisoners
have surrendered rather than fighting to the death or, if captured, committing *hara-kiri*, or ritual suicide.

King Rat chronicles the physical and moral deterioration of men
starved and abused by captors who consider them dishonored barbarians, moral and cultural inferiors. Clavell describes a daily routine of
depersonalized abuse. The prisoners suffer disease and festering
wounds, with Red Cross medication just out of reach. They endure in-
testinal parasites and uncontrollable diarrhea, which creates an inescapable stench, and they do not even have toilet paper. The common pattern
at Changi is a gradual physical decline that comes from an absence of
protein, fruits, and vegetables. Death comes by starvation or by beriberi,
a tropical disease that causes blindness and swells the gonads to the size
of cantaloupes. The men become walking skeletons; they eat maggots,
cockroaches, even rats and an inmate's dog—anything to survive.

Clavell records diverse prisoner reactions to such conditions as fun-
damentally confused POWs, cut off from the familiar and safe, engage
in a Darwinian struggle for food and dominance. Some lose their will to
live and simply roll over and die, others escape into insanity, still others

turn informant, scavenger, or bully and treat their fellow inmates with chicanery and callousness, while an unexpected few rise occasionally to the heroic. In each case, however, motives are mixed, and the heroic or right by normal standards might well be wrong by Changi standards. Old rules don't apply. The seemingly honorable may be dishonorable, given the situation, while the seemingly dishonorable or repugnant might well prolong or even save lives.

At war's end, the arrival of a single Allied soldier, who commands the Japanese prison officials to surrender and who is the first in a wave of liberation helpers to return the dazed men home to normality, initially frightens the prisoners, for in his stunned dismay at their terrible condition the men see for the first time through the eyes of an outsider the nightmare they have endured and the pitiable creatures they have become. Clavell's narrative power is so strong that readers become so absorbed in the reality of Changi that a normal outsider's view is as shocking to them as to the internees. To outsiders, the internees are sideshow freaks, degraded, "worse than animals." The nudity, filth, and public defecation and urination that had been a normal part of their lives make rescuers say that they belong in insane asylums and don't know right from wrong. The prisoner's dream of rescue has become a reality, but the nightmare of a return to normality and to dealing with loved ones and friends after so dreadful an ordeal is upon them, and these survivors' first instinct is to hide, to put off that frightening future.

STRUCTURE

King Rat follows the structure of a medieval morality play: there is a main character, an Everyman, who must decide between two moral positions. He takes center stage, but is pulled by opposing characters, one a "good angel" or good advisor, the other a "devil" or false advisor. Everyman must decide between them, and on his choice rests his future: heaven or hell, blessing or damnation.

In *King Rat*, Peter Marlowe, an aristocratic British Flight Lieutenant, is the Everyman who must choose between two sides. Provost Marshall Lieutenant Robin Grey, a British officer, represents one side; the American corporal, the "King" of the title, the other. Under normal conditions, Marlowe's choice would be clear. The rigid, authoritarian Grey stands for military tradition, rank, honor, integrity, and sharing, virtues that have been instilled in Marlowe since childhood and that he has been taught are always right and always the best choice. In the morality play tradition, Grey would be the good angel. His archrival, the "King," a clever American entrepreneur, would be a devil figure, tempting Marlowe to disobey military regulations, to engage in black-market activities, and to develop a selfish, survivalist code. Many critics interpret the book by this traditional formula and believe that, although Grey is clearly an unlikable human being, ultimately he is on the side of right.

But Changi made Clavell question and then reject the principle of regulated group-good. He begins with a clear-cut moral pattern that provides simple answers and then twists it the way Changi twisted the prisoners. Clavell repeatedly asserts that Changi permanently changed values; *King Rat* records that change. Marlowe, a decent young lad with a strong sense of right, rebels in small ways against Grey's prissy strictures. Warned off by Grey, he nonetheless develops a friendship with the King. The novel records how Marlowe gradually chooses the King's camp, first sharing his food, then offering suggestions for trade, next acting as translator in black-market ventures, and finally joining in the plot to raise rats and serve them to the most despicable of the officers—at cutthroat prices. At the end, with the war over and rescue finally a reality, Marlowe remains the King's friend when everyone else turns on him. This book is Clavell's way of sticking by his American friends and defending the moral lessons he learned in Changi, lessons that those who did not experience Changi might not understand. The novel sets rigid adherence to no-longer-operative past values in opposition to survival, and argues that, amid disease, starvation, torture, and death, survival takes precedence.

CHARACTER DEVELOPMENT

Clavell reveals the personalities, character, and motives of his three key characters (Grey, the King, and Marlowe) through dialogue, interior monologue, and contrasts of behavior, personalities, cultural heritage, values, and philosophies.

Lieutenant Grey is driven by private demons of social and sexual rejection and by personal ambitions: he deserves sympathy but not respect. On the very day he was being shipped off to war, his wife left him for another man. Grey is a toady and a martinet who wants to please his superiors in order to gain commendations and acceptance into the old guard of the military after the war has ended. His every act is with those goals in mind—even his demands for strict adherence to military codes and his passionate opposition to any who challenge that code. Class differences are very important to the English, and they are important to understanding what motivates Grey. He is jealous of Marlowe's aristocratic birthright and accent, for Grey's accent betrays his working-class origins and his overattentive aping of his superiors marks him as an inferior.

His class hatred makes him a willing tool of the Japanese prison guards. Even though Marlowe and the Americans regularly point out that the rules Grey enforces have been put in place by the Japanese guards and that he is, in effect, cooperating with the enemy, he cannot be swayed from his position. He spies on his fellow prisoners and plots to justify the ones he likes least being sent to the notorious Utram Road death camp. Yet he is firmly convinced that he is right and they are wrong, even though what they do benefits their fellow prisoners and what he does injures them. When Grey catches two fellow officers stealing rice with a rigged weight scheme and is bribed out of reporting their theft with the offer of a promotion to captain, it is clear that the supposed voice of right of the morality play structure is corruptible, the voice of a vengeful heart, motivated by anger, jealousy, and spite.

Grey directly opposes the King, the pragmatic American corporal who is determined to survive. George Segal does a fine job of capturing the King's virtues and vices in the movie version of this book. In some ways, the King is despicable and initially seems like the villain of the morality play. Whereas the other POWs are skin and bone, emaciated creatures (like those seen in pictures of Nazi concentration camps), the King is well fed and healthy. Through cunning, he has maintained a normal food intake. Whereas the other POWs wear rags, loincloths, or make-shift sarongs, or are simply naked, the King always wears a freshly pressed uniform. Most go barefoot, but the King wears shoes shined by other men. At the end of the novel, when the concentration camp is liberated, the King's health and vigor, cleanliness, and dress set him apart and, in the eyes of the rescuers, mark him initially as "normal": "Only the King ate like a man, smoked like a man, slept like a man, dreamed like a man and looked like a man" (10). However, as the outsiders see the appalling, skeletal condition of the other men, their bodies nearly nude, ulcerated, and diseased, they see the King as victimizer rather than victim, one whose activities should be investigated and whose survival should be questioned. The men who had depended on him for their own survival turn on him at the end, and their silence is condemnation.

Nonetheless, there is much to like in the King, and both Marlowe and
Clavell pay tribute to him. We don't find out much about him personally,
except that he has had an unhappy childhood, an indifferent father, no
friends, no remaining family, only a tough, survivalist life. In spite of,
or perhaps because of, this background, the King becomes representative
of the American self-made man, classless, democratic, possessed of Yankee ingenuity. Where others have resigned themselves to death, the King
has found a way not simply to survive but to thrive. British officers reject
"doing business" as the mark of class inferiority, but the King, an American, sees trade as the way of the world. He sees opportunities where
others see despair. Clavell takes us into his thoughts as the King engages
in his wheeler-dealer bargaining, and we see a subtle, clever mind at
work. He is a hard-nosed businessman but also a diplomat with an understanding of how to help defeated opponents save face. His black-
market salesmanship to Korean guards, local Javanese, and other
prisoners is a highly crafted but practical art, and through it, he creates
his own economic kingdom of buying, bartering, and bargaining.

The King brings profit to those around him. The American contingent
is much healthier physically and psychologically than the British, thanks
to the King. The men who serve him have more and better food than
other prisoners do. For looking the other way or for actively preventing
interference in the King's activities, those who serve him receive extra
rations. In one case, the top ranking British officer keeps Grey engaged
in conversation so the King and Marlowe can slip out of camp, and eats
better that night for doing so. The King provides a market for the wealth
of the camp (watches, rings, radio parts, and so forth) that would otherwise not exist. He uses his income from acting as a go-between in
exchanges to bring in beans and meat from villagers and to increase the
number of laying hens, and he uses his network of sources to free up
supplies the Japanese have stockpiled but not made available for POW
use (like the medications that save Marlowe). What men like Marlowe
dismiss as insignificant, the King sees as opportunity. Take, for instance,
Marlowe's method for treating cheap, raw tobacco to make it taste like
a high-quality brand. Marlowe sees the process as something to share
with a few friends, but the King immediately recognizes its trade potential and wants to buy rights to the recipe. Marlowe says the process isn't
his to sell, but shares it with the King as a friend. The King markets it
wholesale and sells it throughout the camp until the secret leaks out and
everyone makes his own. Thus the King's action raises spirits, creates a
healthy sense of competition, and spreads around useful information that

might otherwise have gone to waste. In other words, while he does not
intend to be a benefactor, in effect, he is one. Clavell contrasts the frowns
and long faces that follow Grey's progression through the camp with the
smiles of those under the King's protection. "I've never seen so many
smiles in one hut before," says an impressed Marlowe (45). The King is
the prototype of Dirk Struan in *Tai-Pan* and Ian Dunross in *Noble House*
and *Whirlwind*.

Marlowe is decent and honorable. At home in the highly courteous
Malay language, he shares a closeness with the imprisoned Malaysians
that no other prisoner does. He forms a survival triad with two companions (one forages, one guards what has been foraged, and one sub-
stitutes when either forager or guard is unable to act) and loyally shares
what he has, even the King's largess. More importantly, he and his two
companions have, at great personal cost, carried with them, hidden in
their water bottles, the parts of a radio that, at the end of the book, allows
contact with the outside world and brings hope to all the prisoners. Marlowe's altruism makes his decision between Grey and the King pivotal.
Heritage and schooling should sway him toward Grey's position, but his
Asian experiences and his common-sense reasoning that opposing the
enemy and surviving can't be wrong make him judge the King's actions
on the basis of their overall effects. Though put off by the American's
directness, he appreciates his accepting a man for his own worth. "They
think that one man's as good as another," he says with wonder about
Americans in general (339). Slow to make friends, Marlowe finds the
King surprisingly likable and open. The less trusting King suspects ulterior motives, but Marlowe is true, honest, and aboveboard in his
friendship. He gives willingly and is slow to take. Though ridden by
guilt at engaging in trade, he recognizes its necessity. A disillusioned
idealist, he finds in the King hope for survival, not just for himself, but
for the many. At the end, when all have turned against the King, Marlowe waits patiently to thank him for saving his arm and "for the laughter they had had together," though the King only salutes and replies
with a surly "Sir" (337).

Peace brings rescuers whose horrified stares make the skeletal survivors fearful of discarding the insanity of their animal existence: as insane
animals they can't be blamed for their behavior. It also brings a sudden
return to old codes and old moralities. The King is reduced to a beggar,
an ordinary corporal of questionable breeding. Inwardly, he screams,
"what've I done that's so wrong?" (337). He has fed them and helped
them, and now they look at him as though he's not there any more. Our

last image of him is of a sweaty, unshaven, isolated figure, in the back of a truck, despised by his fellows: a lost, faceless nobody, bewildered by fortune's reversals.

Grey gloats that he himself has survived without selling his soul. But Marlowe is not convinced. He asks if it is wrong to adapt, wrong to survive, and wonders what he would have done had he been Grey or what Grey would have done if he had been Marlowe. Finally, he asks the question Clavell himself poses through the novel: "What is good and what is evil?" (351). When Grey contemptuously debunks the King, Marlowe slams his fist into Grey's face and knocks him backward. He alone defends the King's honor, asserting that he changed men, he changed Marlowe, and he taught the camp that "a man's a man, irrespective of background" (350). Marlowe's final defense of the King to Grey is unanswerable: the King prolonged life—"The point is we're both very much alive" (350).

THEMATIC ISSUES

King Rat reflects the thematic interests that dominate Clavell's fiction: (1) human sexuality; (2) father-son relationships; (3) the thrill of danger and risk taking; (4) the impenetrability of Asians; (5) cultural differences; (6) clerical hypocrisy; (7) class hatred; and (8) the value of capitalism over socialism and a sense of the capitalistic entrepreneur-adventurer as hero, in opposition to the rule-bound, authority-oriented supporter of group-think. The first two themes might seem to have no place in a story about prisoners of war. However, memories are the spiritual food that help men find motivation to endure, and memories of family and home give prisoners hope or plunge them into despair.

Human Sexuality

Clavell contrasts what he sees as Western sexual repression with Eastern pragmatism. Part of the psychological explanation for Lieutenant Robin Grey's hate-driven behavior was a bad marriage to a spoiled, narrow-minded woman who played hard to get until he married her and who, even when her husband discovered she was not a virgin, continued to tease him sexually and then to withhold sex. Continually frustrated, Grey grew bitter. His last memory of his wife was of her walking out on him the day he flew off to war. Yet Grey blames his sexual needs for her aversion; "It wasn't Trina's fault," thinks Grey, "weak with self-disgust" (116). Other prisoners have doubts and worries about their wives and lovers—wondering about their fidelity, fearing for their safety, projecting on them their fears and hopes, but Clavell uses Grey's wife as the representation of what goes wrong with Western male-female relationships: sex as a weapon in a battle between the sexes. He contrasts this destructive pattern with the Asian matter-of-factness about sexual needs Marlowe experiences.

Marlowe's experiences are with a woman in a Javanese village where he was hiding from the Japanese and later another in a village where he and the King engage in black marketeering. The chieftain of the first village gave his own fourteen-year-old daughter, Na', to Marlowe to be his sexual partner during his stay in the village. The Javanese believed that a healthy sexual relationship was good for young people and would make the young girl happier with marriage later. Marlowe's sexual ex-perience with Na' was liberating. Marlowe's dreams of Na' later help him cope with the nightmare of prison camp. When he joins the King on a secret trade mission to a nearby village, he and the sixteen-year-old daughter of the village chieftain with whom they are dealing are mu-tually attracted. She is alluring, and, despite his weakened condition from limited food and illness, Marlowe finds himself drawn to her be-cause of his positive memories of Na', whom this girl resembles. He bathes naked in the sea, and she joins him. Corporal King's appearance on the scene prevents any sexual activity, but the desire remains—in marked contrast to Grey's twisted frustrations.

The question of prison camp homosexuality clearly disturbed Clavell. His spokesman, Marlowe, is initially stunned and repulsed that Sean, a close friend and fellow flyer from his squadron, a man whose bravery in the face of battle is undeniable, becomes a transvestite who not only dresses as a female for the camp dramatic productions but continues that role offstage. Men fall in love with him and flirt with him, and he, in effect, becomes a female. Although he had never had homosexual ten-dencies before, in the camp he comes to think of himself as "she" and those around him do too. Many admit that his new role makes life worth living. At the end, of course, when normality returns, the men who had once courted him reject him with all the derogatory words used for ho-mosexuals: "Pansy!", "Bugger!", "Rotten fairy!", and "Homo!", they shout, as Sean strides into the "welcoming" sea and chooses death rather than a lifetime of derision (344). Marlowe's explanation is not clearly worked out, but he finds a partial answer in the Asian concept of yang and yin as necessary opposing natural qualities of hard and soft, of aggressive and passive. The absence of women creates a natural imbalance, yang without yin, and Marlowe concludes that an instinctual drive for balance results in males assuming the "yin" role.

Father-Son Relationships

Another theme is the basic family pattern of a father imposing his principles on his son, who then modifies them based on personal experience. Marlowe's father, like his father before him, was a career military officer who dedicated his life to the service. He instilled in his son high standards of honor, honesty, integrity, service, and the value of understatement and of keeping a stiff upper lip in the face of trouble. He taught his son to downplay acts of courage or of heroism and to do his duty quietly without complaint. Part of his father's attitude included a condescending view of trade or business. Marlowe initially tells his friends that he could not possibly go into business: "Marlowes aren't tradesmen. . . . It's just not done, old boy" (57). Marlowe also believes that an Englishman should be proud to be "killed for the flag" (134); his risking his life to maintain outside radio contact proves that this was a lesson he had taken to heart.

Nevertheless, in the novel, moral lines become indistinct. Marlowe's father's idealism is at odds with the subhuman prison camp conditions, and survival sometimes requires departure from old codes. Military regulations become defeatist when they enforce the enemy's bidding. A stiff upper lip, in effect, signals passive acceptance of appalling conditions. A meticulous sharing of scant rations without grumbling seems to be proper behavior, but Marlowe begins to understand that the career officers who enforce sharing cheat on their own rations and that black-market rations mean that not everyone will die.

As the old moral order breaks up and Marlowe begins to question his father's code, the King becomes a counter–father figure. He likes Marlowe personally, but sees him as an innocent youth who needs to have his eyes opened. The King teaches Marlowe a new code of survival, which is exemplified by the following comments: you have "to have tools to do a job right," "the more time you plan before a deal, the better it is," "buy for a little and sell for more," "with money all things are possible," "a man's got to help his friends or there's no point in any-

thing," you have "to gamble in this life," you have "to look out for
number one" since "no one else does," and "business is business" (153–
54, 134, 78). The King believes in Darwinian adaption to changing circumstances and conditions. His is an American code and a working-class
code. Behind the high-sounding British moral talk of sharing and bearing
up, he sees a nasty reality: the position and privilege of the top ranking
British officers and clergymen assure them better conditions and more
food than the rank and file receive. In spite of the Japanese, the British
class war continues.

In contrast, the King is up front about his black-market profiteering;
he flaunts his better lifestyle and the higher quality and quantity of his
food. However, at the same time, he does what a good soldier should
do, defy the enemy. He also feeds and cares for those under his shelter-
ing umbrella, going to great trouble to get Marlowe the medicine he
needs to save his arm from gangrene. His self-interest promotes group
interests. Caught between competing moral systems, Marlowe feels "un-
clean" and guilty. After he has shared a mouthwatering meal of dog
meat, he feels revulsion. He feels cannibalistic for having eaten a camp
favorite. He understands that his every act involves moral choices and
moral dilemmas. "My God, what a state we've come to," he groans:
"Everything that seems wrong is right, and vice versa. . . . It's too much
to understand. Much too much. Stupid screwed-up world" (241). Yet
Marlowe does not totally give up his father's code. His instincts are still
to sacrifice personal for group needs, but he understands that the King's
code has guaranteed a higher survival rate than otherwise would be
possible, even if only because of the men's consuming hatred for him. If
morality is measured by results, the King's morality, for the time and
the conditions, worked for the greater good.

Risk-Taking

A minor theme related to Clavell's delineation of character is that the
young and the brave are thrilled by challenge, danger, and risk. Marlowe
remembers the pure joy of flying his Spitfire, a World War II single-
engine British plane noted for its power and endurance. He and others
in camp have performed honorably in battle, never thinking of risk, only
of the sheer joy of challenging fate. In fact, Clavell contrasts the simplic-
ity of facing physical challenges with the complexity of facing moral
challenges. Disturbing moral choices make Marlowe wish he were soar-

ing the sky alone in his Spitfire, "where all is clean and pure" and "where life is simple" (136). Like flying, forbidden acts keep life interesting. Marlowe sneaks out of camp and almost gets caught by the Japanese, then sneaks back under the wire and almost runs into Grey, who is desperate to catch him. Marlowe and the King agree that defying authority is "a lot of fun" and that danger stirs the blood and makes one feel like a man (40). Marlowe also risks death because of the hidden radio since getting caught with it means transfer to a death camp. Outsmarting the Korean and Japanese guards and the British camp overseers is a further challenge. In fact, Marlowe's friendship with the King is, in part, stubborn defiance of meaningless rules and acceptance of the challenge of dangerous risks.

Contrasting Asian Cultures

With *King Rat*, Clavell begins his full-length treatment of Anglo-Asian contact. The portrait of the cocky young Marlowe, dressed in a native sarong, fluent in Malaysian, and knowledgeable about Asian forms of politeness in address and in social interaction, sums up Clavell's ideal image of West meets East. Marlowe calls attention to the direct, fast-paced, business-like approach that the King wants to take with the Javanese villagers and the slower, polite patterns of Asian custom, patterns in which friendly personal questions are exchanged, family and weather discussed, and food and drink shared before business can be mentioned. When Malay is spoken, Clavell employs a stilted diction that attempts to render into English syntax the nuances, rhythms, and polite circumlocutions of the Malay language.

Drawing on his war years, Clavell describes the Japanese as cruel, barbaric, ruthless, and sadistic, breaking all the Geneva conventions for treatment of prisoners and systematically torturing prisoners. The deaths the Changi POWs suffered were slow and dehumanizing, and thus worse than the German mass gassings and ovens; at least those deaths were fast. Clavell records bizarre patterns of behavior and swift shifts of mood that make the Japanese guards seem adolescent or even insane by Western standards. For example, one Japanese guard expressed deep affection for his dog and her puppies and cared tenderly for them, but once, angered at a puppy's misbehavior, swung that pup on a leash round and round his head, snapping its neck and choking it to death. Afterwards, he shed tears of remorse. The same soldiers who withheld vital Red Cross supplies and medicines and starved prisoners would pay homage to those prisoners who died honorably at their hands. *King Rat* records the strange combination of dignity and honor, cruelty and childishness Clavell witnessed at Changi.

Clavell's description reflects an understanding of the militaristic dark side of Japanese society that remains unreconstructed by defeat in World War II, the occupation years, and modern democracy. Some modern Japanese intellectuals like Naoki Inose, an historian and media critic, agree: "Many Japanese lack any sense of responsibility for the war and view themselves mainly as victims rather than aggressors" (Yamaguchi, 94). This theory of victimization by Western oppressors, while perhaps defensible in the long and broad view of contact between East and West, is diametrically opposed to the Western understanding of World War II.

Asian indifference to life, the cultural tolerance of cruelty and sadism, the isolationism and distrust of outsiders, and the loyalty to the group rather than to individuals remain themes throughout Clavell's canon.

Contrasting Western Cultures

An interesting section in the opening of the novel emphasizes the ways in which Australians, Englishmen, and Americans can seem superficially alike and yet be totally different. They seem to speak the same language, but the nuances, subtleties, and linguistic cues of that language differ greatly. The British style is more cryptic and indirect than the American, so that voices that seem quite calm and "only a trifle irritated to American ears" are really making a declaration of war. The length of a pause can be a slap in the face between Englishmen, and a quiet and casual "not bad" can be the highest praise. When the King fries Marlowe a tasty egg, a rare and valuable treat, Marlowe pays him "the greatest compliment in the English world" in a carefully contained, flat voice: "Not bad" (33). The impassivity of his voice, by British standards, heightens the compliment. The King is furious and thinks he and his offering of friendship are being insulted. Marlowe is later forced to explain that "not bad" means "exceptional" and is a way of paying a compliment without embarrassing the receiver of the compliment. The King concludes foreigners are decidedly peculiar. The King finds the English underplay hypocritical; Marlowe finds the King's directness embarrassing. The King wants to move immediately to a Christian name basis and calls Marlowe "Pete"; Marlowe is surprised, for among the

English, only trusted friends share Christian names. The Englishman respects privacy and asks no questions; the American is full of questions, many of a personal nature. The linguistic differences represent allegiance to very different codes and sets of values, a different sense of social interaction, and very different friendship-formation patterns.

Anti-Clerical Attacks

Clavell's stance is decidedly anti-clerical throughout his canon. *King Rat* provides clues as to why. Clavell contrasts a self-sacrificing doctor with a hypocritical clergyman. The doctor recognizes the futility of working with only a scalpel and boiled water. His comments are cynical and gruff, but his acts are kindly. He does his best to help the sick and the dying, giving up a portion of his own rations and even bits of his own clothing—complaining all the while. The clergyman, on the other hand, talks piously and admonishes others for their unrighteous behavior while secretly committing deplorable acts. Because of the danger of beriberi, the doctor makes sure that camp suppliers distribute one egg a week to each prisoner. Without that protein, they would go blind. The clergyman repeatedly talks his batmen (military servants) out of their weekly egg, convincing them that donating it is a religious act and giving them his blessing for their contribution. All the while, he knows that they will get beriberi and go blind. They do, and he doesn't care. A clergyman who could so selfishly use his calling to injure those who trust him represents for Clavell the greatest evil he saw at Changi. Given this shaping experience, it is no wonder that each of his books has at least one negative portrait of a religious hypocrite.

Class Conflicts and Class Hatreds

Marlowe admires the American freedom from the class conflicts and class hatreds that separate Englishmen. The King has working-class origins; his father is a salesman. His rank is only that of a corporal, but his ingenuity and strength give him temporary power. However, the moment he is no longer needed, the British, in particular, are venomous in their rejection of him because of their class consciousness.

Part of the contrast between Marlowe and Grey is clearly one of class. Marlowe is unquestionably an aristocrat; Grey is not. Marlowe moves in

the elite circles that Grey longs to be a part of but never can join. The
result is Grey's deep hatred of Marlowe and his determination to trap
Marlowe and destroy him. Grey's fellow officers, in turn, use Grey, but
consider him very much not a part of their circle, for Grey has come up
the ranks but can never rise high enough to be accepted. Despised, he
despises in turn.

Free Enterprise versus Socialism

The major theme of *King Rat* is that capitalism promotes strength that
supports the weak, while socialism encourages weakness and passivity
that injure everyone. Clavell makes this point through contrasting characters: Marlowe versus Grey, the King versus Grey, and Marlowe versus
the King. Marlowe defends the capitalistic entrepreneur-adventurer, the
King, as hero, in opposition to the rule-bound, authority-oriented supporter of group-think, Lieutenant Grey. Thus Changi becomes a battle-
ground of political philosophies and economic ideologies.

Overall, Clavell's argument is that passive acceptance of the status
quo, of starvation food rations, and of daily attacks of dysentery as normal was wrong. It led to needless deaths. The obsessive enforcement of
an equal sharing of outside resources resulted in insufficient individual
benefit to generate the extra effort necessary to acquire more outside
resources. That is, having hard-gained food shared out in such negligible
proportions promoted apathy, a loss of will, despair, and inaction. Without competition, the situation remained a "zero sum," with no new resources created, only scarce ones subdivided meaninglessly.

In contrast, the King provided men with hope, with the possibility
that they could individually overcome the odds. He inspired activity and
action in the face of apathy, decline, and death. He did not steal the
portions of other men; the officers and clergymen did. Basically, Clavell
advances a trickle-down theory of economics. The King inspired those
with gumption to generate an economic flow based on valuables that
would tempt the guards and local villagers to break the rules out of their
own self-interest and that would thereby bring in a steady flow of food
and medicine that would otherwise be nonexistent. These goods would
be shared by those engaged in the plotting or else sold in camp to generate more funds to continue the flow. As a result, some benefited while
others did not. However, this very inequality spurred the passive to consider ways to generate wealth to exchange for food.

If not for the King's black marketeering, Marlowe would have died of gangrene. Instead, the King and his men, out of self-interest, used ingenuity and bribery to get needed medical supplies that would otherwise have been unavailable. In a like manner, the King's bargaining with local villagers for special food purchases brought in protein sources that benefited many. Without such black marketeering, there would have been no protein, except for insects. The plan to breed rats, an "Oriental delicacy" to be sold to Japanese guards and senior Allied officers, was a product of Yankee ingenuity and Yankee humor. If carried out for a long period of time, the breeding plan could have produced valuable protein. Once the King introduced a way of obtaining goods or a supply source, others would imitate his methods and he would need to invent a new pattern. He thus established models of economic opportunism that inspired prisoners to work to survive.

Clavell argues that free enterprise inspires competition and hope that keep men from dying, while socialistic sharing results in apathy, passivity, acceptance, resignation, and death. Grey and the system he defends are thus wrong, and the King and the system he represents are right. Changi made Clavell a staunch defender of capitalism over socialism or Communism. This attitude toward the competing philosophies of capitalism and socialism/Communism is the cornerstone of the rest of his novels.

GENRE CONVENTIONS

King Rat avoids the conventions of many prison camp films and books that show war as heroic, matching wits with prison guards as fun, and escape as feasible. *King Rat* is no *Great Escape* or *Stalag 17*. In Changi, men die from disease and hunger; matching wits with prison guards is a matter of survival; escape from the immediate prison enclosure is possible, but there is only jungle outside the camp—and enemy soldiers and suspicious locals—so escape is futile. Instead, *King Rat* is more like stories of the Nazi concentration camps or the Soviet gulag, the Siberian prison system, described by Aleksandr Soltzhenitsyn in *A Day in the Life of Ivan Denisovich* and *The Gulag Archipelago*.

Like Ken Kesey's *One Flew Over the Cuckoo's Nest* or Joseph Heller's *Catch-22*, *King Rat* builds on the medieval *topos* (common theme) of the world turned upside down. Insanity has become normal; normality is unknown. The POWs, of necessity, have come to accept their plight as

normal and have adapted to its insanity, so that when the real world
intrudes, they run away and hide from their rescuers, who seem oversized, overnourished, overdressed—like some alien species examining
them with disgust.

Another traditional approach Clavell relies on is the delineation of a
microcosm, or miniature world, to suggest a macrocosm, the world at
large. In this case, the microcosm of the POW camp becomes a working
out of the opposition of capitalism and socialism, with the truths learned
in their confrontation indicative of larger patterns at work worldwide.

ALTERNATIVE READINGS

King Rat can also be read as a Darwinian experiment in survival of
the fittest. Only the strong survive. Strength is measured in biological
terms; the young, the healthy, and the fit have a better survival rate than
the old, the diseased, and the out-of-shape. Strength is measured in psychological and emotional terms: men must have the will to survive, the
active determination to endure; the apathetic crumple and waste away.
Strength is measured by intellect: the clever, the ingenious, those capable
of finding alternative food sources and of manipulating the situation to
their ends survive. The slow and dull starve. The most competitive rise
to the top; the least competitive sink to the bottom and are crushed by
their fellows or by their own weakness. Clavell makes this Darwinian
interpretation inescapable through his title, *King Rat*; through the description of the human "rats," the greediest and most selfish of whom
pay a high price for the privilege of eating real rats; and through his
final description of a battle between rats that is clearly meant to represent
the events of the novel. Like the POWs, the rats are locked in their cages
and forgotten by their captors. Like the POWs, their food is limited, and
the weak and crippled die quickly. Like the human King who finds a
way outside the camp to find local food sources, the rat king patiently
attacks his cage until he breaks down the barriers and reaches a new
food supply—in yet another cage. The living feed on the dead, and the
strong fight among themselves and forage. When the rat king finally
loses his will to dominate, a stronger rat takes his place and rules, "not
by strength alone," but by "cunning and luck and strength together."
This final Darwinian image suggests Clavell's own mixed feelings about
events in camp—both a pride and a shame in survival, a sense of being
reduced to the animalistic, but also of having survived through capital-

istic ingenuity, luck, and strength. Clavell praises adaptation and versatility as necessary for survival, but believes the best man is the one who can endure without totally losing his humanity.

Modern readers might also see in *King Rat* a psychological and sociological study of the effects of stress on isolated groups. The "Stockholm syndrome" and Holocaust syndrome of prisoners under stress identifying with their captors explain the psychology of the camp spy who regularly feeds secret information about camp activities to the Japanese. It also explains the peculiar behavior of Grey and his fellows who police the camp for the Japanese. In fact, author Gavan Daws, in his carefully researched book *Prisoners of the Japanese: POWs of World War II in the Pacific* (1994) confirms the factual basis of such behavior, noting that the British took responsibility for POW administration and the Japanese stayed outside the fence at Changi while the British officers did their dirty work, punishing soldiers who broke Japanese regulations and actually sending some of them to isolation holes. Daws's description of the real British officers sounds just like Clavell's fictive one:

> They went strutting around with swagger sticks, demanding military courtesy and formal salutes. They even had their own men doing pack drill for punishment. . . . The British officers treated their own enlisted men like dirt, and in their loftiness they assumed they could treat Americans the same way—they called the transit groups coming in from the Indies *Java rabble*. The Australian enlisted men had no time for British officers. . . . At Changi everyone was a double prisoner, of the British as well as the Japanese. (Daws 1994: 175)

Psychological studies of Holocaust victims like that conducted by Bruno Bettelheim and reported on by him in the article "Individual and Group Behavior in Extreme Situations," published in the *Journal of Abnormal Psychology* in 1943, confirm the reality of this prisoner-master identification and provide further insights into the behavior of the men Clavell describes, and into the feelings of guilt experienced by the survivors. After enduring hell, men like Marlowe find freedom a mixed blessing. They suffer from what is now known as posttraumatic stress syndrome. They are happy to be alive, but blame themselves for having been captured, for not having contributed more to the war effort by fighting, for enduring what others could not, and for surviving while comrades perished.

Another interesting area of investigation is the historical base on which Clavell builds. Daws's book on Japanese POW camps confirms the reality of Clavell's portrait. Parallels include the competing nationalistic divisions in the camp, the educational classes in a variety of languages and academic subjects, the importance of mental games to keep minds active and functioning, the popularity of gambling and games of chance, and the competition for work duty near coconut groves. Perhaps the common British cry to Americans who raided Changi coconuts while on work details, "You can't do that! Those are the King's coconuts!", inspired Clavell to name his Corporal "King" as a satiric insider's mocking of British arrogance about Royal prerogatives. Moreover, a photo of a back view of an American corporal who was an infamous black marketeer at Changi, his well-padded body evidence that he ate better food than his fellows, is included in Daws's account.

Daws also explains the high status of female impersonators, many of whom were not homosexuals, and the general pleasure all the prisoners took in their convincing performances. Daws describes hand-built radio receivers sealed into the bottom halves of canteens, the top halves of which were full of water, like the one Marlowe and his friends carry around, and the tortures that would follow if a prisoner were caught with one. A British dog, a company mascot, was eaten by American soldiers, and many engaged in trade with guards, selling fake Parker pens and fake Omega and Rolex watches with fake trademarks made in camp. Returning POWs cite tales of Japanese soldiers hitting prisoners on the head with sledgehammers, injecting the sick with chloroform for the pleasure of watching them die in convulsions, and crucifying others or throwing them in deep holes and leaving them there or setting them on fire (Daws 1994: 221). The testimony of survivors and the records made by prisoners and by the Allied soldiers who liberated them confirm Clavell's "fiction" down to the last detail, such as the latrine borehole as a center of rumor and as a place of execution for traitors.

CONCLUSION

King Rat is Clavell's shortest novel but also his most powerful. It should make readers understand the plight of the Changi POWs and appreciate their survival tactics. *Christian Science Monitor* critic R. R. Bruun wrote that *King Rat* might have been a "minor classic" if Clavell had been willing to reveal himself more fully (Bruun 1962), not understanding that though Marlowe, Clavell does bare his soul—as much as a former British soldier and a guilt-ridden survivor could. His book is a personal confession of moral confusion and self-doubt, but it is also a tribute to the ability of human beings to endure.

Figure 3.2
Genealogy

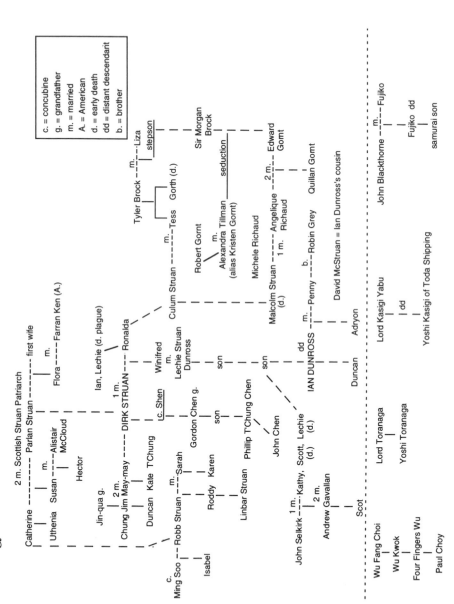

4

Tai-Pan: A Novel of Hong Kong
(1966)

*Since China is the largest unitary mass of humanity, with the oldest con-
tinuous history, its overrunning by the West in the past century was bound
to create a continuing and violent intellectual revolution, the end of which
we have not yet seen . . . the old order was challenged, attacked, undermined,
or overwhelmed by a complex series of processes—political, economic, social,
ideological, cultural—set in motion within China as a result of this pene-
tration of an alien and more powerful society.*
      Ssu-yü Teng and John K. Fairbank, *China's Response to the West*

Tai-Pan (1966), a fast-paced novel of East-West contact and conflict in the
1840s, begins an interlocking series (*Tai-Pan, Gai-Jin, Noble House, Whirlwind*) tracing the fortunes of the fictional Noble House, a business dynasty founded in Hong Kong, extended to Japan, and eventually turned
international. *Tai-Pan*, which was on the best-seller list for forty-four
weeks, sold over two million copies between 1966 and 1986 and was
made into a motion picture in 1986. *New York Times* critic Orville Prescott
praised *Tai-Pan*'s "compelling force" and "unceasing narrative drive,"
its "theatrical gusto," "unflagging ingenuity," freshness, vigor, and "unexpected twists of plot" (Prescott 1966). *Tai-Pan* established an interest
in business, politics, and social-cultural interaction that Clavell pursued
throughout his fiction. A history of early capitalism at its most exploit-

ative, but also its most daring and admirable, *Tai-Pan* glorifies the China traders' business acumen.

PLOT DEVELOPMENT

Tai-Pan unfolds chronologically, moving from crisis to crisis. It begins with problems experienced by Europeans in Canton and Macao and traces step-by-step the establishment of Hong Kong, the political twists and turns that threatened its permanence, and the typhoon that destroyed its buildings but proved its value as a port. It also begins with the dreams and strategies of Dirk Struan, his love affair with a Chinese concubine, May-may, whom he secretly marries, and his conflict with the rival Brocks (Tyler and son, Gorth). It traces Struan's attempts to secure Hong Kong and to build a dynasty. At the same time, it reveals his strategy to bring his English son, Culum, to manhood and to prepare him for his future role as *tai-pan* as well as to launch his Chinese son, Gordon Chen, into cross-cultural enterprises that will link Chinese and British. The plot moves back and forth among three scheming groups— the Struans, the Brocks, and the Chens—with young Culum Struan and Tess Brock torn between feuding families and manipulated to advantage in the strategies of each. While Tyler Brock plans a financial attack on the Struans and Gorth Brock schemes to infect Culum Struan with venereal disease to end his romance with Tess Brock, Dirk Struan strives to protect his son, his family, his colony, and his future descendants from the whims of fate and from mistakes born of ignorance or a failure of daring. The unexpected death of Dirk Struan and May-may amid the violence of a terrifying typhoon leaves the Noble House of Struan as vulnerable as the newly founded Hong Kong colony. However, the concluding action suggests that Culum Struan, despite his youth and self-doubt, has learned his lessons well and, with the firm support of Tess, will indeed try to fulfill his father's dreams. As the individual thrives, so does the group, and the future of Hong Kong looks bright at the end, despite its physical destruction.

THEMATIC ISSUES

Clavell's themes in *Tai-Pan* are as multifaceted as his book, but four dominate: 1) the determination, gamesmanship, and wit that are necessary to establish a colony that will endure; 2) fascination with China; 3) the threat of China; and 4) the importance of crossroads where alien cultures can meet and learn from each other to mutual benefit—with mutual benefit a dominant theme.

Typically, Clavell focuses on a key period of shifting power in East-West relations. *Tai-Pan* begins with the end of an era, a power shift from Macao, where the Portuguese had established a trade center in the sixteenth century, to the newly established, British-dominated Hong Kong. Clavell's focus, however, is not on the end but on the beginning. *Tai-Pan* answers two key questions voiced by its hero: "How do you build a colony?" and "Why is China so fascinating?"

Building a Colony

The novel answers the first question by tracing the building of the Hong Kong colony from the bare rock up and the creation of individual business dynasties, both Chinese and Western. The secret of success in such endeavors, according to Clavell, is a combination of drive, endurance, clever manipulation, competition, and the ability to turn personal peril to public advantage and "to play the Oriental game by Oriental rules" (*Tai-Pan*: 90). Dirk Struan and his rival China traders exemplify the strength of will required for success. Struan is like a sturdy British oak standing the test of time through foul weather. His push to include in the treaty with China a small proviso ceding the island on which Hong Kong is built and his rush to construct buildings rapidly to confirm title are masterstrokes of diplomacy and farsightedness that lay the foundation on which others could build. Furthermore, the early founders of Hong Kong turn ill fortune to their favor. For instance, attacks of malaria lead to the discovery of quinine and a whole new international business shipping cinchona bark (the source of quinine) from South America to Asia. Attacks by armed *tong* gangs justify stronger demands on the Mandarin, the ruler of China. In like manner, careful journalistic coverage turns a typhoon which flattens much of Hong Kong into convincing evidence of Hong Kong's value as a natural harbor in which the British fleet can safely weather any storm. Dirk Struan calls Hong Kong "the key to China," an "island fortress" whose position appeals to an instinctual British sense that a home base should be like England. For Clavell, the founding of Hong Kong illustrates the genius, strength, and farsightedness of the Englishman abroad, and, in particular, of the British sailor-merchant abroad.

China's Appeal

As Clavell's characters struggle for a foothold in China, they illustrate China's appeal to Westerners. To traders like Brock and Struan, China offers the chance to gamble for a fortune in saleable goods, to open China to Western influence, and to found financial dynasties. To government officials far from home, it offers an opportunity to acquire a reputation and a better post back home. The religious can take Christianity to the heathen, test religious values, and perhaps achieve martyrdom. To women like Mary Sinclair and men like Dirk Struan, China offers escape from Victorian sexual hypocrisies to exotic pleasures. To wayward sons of good families, like Richard Cross, it offers a chance to redeem their character and regain their social status. The lawless can find freedom from civilized restraints in pirating and smuggling. To British seamen, China offers a large, reliable port that Hong Kong resident Lo Hsiang-lin calls "a sentinel" (3), guarding not only the entrance to the bay but the entrance to China. To the culturally aware, China offers an ancient heritage from which Westerners can learn about everything from cuisine and art to medicine, business strategy, family loyalty, and time. China thus offers Westerners the potential for change, advancement, escape, and profit.

Contact with the West, argues Clavell, offers China Western technology through trade that increases wealth, betters lives, and provides outlets for the potentially rebellious. Westerners and Easterners alike can escape some of the restrictions of their breeding in Hong Kong. Furthermore, contact with the West provides the Chinese with new models of law, justice, and human rights. Dirk Struan, who undergoes a shift in perspective from parochial Britisher to cross-cultural internationalist, voices Clavell's goal in all his novels as he describes his own secret purpose: he aims "not just to get rich on trade . . . but . . . to use riches and power to open up China to the world and particularly to British culture and British law so that each could learn from the other and grow to the benefit of both" (73). Though Struan calls his goal the "dream of a madman," he is certain that China, "the most ancient and the most populated nation on earth," has something special to offer the world (38). He commits the Noble House to a Chinese perspective of time and vows to bring

China into the family of nations and to help China become a world power. He sees contact with the West teaching the Chinese law, order, justice, and Christianity. Thus, he envisions a crossroads encounter of mutual benefit, with East and West strengthened and enriched, despite hostilities. Clavell's *tai-pan* echoes E. J. Eitel, a late-nineteenth-century Hong Kong resident who observed firsthand the early growth of that city and who, in his book *Europe in China: The History of Hong Kong from the Beginning to the Year 1882* (1895), asserted that Hong Kong would help open China "to the civilizing influences of British power" (Eitel: 569).

The Threat of China

That cultural and ethnic differences evoke fear and hostility is another subtext in *Tai-Pan*. Dirk Struan warns his brother that, with every fourth person on earth Chinese, they will indubitably "swarm out one day" (211). The 1930s avant-garde Polish playwright Stanislaw Witkiewicz, in his play *Insatiability*, voiced the same fear: a "mobile yellow wall" of Chinese soldiers encircle Poland; destroy art, language, creativity, and individuality; introduce mindless bureaucratic red tape and senseless cruelty; and serve rats' tails in a bedbug sauce at their victory banquet in Warsaw. The nightmare Witkiewicz envisions is also Clavell's: unless Englishmen teach Easterners Western values through close contact, they will not only lose their tentative holdings in the East, but will find their way of life endangered. Chinese potentate Jin-qua's dream of control and dominance is set in opposition to Dirk Struan's more altruistic dream of long-term contact for mutual advantage and for shared learning. Clavell encourages his Western readers to think long-term, as the Chinese do, to see in the Chinese of the 1840s the roots of China's role: in the Cold War of the 1960s. Clavell's warning is "know your enemy," but his hope is that prolonged contact can change relationships and that enemies, with time, may become friends.

The Importance of Crossroads

Clavell sees himself not simply as a writer of intriguing adventure novels intended to "delight," but also as a teacher who carries his audience to new worlds and who makes them see hard truths about themselves through contrasting different points of view and ways of life. Political correctness is irrelevant to his depiction of long-seated prejudices and interracial hostilities. His Americans and his British are as bound by the cultural assumptions guiding their behavior as are his Chinese.

Clavell demonstrates how differences separate, but also how, with time and understanding, they can open minds. His novels explain the ancient art of porcelain making, provide insights into Asian poetry, the tea ceremony, Chinese mythology, architecture, and of "the art of war," and teach us to appreciate new skills and perspectives. These lessons begin in *Tai-Pan*. Clavell demonstrates cross-cultural perspectives that could shape the future and reduce the threat posed by modern China, the second largest country in the world in terms of area and the world's most populous nation.

In sum, Clavell's most significant theme is that the contact between East and West epitomized in Hong Kong is vital to the future of both. China needs the idealism, justice, and appreciation of the individual characteristic of the West, and the West benefits not simply from trade but from new knowledge about medicine, art, and science, new perspectives, and the opportunity to influence so large and alien a part of the world's population.

HISTORICAL BACKGROUND

Typical of Clavell's novels, *Tai-Pan* records a turning point of history and is firmly grounded in historical fact. The date, 1841, is significant; with Victoria and Albert on the English throne, Napoleon Bonaparte dead, and England celebrating twenty-six years of peace, the British Empire was at its height. Slavery had been abolished throughout the empire, and the Industrial Revolution was in progress. Factories, canals, and toll roads were being built; mass production and joint stock companies were taking hold. The steam locomotive, the steam hammer, and the steamboat were new to the world, and steamships threatened to end the sailboat as the major form of sea transportation. The first penny post and the first police force had been established, and new laws had broadened voting rights and opened the door to new ideas about government. Change was transforming the Western world. In the East, China resisted change and tried to keep contact with Westerners to a minimum. European mercantile interests, however, saw China as a rich target.

The British silk trade with China, begun in 1699, had included the importation of an herb called *chai* (tea). In a short time, Britain became a nation of tea drinkers. Clavell records the progression that made China's monopoly on tea a central concern to the West as tea became the most popular drink in the Western world and the single major source of internal tax revenue for the British government. However, the Chinese controlled the tea trade by accepting only silver bullion in exchange for trade goods, and by limiting all Western trade to a single Chinese port, Canton. A century of pouring bullion into China critically depleted the British treasury and, says Clavell, "the unbalanced tea-bullion trade was a national catastrophe" (17). The British East India Company, which held a total monopoly on Indian and Asian trade, offered raw materials and industrial goods in place of bullion, but the Chinese emperor, who, like his predecessors, considered China self-sufficient, absolutely refused this attempt at balancing trade.

Because China feared contamination by contact with dangerous Western ideas, it enacted "Eight Regulations" to restrict Western activities even further. The Regulations set limits on both the place and time of contact, which was permitted in a walled-in area called the Canton Settlement during the winter shipping season (September through March). The rest of the year, Westerners were required to leave Canton. Even during the winter shipping season, no families, no women, and no weapons were allowed in the Canton Settlement, and all business and all Western petitions and complaints were handled by a guild of ten Chinese merchants, the Co-hong. The Co-hong monopoly effectively prevented further Western inroads into China.

The English accepted most of the Regulations, but their response to the bullion problem was to seek an illegal way around the trade barriers. By 1810, they had found a way: opium, which British Bengal could produce cheaply and abundantly. The Chinese emperor tried to eliminate the Western opium smugglers by forcefully expelling them from Canton and burning the Settlement. He thereby brought down on himself and on China the full fury of the British Navy. The Opium Wars (1839–1842) were the first major military clash between China and the West, a clash that began a century of British and foreign dominance in China.

The Opium Wars immediately increased British influence in Asia. The unequal Treaty of Nanking granted the British territory and commercial privileges. It opened up five ports, including Canton and Shanghai, to year-round British trade and residence, gave the British extraterritorial rights to try British subjects in China in British courts, and, most importantly, ceded Hong Kong to the British. It also provided for the adoption of the most-favored nation principle, which enabled other Western nations to enjoy the same privileges.

The island of Hong Kong was, at that time, an infertile, inhospitable mountain of stone, bordered by dangerous shoals, in the direct path of yearly typhoons, so its inclusion in the treaty seemed of no significance to the mandarins or to the British. Initial official British reaction was to repudiate the treaty. However, the deep, natural harbor in Hong Kong (later called Victoria Harbor) assured secure shelter for the British fleet. Businesses and homes sprang up almost overnight. Thousands of Chinese in sampans, seeking to take advantage of economic opportunities and British law, moved in quickly, and by the time any official action could be taken to reverse the treaty, strong colonial feelings about Hong Kong and strong commitments to the area had been made by those Westerners already in place. When Sir Robert Peel's Conservatives took over from the Whigs a year after the treaty, the Whig decision to return Hong Kong to the Chinese was reversed; Hong Kong became the center of trade with China and was on course to become the thriving trade center it still is. Today, over one-third of China's imports and exports pass through that port of six million residents.

NARRATIVE PERSPECTIVE AND STYLE

Clavell's scriptwriting skills imbue his narrative with a visual perspective that is like the cinematic eye of the camera, cutting from location to location and character to character, panning in for a close-up, recording dialogue, then pulling back to reveal the full picture. In literary terms, Clavell employs a third-person omniscient voice, which means that his narrator speaks from a distance, recording and commenting on action, events, and characters, providing dialogue (what is spoken aloud) and also internal monologue (what the characters think). The movement from interior musing to exterior dialogue to interior thoughts once again, sometimes with third-person description interspersed to give a sense of place, characterizes the general narrative pattern of the book. Long sections of alternating dialogue with minimal descriptive tags and internal responses require the reader to judge character, motivation, and argument. In the main, the interior monologues of Dirk Struan dominate as he plans strategies and futures, anticipates responses, judges public opinion, and dreams of ways to build and strengthen family, social, and economic ties.

Clavell's prose style in *Tai-Pan* is clear and his metaphors serviceable. He contrasts junks and clippers with cart horses and greyhounds, and describes love as "like the sea, sometimes calm and sometimes stormy ... dangerous, beautiful, death-dealing, life-giving ... ever changing" (451–52). Occasionally, a brief description will sum up a world view. For instance, in a description of a dog fight, the sounds of the death battle, then silence followed by "the furtive growling, scuffling, ripping in the darkness as the victors began to feed," sum up the cutthroat struggles of a "silent press of Chinese" (345). The movie version, with its exotic costuming and sets, its Chinese architecture, elaborately carved and decorated furnishings and sedan chairs, and peculiar water craft, nonetheless makes one realize how little visual description there is. Except for quick sketches of key personalities, broad lines mapping out local landmarks, and an occasional reference to a Chinese clothing style or food, the readers are left to conjure up the setting for themselves. Clavell's description only becomes detailed and visual when recounting hand-to-hand conflict, violence, torture, pursuit (his chase scenes are always fast paced and engaging), storms, and business negotiations. Even the sexual scenes are modestly veiled. What dominates is history, cultural contrasts, and human interaction.

CHARACTER DEVELOPMENT

Through Dirk Struan, Clavell voices his own values and artistic vision. Forwardlooking, innovative, and perceptive, Struan illustrates the risks necessary for high gain, the complex strategies requisite for business success, the obligations entailed by power (*noblesse oblige*), the loneliness of being at the top, and the value of purposefully learning the best Asia offers. Australian actor Bryan Brown, who plays Struan in the film, captures the *tai-pan*'s arrogance, self-confidence, and self-conviction.

Reflecting Clavell's personal experiences with Japanese forced labor camps, Struan deplores slavery. He condemns Japanese slavers for collecting human cargo in China's waters. He criticizes Brock for running slave ships and the Chinese for selling women and children as indentured servants, and predicts failed trade as long as the American South depends on slaves. Struan purchases his Chinese concubine, May-may, in order to free her. The Struans never deal in human cargo, he tells his son, and he is proud that the British led the world in outlawing slavery. Struan's aversion to slavery stems from his experiences as an eight-year-old aboard an illicit slave trader: he recalls the dying whimpers of slaves crushed "like maggots" below decks, "the stench choking him" (556).

Religious hypocrisy is another Struan/Clavell target. Struan argues that the Portuguese priests want one's soul in exchange for kindness. To his disgust, Struan learns that the most pious religious leader in Hong Kong incestuously forced himself on his own dependent sister and that the most respectable community members lead secret lives of sin. Maymay argues the wisdom of an open mind about religion, but notes that the Christian practice of burning heretics is far worse than the Chinese custom of offering the sea god a bar of silver bullion but only tossing over a prayer paper as a gesture. Struan finds her attitudes puzzling but practical, and is revolted by a Chinese Christian fanatic, a self-proclaimed "messiah" who viciously attacks nonbelievers.

Through Struan, Clavell explores generational conflicts, the tendency of youth to distrust the status quo and of empowered adults to distrust change. Struan, like Clavell, believes traditions have a solid historical basis and should be changed only with caution, though it is foolish to avoid change when the evidence demands it. The disagreement between Culum and Dirk Struan about the role of the Chartists in England illustrates generational divisions: the youthful innocent sees only the Chartist ideals and the plight of the poor, while the more politically astute father recognizes the destructive effects of insurrection. The Chartists supported changes that are now solid rocks of British democracy: a vote for every male citizen, vote by secret ballot, and reforms of Parliament (salaries for members of Parliament, equal voice for all electoral districts, annual meetings, no property qualifications). Struan himself uses standard democratic forms of protest to foment change: agitation, argumentation, petitions, lobbying, and public debate. However, the Chartists' assumption that change is good for its own sake, that the ends justify the means, and that violence and revolution can solve social and economic problems disturbs Struan. Culum, in contrast, finds the democratic process too slow to suit his youthful passions and believes it romantic to die for a cause. In Glasgow, the center of the Chartist movement, he led undergraduates in protests against the government, and he secretly carries on the fight in Hong Kong. In capturing a generational conflict of the 1840s, when young people idealistically supported change, even by revolution, and the older generation was more cynical about the means by which change should be wrought, Clavell is commenting on the generation gap of the 1960s in America. Significantly, a trusted friend brings reliable information about appalling conditions in the English mills and about social inequities heightened by a crippling inflation rate and unemployment; when Struan understands that one in every eleven Englishmen is a pauper, he graciously concedes the need for drastic action—even possibly birth control—but not revolution.

Believing Westerners should have learned more about medicine from Easterners more quickly than they did, Clavell contrasts nineteenth-century European ignorance about disease, their reliance on purging and leeching, and their distrust of washing and bathing with the ancient Chinese practice of medicine and the Chinese association of cleanliness with health. Struan lectures his son on the advanced thinking of the Chinese about the connection between excrement and disease and the safety of drinking only boiled water or tea. Westerners had no cure for syphilis, but a secret Chinese remedy saves Culum from infection and ignominy, just as May-may's old Chinese remedy for aborting an unwanted child helps Mary Sinclair reclaim her life. Descriptions of the bubonic plague that caused 20,000 deaths in Scotland between June and September of 1841 and of the malaria that ravaged Hong Kong emphasize the inability of nineteenth-century Europeans to cope with the invisible world of germs. Again, it is the Chinese mosquito net that protects many, and it is a folk remedy, quinine, adopted from Portuguese missionaries, that saves the new colony and that provides the West with a means to fight a long-dreaded killer disease. As a result of his experiences in the East, Struan is obsessed with personal cleanliness, and all Clavell's heroes value good plumbing and long baths.

Dirk Struan is the model of what an Englishman abroad should be: forwardlooking, insightful, tolerant of human differences, open to new ideas and new perspectives, but firmly committed to Western values of individuality, justice, progress, and free trade. He speaks for his creator.

STRUCTURE: UNIFYING CONTRASTS

Despite its chronological progression from January 26, 1841, to the first typhoon the same year and its division into six books, each focused on a pivotal event (Book One, the ship chase; Book Two, the land auction; Book Three, the Struan ball; Book Four, Robb's death from malaria; Book Five, May-may's malaria; Book Six, the hurricane), *Tai-Pan* is loosely structured, as sprawling as China itself. It alternates between conflicting perspectives and cultures and between intimate tête-à-têtes and public confrontations. Contrasts between main characters, between cultures, between father-son relationships, and between male-female perspectives tighten the structure.

Contrasts between Main Characters: Dirk Struan and Tyler Brock

Clavell's novels usually involve two key characters at odds with each other, Marlowe and Grey in *King Rat*, Dunross and Gornt in *Noble House*, Struan and Brock in *Tai-Pan*. Brock and Struan are both China traders, both devilish rascals willing to break the rules and challenge fate, yet they embody opposing principles. Brock is ruthless and his goals are selfish, while Struan has a vision for the future and a respect for family and community. Brock has been a slave trader; Struan abhors the slave trade. Brock's perspective is short-term and immediate, limited to instant gratification and gain. Struan's perspective is long-term; he has a vision of future betterment, not simply for himself or his son, but for future generations, for his community, and for his nation. Brock grooms his son to be just like himself: brutal, tough, and underhanded. Struan tries to teach his sons through adversity to discover their own inner strength. Brock's attitudes toward male-female relationships are highly conventional (women are either wives, mothers, or daughters to be strictly controlled, or they are whores to be used and abused), while Struan's views are more modern and more tolerant, as his support of Mary Sinclair and his marriage to May-may both indicate. Whereas Brock takes advantage of the China trade but keeps himself apart from the Chinese, Dirk Struan immerses himself in Chinese culture and becomes a strong interpreter and defender of Chinese ways. The conflict between these two perspectives, these two men, and these two families unites the book, as they compete for gold in Book One, land in Book Two, social clout in Book Three, and control of the next generation in the remaining books.

Contrasts between Cultures: Chinese and British

Clavell's novels always provide interesting studies in culture and are structured on movement between cultures. In *Tai-Pan*, a European section alternates with a Chinese one. *Tai-Pan* depicts British colonial, Hong Kong Chinese, and mainland Chinese family relationships, manners, mores, business strategies, and political maneuverings. It explores the Chinese concepts of "face" and "*joss*" (fate) and the Oriental sense of long-term familial obligations passed on from generation to generation. All this is contrasted with the short-term business vision of Westerners. Some of the differences are only surface curiosities, differences that are simply a matter of taste or fashion, but others are essential, affecting livelihood, attitudes toward human worth, and the future.

Clavell's depiction of the British and the Chinese sense of superiority is tongue-in-cheek, for both sides are blind to the limits of their perspective. Both groups believe themselves truly civilized and all others barbarians. Gordon Chen, though half English, considers most Westerners "savages" and is grateful to have been brought up Chinese, not European. May-may muses on the naivete and ignorance of Western males, while Jin-qua, the rich and powerful mainlander representative of the Mandarin, thinks Europeans are "hairy," "apelike" barbarians, their smiles "repulsive," their manners "ugly" or absent (139). This sense of superiority extends to ideas about manners and social graces, food and sex. Culum calls the Chinese "ugly, repulsive heathens . . . impossible to tell apart" (252). Despite European pride in a 500-year-old culture, the Chinese, says Struan, have had 5,000 years of civilization—of "books, printing presses, art, poets, government, silk, tea, gunpowder and a thousand other things" (101). May-may adds that Jesus is a new god, only 2,000 years old, whereas the more than 630 Chinese gods are 5,000 to 10,000 years old.

The English are sickened by the Chinese willingness to eat anything that normally moves with its back to the heavens, including insects, but the Chinese, proud of their healthy and varied cuisine developed over centuries of experimentation, are appalled at what the English call "solid" fare: the monstrous quantities of half-raw meats, blood gravy, and tasteless, boiled vegetables. The English mock the Chinese fastidiousness; the Chinese pride themselves on their cleanliness. The Chinese take joy in gambling; the Europeans feel some degree of guilt at engaging in it. The Chinese revel in lengthy titles, the English find them pretentious, and the Americans reject them altogether. The Western funeral is a brief, somber affair, with solemn, silent mourners dressed in black. The Chinese funeral is loud and colorful, with professional mourners dressed in white, shrieking and moaning, pounding drums, shaking rattles, waving banners, and tearing their clothes for as long as one hundred days of mourning, ending with a feast and the burning of a tablet so the soul will be reborn. Westerners bury a body at sea; the Chinese bring the body home to relatives for a proper mourning and burial.

Some of the differences reflect opposing attitudes about the value of human life. In so poor and so highly populated a realm as China was and is, life is cheap and survival is a battle won by the fittest. Struan sees Chinese sailors watch men drown and not lift a hand because life and death is a matter of *joss*. By modern standards, the nineteenth-century Europeans seem bloodthirsty. A fistfight between representatives of the Royal Army and the Royal Navy is vicious and uncompromising, a fight almost to the death. The fights between Struan and Gorth Brock and between Struan and Tyler Brock are equally bloody and violent. The traditional European forms of punishment—flogging, keelhauling, hanging—also seem cruel and harsh, but at least they were quick. The Chinese forms of torture—thumbscrews, blinding, mutilation, amputation, flesh slicing, genital crushing—were slow and terrible, defying modern Western comprehension. The slow torture of Scragger makes this point most forcefully. Secretly told from day to day that rescue is on the way if he can only endure, Scragger is slowly dismembered, a piece at a time; each stub is coated with tar, and as it begins to heal, the victim is forced to choose which part will be the next to go.

The differences in attitudes about human worth are reflected in the differences in attitudes toward the value of women in society. As is still true today on mainland China, as the one child per family controversy has so openly confirmed, sons bring a family pride; daughters have little value. In *Tai-Pan* even the poorest fisherman values sons above daughters and carefully ties sons inside the boat, but not daughters; if one falls overboard, it is no real loss. Impoverished parents give away daughters in payment of debts or sell them into concubinage to help support the family. Rich parents use daughters for political gain: a daughter strategically placed in a rival's household can bring a family wealth and security. May-may is so placed and takes pride both in her liaison with Struan and also in her service to her grandfather, Jin-qua, passing on to both of them vital information that affects East-West relationships.

Clavell plays on Western disapproval of Chinese attitudes, but near the end of *Tai-Pan*, suggests Western hypocrisy by demonstrating that nineteenth-century Europeans also valued women less than men, although not as openly as the Chinese. As John Stuart Mill pointed out in "On the Subjection of Women," perceptions of attitudes shape reality: the nineteenth-century Englishman could see the wrongs of slavery (which only a century before had seemed a natural activity), but not the wrongs of subjugating women, which was as unnatural as slavery. In his portrayal of male attitudes toward marriage, Clavell shows Struan shocked when May-may buys him a beautiful young girl for his birthday, but Struan also considers marriage with a lovely girl from a respectable American family, Shevaun, because of her youth, her "useful dowry," and her "interesting political connections" (345). He likewise considers marrying the daughter of some lord or earl or Cabinet minister to help strengthen his power base and is not shocked when Shevaun's father arranges a marriage for her to gain Cooper-Tillman shares. Shevaun's protest that she is being sold for shares and her request that Struan buy her instead, as the Chinese bought concubines, does shock him, and his protest that buying a marriage partner is against the law seems feeble in the face of the realities of Shevaun's situation. Shevaun may seem better off than May-may, but Clavell makes it very clear that she is also trapped by family, by society, by convention.

Unlike nineteenth-century Europeans affected by the restraints of the Victorian age, the Chinese talk openly about sex and, in fact, describe it as natural and as regular an occurrence as eating; one characteristic of the Chinese throughout Clavell's canon is their very racy daily conversation, filled with sexual puns and metaphors to describe the world around them. May-may teases Struan about his embarrassment when she talks about sex although he is not embarrassed to engage in it. Struan says that there is no Chinese equivalent of Western words like "love" and "adore." Sex is a practical matter, having to do with duty, station, and appetite. Related to the Chinese openness about sexuality is a more general cultural attitude toward public space versus private space. The Chinese servants walk in without knocking and converse with Struan while he bathes, a cultural behavior pattern modern visitors to China like Mark Salzman, the author of *Iron and Silk*, confirm. Clavell clearly approves of the Chinese attitude toward sex and is contemptuous of what he sees as culture-bound Western sexual restraints that lead to perversions. Culum, in love with Tess, turns self-righteous and condemns lust as a sin, but this doesn't stop him from visiting prostitutes before his marriage. Gorth is a murderous sexual pervert, who beats prostitutes to death for his sexual satisfaction. Mary Sinclair's preacher father gains sexual satisfaction from beating her, and her self-righteous brother cannot control his sexual obsessions with his own sister.

Because the Chinese culture is a carefully ranked culture, with wide divisions between those with power and those without, forms of subservience disturbing to Westerners are inevitable. May-may continues to kowtow, that is, to kneel and touch her forehead to the floor eight times, to show obeisance to a superior, and she expects corporeal punishment for mistakes. When Struan purchased her, May-may had bound feet, only three inches long. Horrified, Struan cut off the bandages only to discover that she could not endure the pain caused by the removal of the bandages. To his greater horror, he learns that she takes pride in this crippling, physical deformity as a sign of her value and worth, for to the Chinese of the nineteenth century, foot binding was a physical demonstration of rank and desirability. To be a woman with "lotus" feet was to be a desirable and worthy possession, and men who could afford a woman too physically crippled to do anything but look beautiful had a visual confirmation of their wealth and power.

Clavell wants Westerners to think of time as Asians do: long-term. Struan says that to the Chinese, "immediate" means "anything up to a century" (92). Thus, when Struan is forced to borrow five million dollars in silver from the Chinese tycoon Jin-qua, Jin-qua's repayment demands affect *tai-pans* for the next two hundred years: Jin-qua and his descendants will hold (or hand on to others, as they see fit) four half-coins. When a half-coin is presented to the *tai-pan*—to Struan himself or to his descendants—it must be matched to a half-coin held by the *tai-pan*. The *tai-pan* will then grant any favor, irrespective of the law. Another far-sighted demand made by Jin-qua—that one of his sons be educated in London—anticipates the permanent joining of the fortunes of China and of Britain. Later the pirate king Wu Fang Choi, who has been given one of the coin halves by Jin-qua, demands that Struan train nineteen of his lads, one to be assigned to each of Struan's clipper ships for training as captains, and that Struan oversee the education of three boys destined to be future leaders. In each case, immediate gain is set aside for anticipated gain twenty, thirty, even a hundred years later. When Struan draws up the regulations to be adhered to by future generations of Struan *tai-pans*, he demonstrates how well he has learned his Chinese lessons.

After particularly trying negotiations, Struan muses on the Chinese mind and is awed by its "subtlety" and "diabolic cunning," its "majesty" and "ruthlessness" (138). Where the English sense of one-upmanship is bold (beating an opponent in a fight, or winning a contract or a woman an opponent wants), the Chinese find significance in the smallest act in a much larger game, as in Wu Fang Choi and Struan's unspoken competition to prove superior mastery of chopsticks or the serving of *dim sum* at an inappropriate time to indicate displeasure or contempt. In another instance, May-may's exchange with Gordon Chen about having Gorth Brock murdered is so cryptic he almost doesn't understand. Struan's use of the Mandarin, Cantonese, and Hoklo dialects marks how deeply immersed he has become in Asian culture and in the linguistic conventions that reflect the subtlety of social interaction.

A conversation between Struan and May-may lends the structural pattern of alternating cultures thematic significance. May-may challenges Struan: "Learn from us, from the lessons of China, Dirk Struan. People never change." He, in turn, challenges her: "Learn from us, from the lessons of England, lass. The world can grow into an ordered place where all are equal before the law. And the law is just. Honest. Without graft." To her question "Is that so important if you are starving?", he pauses a long while, but then answers yes (199). Struan meets the challenge of the East. However, while Struan sees his training of Wu Fang Choi's men as spearheading a Western advance "into the heart of China," Jin-qua, through May-may, sees himself civilizing "the barbarian earth" by teaching Struan "civilized ways," though, of course, both men understand the danger of education: "The student may learn too well, and before you know it, the student will rule the teacher" (323). Education could possibly backfire, but both men consider the benefits worth the chance.

Struan's secret marriage to May-may, their death in each other's arms, and their burial together unites the alternating movement between Chinese and European in a final amalgam that is Struan's (and Clavell's) dream for the future: a merging of the best of both cultures into a hybrid, the Eurasian.

Contrasts between Father-Son Relationships

Tai-Pan explores four main father-son relationships, those of Tyler Brock and his son Gorth Brock, Dirk Struan and his English son Culum, Dirk Struan and his Chinese son Gordon, and the English pirate Scragger and his son Fred. Clavell depicts the sons struggling for self-definition in the face of parental expectations, yet reflecting their fathers.

A key conflict between Clavell's fathers and sons results from the fathers having had to struggle from an early age to reach where they are, whereas their sons were born into wealth and success. Brock wants to make sure that his son works hard and understands by direct experience the ruthlessness that has made his father who he is. As Gorth matures, Brock leaves the dirty work of the business to him: the lawbreaking, the plots, the killings. For example, Brock goes below deck and leaves his son to ram the Struan bullion ship. Cynically, he wants to be able to honestly deny responsibility, but also he takes a perverse pride in his son's exploits. In the midst of a Co-hong attack, Gorth tries to assassinate Struan, but hits the Russian archduke Alexi Zergeyev instead; later, Gorth conceives and carries out the plot to turn Culum against Struan and to infect Culum with the "pox." The more devious Gorth's schemes, the greater his father's pride. In the miniseries version, Brock calls Gorth his " *joss*." However, since the father-son relationship is built on naked power and force, as Gorth gains strength, he challenges and then defeats his father. Gorth prides himself on the ruthlessness his father taught him and on his knowledge that "in truth he could crush him, man to man" (543). The two are a deadly duo for whom might makes right.

The relationship of the Struans in some ways parallels that of the Brocks. Dirk Struan can never forget the anguish of having had no money, no food, no warmth, no roof, and no hope and of "the bloated heaving stomachs of the children," "their cries on a starving wind in a cesspool of a street" (71). His sons have never been deprived, and Culum disapproves of his father's philosophy of life as "a never-ending battle" (113). Dirk Struan determines to teach his untested English son hard lessons about the iron discipline demanded of a *tai-pan*. He begins by providing Culum with the means to cross him publicly and gambles that his son is man enough to do so. Once Culum has demonstrated his rebellious strength publicly by setting aside for the church the knoll everyone knows Struan covets, Struan explains his strategy: he couldn't afford the high price the Brocks would have forced him to pay for the knoll and has used Culum to save face. Culum's victory turns into a lesson in strategy. Such tough lessons strengthen Culum but alienate father and son. Struan tells Culum that he is the only man on earth his son can completely trust, but when he hedges that statement with the truth, "providing you dinna, with calculation, go against the house" (309), he loses his son's trust and affection. Despite all Struan does to further his son's interests, Culum understands that he will always be his father's tool and that he cannot lead his life the way his father wishes. He tells Struan that he is tired of trapping people and using them and that he is not like his father and never will be (640). Struan loves his son in a way Brock does not, and he tries to do his best by him. He is proud of the way Culum matures, and he vows revenge on Gorth for his plot to destroy Culum; if May-may had not anticipated him by hiring an assassin, Struan would have fought Gorth to the death. Culum, in turn, is morally repulsed by his father's past as pirate, opium smuggler, murderer, and adulterer. His father's Chinese mistresses and mixed-blood offspring offend him. But despite his dislike and distrust, Culum cannot give up his father's vision of the future and of the family destiny.

Struan's relationship with his Chinese son Gordon is very different. Dirk Struan had Gordon adopted at an early age, by a powerful ally, and protects his personal reputation in the European community by not openly admitting the relationship. However, he watches out for Gordon's interests and puts opportunities his way. Because Gordon has been raised with the Chinese tradition to expect nothing and to appreciate sophisticated strategy, he has a greater emotional distance from his father than Gorth and Culum have on theirs. When his father gains face in the community, so does Gordon. Furthermore, the training Struan has provided him has helped him become the greatest landlord in Hong Kong. He is very much his father's son in his business acumen and his entrepreneurial spirit. Struan's vision of British power taking hold in the Far East is matched by Gordon's pragmatic concern for family profit. Gordon owns buildings, sedan chairs, laundries, sampans, apothecary shops, restaurants, shoeshine stands, clothes and shoe shops, jewelry stores, and a large money lending business. Both of Struan's sons join secret societies, but Culum does it to assert his manhood while Gordon does it as part of a long-term scheme to separate Hong Kong Chinese from mainland controls. Gordon's reaction to his father is one of gratitude and admiration. In fact, even when Struan is not being clever, Gordon reads his actions as if they were carefully contrived strategy and takes pride in their subtlety and sophistication.

The fourth father-son relationship, that of Scragger to Fred, parallels that of Dirk Struan to Gordon. Scragger is a pirate and a rascal, but his love for his son leads him to send his son away—for his own good. As part of the deal made between the pirate king Wu Fang Choi (Scragger's employer) and Dirk Struan, Scragger helps arrange for the Struans to take on his son: to clothe and educate him, to send him to the best British schools, to train him to be a gentleman. As a farewell inheritance, he gives his son a fortune in pirated jewels. He knows he will never see his son again, but it is his son's survival and future welfare that drive him, and he provides for him as best he can.

In all four relationships, the fathers teach their sons that a man without a birthright or power is defenseless, but each has a different view of what that birthright consists of and how that power should be passed on.

Contrasts between Male-Female Relationships

Clavell often clarifies cultural contrasts through sexual liaisons. His central character is usually attracted to a beautiful young woman who proves as enigmatic as the culture she represents, so that male and female indeed seem like separate races: intriguing, challenging, possessable, but forever alien.

Glessing, a minor official, sums up the European values for a wife in his description of Mary Sinclair: "She's the toast of Macao. She runs the Sinclair house impeccably and treats Horatio [her brother] as a prince. The food's the best in town and she rules the servants beautifully. Plays the harpsichord like a dream and sings like an angel" (24). That he thinks she likes him is a bonus, but not a prerequisite. The downside of such a wife is that she has no income, her parents are dead, and she has not spent time in Europe. But Clavell also describes the hidden side of this ideal mate: she is a victim of beatings by her father and rape by her brother, and she has a secret history of sexually servicing rich Chinese.

The marriages in *Tai-Pan* demonstrate the dangers of conventional calculations concerning ideal unions. For example, Robb Struan, the *tai-pan*'s brother, is trapped in a loveless marriage in which man and wife had little in common to begin with and have grown further apart with time. Social expectations and an unenlightened legal system that permits divorce only by an act of parliament keep them together. As a result, both suffer. Robb's wife, burdened by an unwanted pregnancy, becomes half-crazed with hate, nags her husband to distraction, denigrates his successes, and tears the family apart. Even worse is the marriage of Aristotle Quance, a kind-hearted painter and libertine whose termagant wife determines to break his spirit and force him into her mold.

The marriage of Culum Struan and Tess Brock seems one of mutual attraction, but even it has its negative side. Tess is only sixteen and her parents are anxious to marry her off because of a disturbing "incident" with one of her father's sailors. Both sets of parents manipulate the young couple for personal and business goals. Culum can only be strong if he can separate his wife from her family; Tess must reject her parents if she is to support her husband. At the end of the novel, Tess has already unthinkingly revealed dangerous secrets to her father, and Culum has resolved to break ties with her family forever. Such a beginning promises troubled times ahead.

Mary Sinclair complains of a double standard whereby European males can have Chinese mistresses and remain socially acceptable, but a European woman who takes any kind of lover is a social pariah: "You men do what you please, but we women can't" (53). Consequently, Mary is forced to play a hypocritical game. On the one hand, her public image is that of the sweet, innocent virgin who makes "silly conversation," adores the church, and spends her time playing the harpsichord, singing, and doing needlework. On the other hand, her private self is a woman who resents male hypocrisy, who does as she pleases, who can speak Cantonese and Mandarin, and who sells her body to rich Chinese lovers. Struan is offended by her violation of his definition of a European woman, but when her information proves essential to gain Noble House a monopoly on the opium trade and to stop the Brocks, he swallows his condemnations and gives her the support she needs. Mary's pregnancy and abortion captures her dilemma: respectability at the price of conventionality and submission, or freedom at the price of disgrace and ostracism.

Clavell contrasts his European women with May-may. As the granddaughter of Jin-qua, she was chosen to teach the *tai-pan* "civilized" Chinese values and, on pain of being cast out of the family forever, told to accept her fate as concubine. She is proud of her uniqueness: at twenty she can read and write English and Chinese and speak English, Cantonese, Soochow, and Mandarin. She has accepted her place in life and made the most of it. By Western standards, her situation is unspeakable; by Chinese standards, she has a good life. In doing as the men of her family wish, she pleases herself, and her secret knowledge and secret powers give her respect that allows her to feel much better about herself than Mary Sinclair, Shevaun, or Tess Brock do about themselves.

GENRE CONVENTIONS

Tai-Pan is a fictionalized history, dramatizing the founding of Hong Kong and bringing to life the men and women who created that city. To capture effectively the broad scope of this historical moment, the novel draws on a mix of genres. It is an historical romance, tracing the affairs of Hong Kong's founding fathers; a dynasty story, of extended families gaining wealth and power through trade; a sea adventure, with a night-

time chase and pirate attack; a medical story, about malaria and a cure
that may be only legend; and a spy story, with May-may helping her
influential grandfather plot the course of Chinese-British relationships. It
is also a maturation story, with young Culum Struan learning humility,
tolerance, and the value of his heritage, and discovering the inner
strength to succeed as *tai-pan*.

ALTERNATIVE READING: THE HISTORICAL ACCURACY OF *TAI-PAN*

One critical approach to fictionalized history is to investigate the historical base on which an author builds and to determine the accuracy of
the facts presented. A related historical-critical approach is to investigate
the research sources themselves, the printed, factual materials an author
uses. Good historians, in general, search for clues to find meaning behind
bare facts and to form an accurate understanding of past events. They
search for facts in the physical remains of the past, documents such as
wills, birth certificates, land titles, government records, court proceed-
ings, and the newspapers of the time, as well as the diaries, letters, and
memoirs of eyewitnesses. They also draw on family histories passed on
orally from generation to generation—genealogies and histories of family businesses and of past events.

Once the information is collected, the historian must be a judge. Where
there are no facts available and the witnesses are silent, the historian
must evaluate related facts and make an intuitive guess about what is
missing, what has been covered up, and what really happened. Where
there is a disagreement about facts, the historian must decide which of
the sources seem most accurate or most reliable. In addition, the historian
must be an interpreter of reality, for bare facts are meaningless without
broader, more abstract patterns to give them significance and to place
them in an interpretive pattern that helps readers judge their past importance and their value to modern life. Facts that don't fit the pattern
are often subordinated or left out because of little interest, whereas facts
that do fit the pattern are sometimes given much greater emphasis than
they had at the historical moment in which they occurred. For example,
the miniscule clause in the treaty with China that gave a tiny barren
island over to Western dominance seemed insignificant at the time both
to the Chinese and to most Westerners, but looking back, with the perspective of time, historians agree that it was a pivotal event that greatly

affected East-West relationships thereafter. In addition to judging which facts are pivotal and which are irrelevant, the historian, and in this case the historical novelist, must also organize those facts into patterns or plots that make interesting, informative reading for people of our age. It is in the decisions about which facts are pivotal and which best interpret past events that disagreements occur.

Because the reporting of history is determined by culture and by theories of interpretation giving meaning or pattern to details and "facts," what one culture considers "historically accurate" another culture will deride as "distorted," "biased," or "slanted." Therefore, we will judge Clavell's historical accuracy from three perspectives: that of the West, that of China and Hong Kong, and that of Marxism. Westerners inevitably view Western involvement in China and the founding of Hong Kong as positive, perhaps a bit aggressive because of the stubborn isolationism of the Chinese, but basically progressive, forward looking, and mutually beneficial; Hong Kong's commentators value the resultant cultural mix and balance the Chinese perspective with the Western perspective, noting the enormous Chinese contribution to the development of Hong Kong that Western historians might downplay; and Marxists view Western involvement in Hong Kong negatively, as the aggressive and oppressive imposition of capitalistic patterns on a subjugated and unwilling local population. Clavell's view is that of a Westerner, but he tempers that view with an earnest attempt to capture the Hong Kong Chinese perspective and to give the Chinese their due in the history of a colony dependent on a large Chinese population. However, Clavell is diametrically opposed to a Marxist interpretation of events, and counters Marxist accusations of exploitation with a "tu quoque" ("you're another") argument attacking Russian Marxists as more aggressive and more exploitative than other Westerners.

Clavell is not exclusively an historiographer. He does not claim to write accurate history, but instead sees his role as an interpreter of history, as one who distinguishes clear patterns and movements behind the facts. As a writer of historical fiction, he is subject to the judgments of historical criticism. One basis of judgment is the quality of his research. Clavell proved himself a careful researcher by reading exhaustively about the history of Hong Kong before writing. He had lived in and around Hong Kong in his youth, and much later he and his wife spent a year there researching *Tai-Pan*, talking to residents and experts, and reviewing histories of the city's founding fathers. In other words, he had personal experience with people and place, and he augmented this per-

sonal knowledge with local sources of historical information rather than
being content with the limited materials available elsewhere. He drew
on oral tradition as well as historical record.

Overall, Clavell's portrait of movements and patterns agrees with that
of Hong Kong historians. Lo Hsiang-lin of the Department of Chinese at
Hong Kong University writes in *Hong Kong and Western Cultures* that
little attention has been paid to Hong Kong's very significant role in "the
interchange of Chinese and Western cultures" and that Hong Kong's
contribution to and influence on the new cultural movement in China
has been sadly underrated (Lo 1964: 1). Lo's goal is to rectify that error,
just as Clavell's is to do so through fiction. Lo points out that since 1842
Europeans and Americans coming to China as traders or missionaries
came to Hong Kong first to acquaint themselves with conditions on the
mainland, just as Chinese going abroad dipped their toes into that West-
ern-influenced city before sailing to foreign lands. He further notes that
successful Hong Kong Chinese industrialists and merchants patronized
the arts of China and imported tutors to train their descendants in the
best of their ancient heritage, while British colonials sent their sons home
to England to learn about their heritage and to bring back to Hong Kong
the most modern Western technological advances. The result was what
Clavell's characters call "the cream" of two cultures meeting, flourishing,
taking root, flowing into each other, and, as Lo says, forming "a conflu-
ence" that had "far reaching influence" (6). With Hong Kong as the hub,
Westerners absorbed Chinese culture, and Chinese imbibed the essentials
of Western culture. Clavell takes as his goal the dramatization of this
give-and-take.

Historical figures, both Chinese and British, confirm the amalgam
Clavell depicts. Typical is historian James Legge, a Scotsman and "a
Western scholar of the Confucian school" (Lo 1964: 30) who translated
Chinese classics into English and advocated recruiting Hong Kong Chinese to the police force. Jung-fang Tsai, in *Hong Kong in Chinese History*,
describes the entrepreneurial activities of the brothers Li Sing and Li
Leong, who diversified their investments to include "the money changing business, shipbuilding, trade, opium monopoly, gambling and coolie
labor brokerage" (Tsai 1993: 56) and who identified their interests so
closely with the British that they secretly funded the British against the
mainland. The history of such real families closely parallels that of the
fictitious Chen family.

Tsai confirms that a large number of secret societies, bandit gangs, and
urban bands of beggars grew up quickly in Hong Kong (21), and his

history suggests that Clavell's record of the growth of the Chinese tongs or triads (secret, militant underground organizations committed to unified action in trade and in politics) is quite accurate. China had had centuries of revolts and insurrections caused by famine, oppression, and discontent. Peasant revolts had been savagely put down, but the secret societies that helped foment them had survived. Clavell places one of his characters, Gordon Chen, at the heart of one such clandestine revolutionary group. He makes Chen a supereffective, capitalistic entrepreneur who adeptly uses Western and Eastern connections to remake his world.

Tsai also describes Chinese entrepreneurs who prospered and became important community figures, like Clavell's Chens. One such real figure, an outcast boatman named Loo Aqui, operated a gambling establishment and brothels, held the opium monopoly, was a slum lord, and was rumored to be a pirate "sea king," who demanded tribute from those who sailed his waters. Yet Loo Aqui used his wealth wisely; he built a theater and a temple, and, says Tsai, he inspired the fear essential for respectability in "a rough frontier society" (44). Tsai records the fluidity of Hong Kong society, which allowed daring adventurers who had acquired wealth by not-so-respectable means to attain social respectability and a place as community leaders through judicious spending (43). This fluidity lies at the heart of Clavell's portrait of Hong Kong.

Clavell also mentions the Portuguese Jesuit missionaries who established churches and missions where others dared not go, and the English missionaries who settled in Macao in the early 1800s, translated the Bible into Chinese, and founded mission schools and orphanages. However, he downplays the role of the church and of missionaries in opening up China to the West and instead credits the adventurers and traders for establishing Hong Kong as a Pacific Rim trade center. In other words, his personal dislike of organized religion affects his interpretation of the role of the church in opening China to the West. Furthermore, to meet his fictional needs, he takes other liberties with facts and changes the historical record in a number of minor ways.

Clavell regularly combines several historical figures into a single character. In historical fact, an Englishman and a Chinese worked together to secure English rights to Hong Kong, but were eventually dismissed from their posts, the first for getting a bare island of little worth, the second for not asking sufficient concessions for yielding a strategically placed island with a valuable harbor (Rogers 1966: 39). Clavell makes these two a father and son (Dirk Struan and Gordon Chen), and endows them with greater manipulative powers and a more extended period of involvement than their historical counterparts. Dirk Struan is a China trader whose wealth depends on opium smuggling; Gordon Chen is an ingenious entrepreneur with a golden touch, blessed by Yankee ingenuity and Chinese business acumen. In addition, Clavell makes Struan the force behind the historical scene who advises the Navy on their line of attack. Struan manipulates the Crown representatives to include Hong Kong in the treaty and to invest in that barren rock as a gateway to Asia. Struan persuades the British plenipotentiary to ask for British law for British subjects in Hong Kong, British citizenship for Chinese residents of Hong Kong, and the banning of Chinese officials and customhouses from Hong Kong. Struan finances the first newspaper, establishes the first jockey club, and encourages the building of a race course. His son and heir, Cullum, makes sure a church is established on the highest hill, and Struan's friends and supporters in Parliament push for ratification of the treaty granting Hong Kong to Britain. Likewise, the behind-the-scenes action of Gordon Chen sums up the Hong Kong Chinese commitment to freewheeling, capitalist-style business and to huge profits, safe from mainland control.

Thus, Clavell takes the actions of many real people who founded Hong Kong and synthesizes them into his fictitious heroes, mostly into Dirk Struan. This is a weakness of the book, for Struan comes across as bigger than life. He is a privateer, a smuggler, a man respected by British and Chinese alike, knowledgeable about human weaknesses and strengths, and capable of manipulating them to serve his private ends, but he is also motivated to aid others and to act in the best interests of the colony and of future generations. Clavell, not content with such monumental achievements, also depicts Struan as a survivor of the naval battle at Trafalgar (where he was a powder monkey at age seven) and as the inventor of binoculars!

Despite such exaggeration and despite some anachronisms, Clavell faithfully depicts key historical events and captures the spirit of the times: the fears, the hopes, the conflicts, and the gutsy determination of the Westerners who transformed a rocky island into a Western base, Hong Kong. At the same time, he provides diverting, interesting, and unexpected historical tidbits, for example, the history of venereal disease, the condom, and the can-can, the conflict in the Dardanelles, the mutiny at Botany Bay, Captain Cook's cure for scurvy, the destruction of China's monopoly on tea, the death of the China clippers, and the development of a ship's chronometer. His characters struggle with the conflicts of their age: they face up to Darwinian ideas of the survival of the fittest, debate economic concerns originated by Marx and Engels, and, to a lesser degree, toy with Freudian interpretations of their motivations. With bold splashes across a huge canvas, Clavell captures an age and a moment in history. His perspective is that of a modern man looking back and interpreting past events in the light of effects that came long after them. He manipulates and compresses time, facts, and figures. Nonetheless, the final result, *Tai-Pan*, is a highly effective, panoramic, impressionistic image of the spirit of the times. His view fits the historical record of most Western nations and, to some degree, of the Hong Kong Chinese.

A Marxist interpretation of this history would, however, diametrically oppose Clavell's interpretation. The Marxist view interprets historical events and institutions in terms of class struggle and patterns of economic inequality that precipitate revolution. For the Marxist, history is a drama of class competition for power, and capitalism is the archvillain, preventing workers from enjoying the fruits of their labor. Marxist historians would deride the capitalistic ventures Clavell praises as, instead, indicative of the territorial imperative of an acquisitive, imperialistic colonialism dependent on the exploitation of native populaces to bolster a weak economy, and the Chartist movement as indicative of the natural urge to revolution of the exploited masses. It would focus on the class struggle in England between wage slaves and industrial magnates, and the economic competition driving East-West relationships. In fact, A. N. Khokhlov, in the entry on Hong Kong in the *Great Soviet Encyclopedia*, typifies the Marxist view of the history of Hong Kong. He blames "China's financial enslavement by the imperialist powers" on capitalists who "imposed on China" a ninety-nine year lease of the New Territories and who made Hong Kong "a bastion of British imperialism in China." Khokhlov reminds readers that the People's Republic of China considers Hong Kong a territory that has been "torn away" and that the working class of Hong Kong, "the Chinese proletariat," has repeatedly "defied the imperialists" with large strikes (Khokhlov 1980: 66b).

How readers judge the historical accuracy of Clavell's portrait, then, depends on their personal perspectives and the larger philosophic and economic patterns to which they give credence.

5

Shogun: A Novel of Japan
(1975)

> *The Japanese . . . were the Westerners of the East. Curious though their*
> *customs might be, and slightly exotic their appearance, still they seemed to*
> *honor,* au fond, *the virtues then most admired in the West: diligence, loy-*
> *alty, patriotism, the stiff upper lip, and never-say-die.*
> Jan Morris, in *Japan: Photographs, 1854–1905* by Clark Worswick

Shogun (1975) took the literary critics by storm. Praise ran high: *Shogun* was described as "irresistible," "marvelously engrossing," "surging with action, intrigue and love," "vast and dramatic," "stunning," "savage," "beautiful," "extraordinary," and "so enveloping you forget who and where you are." *New York Times* book reviewer Webster Schott wrote, "Clavell has a gift. . . . He breathes narrative"; his hero is not a person but a place and a time, "medieval Japan on the threshold of becoming a sea power" (Schott 1975). The novel seized the popular imagination, and Blackthorne, Toranaga, Lady Mariko, *arigato*, and *konnichi-wa* became household words among readers.

Book sales exceeded seven million, and in response to such popularity, NBC sponsored a miniseries adaptation of the book. Clavell took part in every phase of the production, including casting and direction. Richard Chamberlain played Blackthorne, noted Japanese actor Toshiro Mifune took the role of Lord Toranaga, John Rys-Davies was Rodrigues, and Yoko Shimada played Lady Mariko. The television miniseries was fol-

lowed by the printing of two and a half million copies of a Dell paperback edition of *Shogun*; the publication of a book called *The Making of
James Clavell's "Shogun,"* which provides insights into the production of
the miniseries; a Japan Society booklet called *Learning from Shogun*, which
enumerates the intercultural lessons of both the miniseries and book; and
a two-and-a-half-hour theatrical version of *Shogun*, filmed simultane-
ously with the miniseries and released internationally as a motion picture. Eric Majors, a personal friend of Clavell's associated with Hodder
and Stoughton publishers, explained the huge popularity of the book by
saying: "It took the Western mind into a completely different world. It
was the first time that one began to understand the Japanese." Indeed,
Shogun is one of the most effective depictions of cross-cultural encounters
ever written.

   Shogun is a detailed portrait of feudal Japan in the process of becoming
a nation-state dominated by one ruler. It depicts the very different attitudes of seventeenth-century Japanese and Europeans toward sex, food,
drink, and bathing, and the very different perspectives that allow each
to learn from the other. The novel is Clavell's finest effort, a forceful,
gripping portrait of gradual acculturation; we see the European sea captain Blackthorne slowly coming to see the Japanese first as humans, then
as equals to Europeans, and finally as superiors. The psychological pre-
cision of Blackthorne's education and gradual acculturation is one of
Clavell's most praiseworthy literary achievements, especially since at the
end of the novel we come to see Blackthorne, "our" European "stand-
in" throughout, for what he really is: a pawn of a clever warlord, an
Englishman limited and bound by fading memories of his former culture. *Shogun*'s sophistication about the clash of cultures has much to
teach modern readers and would make Clavell an important writer quite
apart from his other efforts. However, his striking image patterns, the
tensions between his personal history as a war-time prisoner of the Japanese and his urge for fairness, the detailed descriptions that vividly
bring to life an historical moment and yet make a modern statement, his
masterful control of perception, and, most of all, his in-depth psycho-
analytical study of characters distanced by both time and culture yet
endowed with life and spirit make this his finest work—one that deserves closer critical attention than it has received.

PLOT DEVELOPMENT

Set in the feudal Japan of the 1600s, *Shogun* traces the fortunes of the Elizabethan English seaman John Blackthorne (Pilot-major of five Dutch galleons) and his crew. Defying the geographical limits of their age, they have rounded Cape Horn and crossed the Pacific, guided by a priceless, stolen Portuguese rutter (a ship's pilot's guide), which spells out in detail the trade route to the Japans, as Japan was then known. During the voyage, they have lost four ships and most of their crew. Blackthorne brings his remaining ship to safe harbor in Japan in the spring of 1600. However, his ship needs repairs before it can sail, and he and his eleven-man crew, suffering from scurvy, must wait. Initially, they are treated well by local villagers, but when Yabu Kasigi, the headman or *daimyo* of the area arrives, he treats them as prisoners. He has them tossed into a deep pit and has containers of salt water and rotting fish emptied over them. Before they will be freed, they must choose a victim to be executed from among themselves. When they attack their jailers instead, Yabu has a prisoner slowly cooked alive; his screams shatter the night. A samurai who is pulled into the pit is granted the mercy of a knife with which to commit *seppuku*, suicide by slashing open his own belly. This is the Westerners' initiation into a new and puzzling world, the world of feudal Japan.

The novel captures the feudal nature of relationships. Just as the feudal hierarchy requires his retainers to submit to Lord Yabu, so Yabu must yield to his superior, Lord Toranaga Yoshi, president of the Council of Regents, who demands that the Dutch crew and galleon be protected and the pilot and all booty sent to Osaka aboard an oar-powered galley captained by the Portuguese pilot Vasco Rodrigues. Where the Westerners have a certain sense of independence and equality based on shared competence (Rodrigues lets Blackthorne pilot the oar-powered galley through a rough storm), the Japanese are bound by feudal obligation. For example, Blackthorne initiates a search for Rodrigues, who has gone overboard in the storm, out of a personal sense of obligation; Lord Yabu, in contrast, braves a steep cliff and an incoming tide and several close calls with death to save Rodrigues, because of his duty to Lord Toranaga. At Osaka fortress, Lord Toranaga is equally bound by feudal regulations that put him in danger from his archrival Ishido and that make him as much a prisoner as Blackthorne, though he commands his section of the castle. Lord Toranaga has friendly relations with the heir apparent, Yaemon, whose official guardian he is, and with Yaemon's grandmother, Yodoko, the widow of the Taiko or former leader. However, feudal law defining obligations compels Lord Toranaga to attend an official meeting of the five regents charged with the protection and care of the heir. Because that meeting is purposely and repeatedly delayed with various pretenses, Lord Toranaga is, in effect, a prisoner, bound by duty inside a fortress commanded by forces anxious to reduce his power and perhaps end his life.

Blackthorne's arrival threatens to disrupt a delicate balance of power. He meets key Japanese and Jesuit figures, including Father Alvito, who serves as translator and who is dismayed at how much Blackthorne reveals to Toranaga about European politics, the Pope's division of the world into spheres of influence for plundering, and the revenues the Jesuits are earning. Toranaga realizes he has a gold mine of information in Blackthorne, but that he must use him with seeming indifference. Therefore, he has him imprisoned in a claustrophobic hellhole, but in the company of a Dominican priest, Friar Domingo, and with protectors among the prisoners, though Blackthorne does not know this.

Friar Domingo, happy to see a European after years of imprisonment, begins teaching Blackthorne Japanese and educating him about the Portuguese trade and the Jesuit secrets, including their master plan for Japan. When Blackthorne is finally led out, it is not to crucifixion, the fate of the other prisoners, but back to Toranaga, though he must first survive armed encounters between Ishido's and Toranaga's forces and what seem to be lawless *ronin* (leaderless samurai) kidnappers. Since Friar Domingo died of a heart attack when Toranaga's guards came for him, Toranaga assigns Lady Mariko to interpret for Blackthorne and to teach him more about the Japanese language and customs, while Toranaga himself questions Blackthorne and has him make maps depicting a European view of the world and of key trade routes used by Westerners. Friar Domingo has given Blackthorne a solid grasp of Japan's situation, which he uses to advantage in winning Toranaga's trust and making him distrust the Jesuits. When Blackthorne helps foil a possible assassination attempt on Toranaga, a friendship between Toranaga and Blackthorne is established.

When Toranaga arranges for his consort of many years, Kiritsubo, to leave Osaka castle, it is actually an escape plan for himself. His younger consort, Lady Sazuko, who is pregnant with Toranaga's child, creates a distraction by falling, so Toranaga, in disguise, takes Kiritsubo's place. Blackthorne, who has seen the exchange, understands the danger when

Ishido himself stops the procession at the castle bridge and insists on giving Kiritsubo (Toranaga in disguise) a personal message to take to Yedo. Blackthorne endangers his own life, playing the madman and crying out that it is "bad luck" for a prince to deliver a message himself, to distract Ishido from this act. His ruse is successful, and the escape party moves on, only to be ambushed by Ishido's forces, who are disguised as *ronin*, and then to be foiled again by Ishido's gray-uniformed samurai, who guard the dock where Toranaga's ship waits. Again, Blackthorne, aided by Lady Mariko, assures Toranaga's escape by sending Ishido's major force away on a wild goose chase to "rescue" Toranaga's party from attackers, by quietly informing Toranaga's brown-uniformed naval troops that their lord will be boarding, and by launching the attack on the few remaining enemy guards.

Their escape ship freed, they must next face a barricade at the harbor's mouth, and again it is Blackthorne who suggests that cannons from a nearby Portuguese ship are vital to their breaking through the enemy line. Thus Toranaga boards the Portuguese vessel and makes a deal with the Portuguese leaders, Father Alvito and Captain Ferriera. Toranaga agrees to allow the Jesuits to build a cathedral in Yedo and to leave Blackthorne for Ferriera to question in exchange for cannons. Blackthorne, who has missed Western food, eats and drinks himself senseless while his life is bartered for Toranaga's. Rodrigues, who understands the pact with Ferriera will cost Blackthorne his life and who feels obliged to Blackthorne for saving him from drowning, tosses Blackthorne overboard in feigned disgust and sends a trusted underling to get Blackthorne back aboard Toranaga's vessel. An exciting sea chase ensues with Rodrigues seeming to threaten Blackthorne and his galley but with the two actually working in concert so that the Japanese galley storms the blockade in tandem with the Portuguese vessel. The danger safely passed, Toranaga reboards the galley and they sail to Yedo.

The rest of the book records Toranaga's manipulation of all those around him as he plays opposing forces off against each other to gain time to prepare for war and to escape a number of traps set for him by both his opponents and his allies. Like a puppetmaster, he controls every action of those around him. He uses their strengths and weaknesses to attain his goals and, at the same time, gives them what they want or need, even when they themselves are unaware of that need. He tempts the Jesuits with the promise of concessions and the possible conversion of his son; he pries valuable secrets from a "willow world" *mama-san* with ambitions for a special "floating world" red-light district, samurai status for her son, and a change in status for geishas (the right to be purely artists, not prostitutes); he offers his treacherous brother his blessing for an advantageous marriage to Lady Ochiba, the mother of the legal heir, Yaemon. Cynically, he then increases his own power and betters his position by offering Lady Ochiba marriage to himself and adoption of her son before his brother has time or opportunity to propose. Toranaga's offer would give the heir the protection of the most powerful warlord of the age and would give Toranaga influence over the heir and access to the throne: his adopted son would be king.

Blackthorne considers himself master of the sea and an experienced politician. However, his Japanese experiences teach him that he is a naive barbarian compared to the Japanese samurai and warlords. Deluded into thinking he is in control of his fate and promised an opportunity to attack the Portuguese Black Ship and to initiate English trade with Japan, Blackthorne is cleverly exploited by Toranaga and his associates, who draw him into plots and counterplots as they tap his knowledge of ships and shipbuilding but at the same time help transform him into an honorable and courageous samurai. *Shogun* is a record of that transformation. Blackthorne saves Toranaga's life on at least three occasions; he adopts Japanese patterns of courtesy, of obliqueness, and of duty; and his developing sensitivity to human relationships helps him read nuances of character.

Lady Mariko, who is unhappily wed to the brutish samurai Buntaro, teaches Blackthorne the Japanese language and Japanese culture and, with time, love, though their physical enjoyment of each other is limited to a few occasions. Their dalliance on their trip to Osaka is bittersweet, since Mariko knows she will die there. The cruel Yabu proves treacherous, betraying Lady Mariko to Ishido and his *ninja* assassins and informing Toranaga's opponents of what Yabu thinks are Toranaga's plans. Toranaga, who has feigned weakness and indecision to gain time for his plots to work, surprises even his allies at the end with a sudden attack that results in his complete political control and in his investment as Shogun of the Japans.

STRUCTURE

Shogun depends on four structural patterns that provide unity and interlock characters and events. The most obvious structural device is chronology. Events move forward in time from the spring of 1600 to

November 21 of the same year. Clavell notes the dates at the beginning and end, mentions the time of Blackthorne's imprisonment with Friar Domingo as May 1600, and has Mariko promise the renewal of her marriage with Buntaro and a return to Blackthorne in August, when she knows she will be dead. Events move inexorably toward a pivotal moment in history: Toranaga's confrontation with his fellow regents and the implementation of his war plan, "Crimson Sky." In that short period are crammed the experiences of a lifetime as Blackthorne reevaluates himself and his culture and learns a new perspective and as Toranaga overthrows forty years of Portuguese and Jesuit dominance and opens up a new era for Japan. Past events are filled in through the memories and dreams of Blackthorne and through Blackthorne's conversations with Friar Domingo, Father Alvito, and Lady Mariko, who relate personal, church, and state histories.

A second structural pattern is a division of the action into six books, each of which involves parallels and contrasts. Book One (chapters 1 through 9) establishes the situation, records the initial encounter, and ends with a turning point, the Japanese discovery of Blackthorne's value as a highly skilled ship's pilot and Rodrigues's obligation to Blackthorne for saving his life. Book Two (chapters 10 through 29) introduces Lord Toranaga and the complex political situation in which he operates, and marks a period during which Blackthorne begins to seriously learn the Japanese language and culture. It begins with despair as Toranaga has Blackthorne imprisoned, but ends with hope as Blackthorne helps Toranaga escape imprisonment. Book One ends with Blackthorne saving Rodrigues's life; Book Two ends with Rodrigues returning the favor. Book Three (chapters 30 through 46) records Blackthorne's language and culture lessons and the changes he undergoes. Initially, Blackthorne is so outraged when he learns that an entire village must make sure he learns Japanese within six months or else all the villagers will be executed that he attempts *seppuko*, or Japanese-style suicide. Although a samurai deflects Blackthorne's blade at the last moment, Blackthorne is so changed by the experience, and the Japanese so stunned by such "civilized" and honorable behavior, that this marks a turning point in his understanding. This initial reaction is balanced with a later reaction: Blackthorne recognizes the Japanese logic that requires the execution of his aged gardener for breaking his thoughtless command that a rotting pheasant, which was offensive to the community, be left in place; he accepts personal responsibility for that death and honors the self-sacrificing community spirit of the dead man. The first proof of his change is his friend Rodrigues's attempt to kill him. The second proof is his reencounter with his crew, in Book Four (chapters 47 through 51), and his revulsion at their stench, their loutish behavior, and their association with *eta*, Japanese who are social outcasts because they break Buddhist law by butchering animals. In Book Four, Blackthorne's hopes that he can use his refurbished ship *Erasmus* to fight for Toranaga, to defeat the Black Ship, or to begin trade are dashed by its destruction in Book Five. Books Two, Three, and Four record the deceptions and illusions perpetrated by Toranaga, while Book Five (chapters 52 through 61) begins to expose the strategy behind the illusions and to test the mettle of Toranaga's supporters. Book Six is a wrapping up, with Toranaga at last exposed as puppet master and the events of the preceding chapters explained in terms of his master game plan. The pieces of the puzzle fall into place and the denouement occurs.

A third, and perhaps more significant, organizational pattern depends directly on the key character, John Blackthorne. *Shogun* is organized around the four stages of culture shock he undergoes: (1) delight in the new culture; (2) horror, shock, revulsion, and resistance; (3) gradual accommodation; and (4) immersion and acceptance. The delight is short-lived. His reaction is partly joy at surviving and at accomplishing the seemingly impossible goal of sailing to the Japans, and it is partly a pleasure in at last having fresh fruit and vegetables and at imagining the possibilities for gleaning wealth with the aid of what seem like simple, kindly villagers, who are awestruck by his blue eyes and striking sexual equipment (they bathe him). However, his delight is cut short by the arrival of Lord Yabu, who teaches Blackthorne and his crew the reality of their situation. Blackthorne is angered at and disturbed by the cruelty of the Japanese, by their willingness to commit suicide and to kill instantly, without thought, and by their casual attitudes toward human sexual appetites and the human body.

Blackthorne's accommodation phase begins when he gets help from Lady Mariko. Like Dante's Beatrice, who inspires the pilgrim Dante toward Paradise, Mariko is the perfect guide, helping Blackthorne move past his outrage and disgust to achieve a gradual understanding and appreciation of the Japanese way of life. In her own quiet way, she brings alive for him the discipline, loyalty, and deep-rooted sense of obligation and of honor that motivates her, and, by extension, Lord Toranaga and others. Blackthorne's comments on the courage and competence of people he had previously regarded as heathen sadists mark this change. As his understanding grows, so does his appreciation, especially as he begins to recognize the subtlety and skill of Toranaga's manipulation of those around him. Finally, he reaches the highest level of cultural adjustment, at which he begins to think like a Japanese and to view Europeans as his new Japanese friends once viewed him. He is proud of having achieved samurai status, of being adept enough at Japanese manners to have Lady Ochiba praise him as a courtier. The cruelties that once seemed inexplicable still bother him, but he has adjusted to them and now sees their justification and responds to the philosophical attitude toward life that provokes them. His transformation is summed up in his response to Fujiko: What had once seemed ugly, repulsive, and alien has now acquired a special beauty bound up with duty, respect, and admiration.

A final organizational pattern, which is virtually Shakespearean in nature, is the investigation of a multifaceted topic or idea, like "love," through its demonstration in contrasting characters, "foils," from different social levels or different value systems. Thus, Lady Mariko's illicit, romantic love for the barbarian John Blackthorne parallels the samurai Kasigi Omi's inappropriate, romantic love for the courtesan Kiku. The depth of Lady Mariko and Blackthorne's physical and spiritual attraction is played off against the lighthearted love affairs of Toranaga, and against Toranaga's long-lasting friendship with good-humored past lovers like the loyal Kiritsubo, against the ambitious lust of Lord Ishido (Toranaga's key rival) and Lord Zataki (Toranaga's brother) for Lady Ochida (widowed mother of the heir), and against Lady Ochida's illicit sexual encounter with a peasant who is the real father of the heir. Rodrigues's protective love for his Japanese wife parallels Blackthorne's love for Mariko and his sense of responsibility for and obligation to Fujiko, but contrasts with the animalistic couplings of Blackthorne's crew with *eta* prostitutes and with Yabu's perverted sexual need for both a male and a female prostitute after the pleasure of the kill.

THEMATIC ISSUES

Shogun provides a valuable lesson about the courage, determination, and even madness it took to face the unknown in the hope of discovering a new world of wealth, and of earning fame. One of Clavell's main themes is the power of extraordinary men to inspire and compel the ordinary to achieve beyond their capacities. In some small way, *Shogun* is a tribute to the spirit of the Renaissance that opened minds to possibilities inconceivable before that time; to the early Portuguese who sailed uncharted waters; and to the English Queen Elizabeth, who sent sailors like Drake and Hawkins into the unknown for trade and plunder, but ultimately for the advancement of us all. Clavell's powerful descriptions of the dangers Blackthorne and his crew encountered, the storms they braved, the diseases they suffered, and the harrowing treatment they endured at the hands of their captors makes clear what Clavell's daughter's textbook meant when it said, "In 1600 an Englishman went to Japan and became a samurai" (*The Making of James Clavell's "Shogun,"* 1980: 14). Blackthorne's spirit of adventure, his competence and skill, his endurance, adaptability, and pigheaded obsession with his ship are virtues Clavell means readers to admire and respect, as the Japanese of the story come to do.

However, *Shogun* is more than a tribute to the spirit of an age. Elizabethan Sir Phillip Sidney, echoing Horace, said that a work of art should both "profit" and "delight." The "delight" of *Shogun* rests in the adventure story: the excitement of a sea confrontation, the pleasure of a secret romance, the shock of armed encounters, the terror of shadowy assassins, the bravery of a samurai woman taking up the sword in defense of her lord. The "profit" rests in the themes. Clavell teaches readers the value of teachers and teaching, the duplicity of Jesuits in Japan, the shock of cultural differences, and yet the human spirit beneath those differences that allows men and women from alien cultures to find common ground, peace, and understanding. Related to these last two themes and to the teaching theme is a broader theme, the nature of perception, which will be further explored in the section on character development.

The Value of Teachers and Teaching

A recurring theme that unifies *Shogun* is the importance of teaching to pass on knowledge and skills. Blackthorne repeatedly draws on the wisdom, advice, and lessons of Alban Caradoc, under whom he was apprenticed and learned the skills of sailor, pilot-navigator, and shipbuilder. In times of trouble, he can hear the warnings of his first teacher: "Get your wits about you boy. . . . When the storm's the worst and the sea the most dreadful, that's when you need your special wits. That's what keeps you alive and your ship alive . . ." (53). Caradoc had sailed with Francis Drake and Admiral Hawkins and his lessons were born of experience. As a result of that apprenticeship, even the Portuguese recognize Blackthorne as "the best Protestant pilot alive" (133).

In Japan, his teacher is the Portuguese pilot Rodrigues, who, despite their rivalry, warms to him as a fellow pilot. Rodrigues teaches Blackthorne a few key Japanese words and, more importantly, gives him advice about Japanese manners and attitudes: Japanese are "six-faced" and "three-hearted" (136). His recommendation that Blackthorne act like "a king" (144), though it might get him killed, improves Blackthorne's status and wins him better treatment. Rodrigues is initially hesitant about teaching an Englishman, but while recuperating from his injuries, he provides information vital to Blackthorne's safety. Blackthorne's next teacher, Friar Domingo, mistakes him for a Spanish Catholic. Domingo teaches him the Japanese language and culture and informs him of the dirty dealings of the Jesuits in India, China, and Japan, of their enormous profits from the silk and tea trade, and of their plots to expand Christian influence in Japan.

Lord Toranaga provides Blackthorne with his most important teacher, Lady Mariko, who teaches him not only Japanese but a way of life and a value system worthy of respect. She inspires him to see with new eyes, to discover inner harmony, to be stoic, and to learn the Zen way of mental control—of compartmentalizing problems, of concentrating so intently on the world of the mind that he can watch a rock grow or savor imaginary tea from an imaginary cup. She, in turn, learns from him a Westerner's sense of justice and right, of Christian love for fellow human beings, even for peasants, of conscience and guilt. Though she can never really practice it, she also learns the virtue of his open-hearted directness. What began as Mariko's duty becomes pleasure as sharing diminishes differences.

Ironically, Blackthorne contemptuously dismisses as devious schemers with ulterior motives the genuine teachers in the book, the Portuguese Jesuits, who set up schools, write a Japanese grammar, develop Japanese-English, Japanese-Portuguese, Japanese-Spanish, and Japanese-Latin dictionaries, and teach Roman Catholic religious values. Their Catholicism and the historic antagonism between England, Portugal, and Spain make him distrust their motives. By the close of the novel, Blackthorne trusts the Japanese more than he does these fellow Westerners. Nonetheless, Blackthorne could not progress as rapidly as he does without Jesuit books, for books, Clavell teaches, are the essence of what others have learned through long years and hard experience. They are a shortcut to knowledge and wisdom, just as the navigator's rutter is a mariner's shortcut to navigation.

However, there are no easy shortcuts to learning in Clavell. Yabu and

Omi's attempts to force rapid learning by placing a village under sentence of death unless the villagers teach Blackthorne to speak Japanese fail. Clavell depicts repeated correction without explanation or clarification as ineffectual and suggests instead that the best combination for learning is self-motivation, good books, and a sympathetic guide who takes the time to provide reasons, not just corrections.

Blackthorne becomes a teacher, initially lightheartedly teaching Toranaga to dance an English sailor's hornpipe, to dive in an English manner, and to swim with an English stroke. He also teaches Toranaga, Yaemon, and Lady Mariko about Europe and Europeans, about his personal travels in North America and his encounters with Laplanders, and about the Pope's line of demarcation dividing the world between Spain and Portugal. He gives geography lessons by drawing a map of the known world and of the routes he has sailed. Toranaga realizes Blackthorne's value as a teacher who can open up for the Japanese the ideas and strategies of Westerners, their customs, values, and methods of waging war, shipbuilding, and sailing.

Clavell's final point about education is that it does not simply pass on information, it changes perception and opens learners' eyes to what was hidden. Studying the Japanese language, history, and culture transforms Blackthorne; he can never again be the man he was. He sees his crew with new eyes, and he interprets events with a deeper understanding. The more one learns the more there is to learn. Blackthorne has learned to look deeply into the heart of the Japanese, but there are realities and truths he is yet unable to perceive. The reader is left to speculate about how many more years of learning it will take before he can see as clearly as Toranaga does—if ever.

Clavell is the teacher behind the scenes, using his own experiences and historical facts to provide readers a valuable "rutter," a guide to understanding the Japanese. *Shogun* is that rutter, Clavell's record of a voyage of discovery he himself sailed in his relations with the Japanese, one that teaches readers to make their own voyage into a world Westerners initially find incomprehensible.

Jesuit Duplicity

Clavell concentrates his anticlerical attack on Jesuits. Blackthorne, as an Elizabethan Englishman from a Protestant heritage and a nation at war with Catholic Spain (of which Portugal was then a part), automatically suspects any Catholics, but most especially the Portuguese Jesuits, whose campaign as soldiers of Christ was being conducted against Queen Elizabeth in England, and whose reputation for duplicity he finds confirmed by tradition ("Hang a Jesuit, and he will steal your rope.") and by the Dominican Friar Domingo. Friar Domingo blames the Jesuits for plotting against the other Catholic orders to keep Japan totally in Jesuit hands and for inciting the Taiko to crucify twenty-six Franciscan fathers at Nagasaki. Friar Domingo calls Jesuits "traders, gun runners, and usurers" who deal in gold and smuggle guns to further their interests (233) and blames them for meddling in politics, pimping for kings, lying, cheating, bearing false witness against other orders, and spreading poison against Spain. He denounces them as devils who "hide behind a net of poverty and piousness," but who, underneath, serve only themselves, lusting for power at any cost, feeding like kings, and amassing great wealth (239). Friar Domingo's diatribe seems confirmed by Fathers Alvito and Dell'Aqua, who curse Blackthorne's honest description of the line of demarcation and his use of Friar Domingo's insider knowledge to change Toranaga's view of Jesuit activities, who keep Japanese Catholics from becoming priests, and who declare Mariko a church martyr to exploit her noble samurai lineage. Given this context, Rodrigues, a Catholic himself, who remembers the *auto da fé* of the Inquisition and the two thousand witches burned in Portugal alone the year he sailed for Asia, is nonplussed by the Jesuits' politically self-serving declaration, "Thou shalt not kill."

Blackthorne's experiences with Toranaga confirm the power of the Jesuits. As the main interpreters between Japanese and Europeans, they have multiple opportunities to manipulate information. They move freely throughout the land, despite laws confining European activities to Nagasaki. Toranaga's concessions to church power win him their secret support. As an advocate of free trade, Clavell sees the Jesuit willingness to mix trade and politics with piety not simply as cynical and hypocritical but as historically unforgivable.

Cultural Differences

Shogun takes Westerners into the Japanese mind in a way that sociological studies or mere histories do not. In doing so, it follows the progression Clavell himself must have experienced, from his first shocking contact with the Japanese, the incredible cruelties and indifference to human suffering he saw firsthand at Changi, to his later experiences, through which he gained a gradual respect for the Japanese sense of duty, loyalty, and honor and finally, an understanding of the alien philosophies that compel the Japanese vision of the world.

Clavell's concern with Japanese cruelty is natural, given his Changi experiences. His initial image of Yabu gaining sexual pleasure from the cries of an English sailor being slowly boiled in a pot, and composing a poem and dedicating a very special stone for his host's Zen garden to celebrate the occasion, seems indescribably alien and barbaric. Throughout *Shogun*, Clavell describes samurai laughing as they hack people to pieces, torture victims, and crucify prisoners. Rodrigues tells Blackthorne of a fifty-foot mound containing the noses and ears of conquered Koreans. Though Clavell can never forgive Japanese indifference to human life, in some cases, like that of Yabu, he presents the sadism as the perversion of a specific person. But Clavell also gives cultural explanations for some actions. A samurai flinging himself over a cliff to his death to gain the attention of his superior, Lord Yabu, who is in danger, stuns Blackthorne, but he is told that in forty days the samurai will be reborn with higher status because of his deed. When a carefully coached assassin armed with secret passwords breaks in to Toranaga's section of the Yedo fortress, the guards in charge calmly face decapitation, believing it an appropriate punishment for dereliction of duty. Clavell had plenty of examples of extreme cruelty available in the historical records. For instance, a common means of executing Christians was to hang the victims head downward on a gallows and let them slip slowly into a pit filled with the drainings from a manure heap (Plattner 1952: 98). On the last page of the novel, Toranaga does what his historical counterpart Tokugawa did: after his men have taken 40,000 heads in battle, he has his rival buried with only his head sticking out of the earth and invites passersby "to saw at the most famous neck in the realm with a bamboo saw," a lingering death that took three days to accomplish (121).

Neither Clavell nor his representative Englishman, Blackthorne, feel comfortable with such cruelty, but references to Spanish and Portuguese cruelties—the burning of infidels and heretics at the stake, the use of the rack and other instruments of torture—place Japanese cruelty in a wider context. Moreover, Blackthorne eventually comes to see cruelty as inseparable from the stoicism of the Japanese and from their Spartan lifestyle. Clavell depicts a system that cultivates bland indifference to pain and suffering as a prized characteristic, that considers *seppuku* or ritual disemboweling as the death of choice, and that values a willingness to face torture and death as proof of true nobility. In such a context, cruelty is reduced to policy and to a demonstration of stoic indifference and endurance. Rodrigues points out that while the Chinese value the scholar and the art of negotiation, the Japanese have historically valued the soldier, the samurai, the military leader, above all others, and have made the art of war their study. Their proud sense of honor makes death a small price to pay for insult.

Though the cruelty of the Japanese shocks Blackthorne, their cleanliness amazes him. His first experience with cleanliness is when he is forced to bathe. Elizabethans believed a bath could kill, so many went their whole lives without bathing. However, the Japanese, repulsed by the stench of Westerners, insist on cleanliness, and Blackthorne comes to appreciate their perspective, and to be equally repulsed by nonbathers. Blackthorne is also impressed by the cleanliness of Japanese doctors, who recommend fresh air for a speedy recovery from illness, whereas their European counterparts would shut up all windows for fear of contagion being carried in the air. Most of all, Blackthorne is impressed by the incredible cleanliness of city streets. In London and European cities of that time, offal, feces, urine, and garbage were cast into the streets to be scavenged and often piled up so high that pedestrians and carts could not pass; herds of swine were driven through the main thoroughfares at night to eat the waste. Londoners let rats, wild dogs, cats, maggots, rain, or the occasional fire cleanse their streets. In contrast, Osaka and other Japanese cities far larger than London seemed swept clean, sparkling and neat. In Osaka, no beggars, cripples, or wild, loutish youths preyed on travelers. Instead, all was orderly, clean, and peaceable—virtues both Blackthorne and Clavell have come to value. In fact, all Clavell's novels emphasize that Easterners valued cleanliness long before Westerners did.

Shogun also contrasts Japanese group and family loyalties with Western personal loyalties. Western readers, schooled in the importance of loyalties to individuals, expect Blackthorne's growing friendship with Toranaga and his having saved Toranaga's life on several occasions to result in a loyalty that would make Toranaga protect Blackthorne as his personal friend. Yet Toranaga uses Blackthorne as a bargaining chip time and again. When Toranaga fears assassination, he lets Blackthorne use his room, knowing the attackers might kill him. When the cruel Ferriera demands that Blackthorne be turned over to him as his price for helping Toranaga escape, Toranaga agrees. He sends Blackthorne into the heart of the enemies' fortress, knowing he might not return. From a Japanese perspective, Toranaga is a wise lord who uses the loyalty of those under him to best serve his own long-term family and group interests. If this means that Blackthorne or Lady Mariko or any other vassal must be sacrificed, so be it. One reason Toranaga eventually gives the lovely Kiku to Blackthorne is that her beauty distracts Toranaga from his duties, and duty comes first.

Westerners might expect romantic lovers like Blackthorne and Lady Mariko to find their life and meaning in each other, but Clavell guides Westerners to understand Mariko's choice of duty over love. She has no choice: to act otherwise would be a betrayal of love. Blackthorne realizes this and loves her the more for her bravery, which wins her the respect of friends and foes.

Cultural Understanding

Clavell provides a Japanese perspective. Acts that seem insane in one culture might be normal within another. When Blackthorne understands Japanese self-sacrifice for community good and appreciates it as a valuable act, his perspective has truly changed. Clavell's theme, then, is change. Because of his bicultural perspective, Blackthorne can choose the best of both worlds: the Christian compassion, independent spirit, technological skills, and personal loyalties of the West, and the duty to group, obligation to community, and sense of honor of the Japanese. If Clavell's overall message is the value of education, of teaching and of learning, then perspective is the key to this learning. By developing the ability to see through the eyes of the Other, one can more clearly examine one's own culture and choose the best of both worlds.

CHARACTER DEVELOPMENT

Clavell does not highly individualize Blackthorne's Dutch crew. Jan Roper stands out for his anger, bigotry, and religious fanaticism as he denounces all papists as devils and all Japanese as animals, and eventually dies in a fit at the thought of having to stay among them any longer. But Clavell does highly individualize even minor Japanese characters. It is almost as if he is countering, with distinctive Japanese and homogenous Europeans, the Western cliché that all Asians look alike.

There are memorable portraits of a number of Japanese figures. Some of these portraits gain significance from contrasts: for example, those of the Taiko and his son and heir; of Toranaga's aging right-hand man, Hiro-matsu, and his son, Lord Buntaro; and of Toranaga and a number of his sons, some alienated, some loyal. The good-hearted, willing Naga is a foil to his brother Sudara, who, except for his deep love for his wife, Lady Genjiko, is as icy, calculating, and capable of intricate gamesmanship as his father, Toranaga.

Other characters stand out. To prove his courage, Yabu accepts Blackthorne's challenge to climb down a sheer cliff to bring back Rodrigues; then, with the tide coming in and the cliff unscalable, he meditates on his death poem with stoic acceptance; when there is a chance to escape, he risks his life again to drag the unconscious Rodrigues to safety. A man of contradictions, he protects Toranaga against Ishido's plots, arranges for the poisoning of Toranaga's key enemy, and loyally defends Toranaga with his life, yet he negotiates with Ishido against Toranaga, leaks secret information about battle strategy, and lets in the *ninja* forces that kill Mariko. He is indifferent to his own death and to the deaths of others, yet he enthusiastically envisions and strives for a Japanese fleet "filled with samurai, piloted by samurai, captained by samurai, sailed by samurai" (177). After efficiently settling family matters for his betrayer, he meets his death honorably, by *seppuko*. In life and in death, Yabu remains inscrutable to Westerners.

In *Shogun*, as in *King Rat*, three key characters dominate the action. The first is, of course, Blackthorne, through whose eyes we see the Japanese as a European would. The second is Toranaga, whose subtlety and clever machinations mark him as a superior whom Blackthorne learns to respect, honor, and love. The third is Lady Mariko, who helps Blackthorne and Toranaga appreciate their value to each other and bridge the linguistic and cultural differences that initially separate them.

We first see Blackthorne as highly competent and aggressively in charge, at the helm of his ship. However, on land, in the alien environment of Japan, Blackthorne is like a child—reduced to childish rages and tantrums. Thus Toranaga and his fellow samurai find Blackthorne a cryptic anomaly: "One moment so brave, the next so weak. One moment so valuable, the next so useless. One moment killer, the next coward. One moment docile, the next dangerous" (399). Like anyone learning a language and culture, he is like a toddler, a two-year-old, dependent on Mariko as a kind of mother figure. As he learns the language and learns from Mariko the rationale for behavior that had previously seemed incomprehensible, he gradually "grows up" in Japanese culture. After his attempt at *seppuku*, he is reborn a changed, matured man, no longer fearful of death, more understanding of the values of the society in which he has been thrust. By the end of the novel, Blackthorne has proven himself worthy of his *hatamoto* samurai status. His loyalty is no longer to his English queen but to his Japanese master.

It is Toranaga who began the process that transformed Blackthorne, and it is Toranaga again who sets him on a new course and new ambitions: to rebuild his ship in Mariko's honor, to call it "The Lady," and to sail against the Portuguese Black Ship to win wealth and honor for Toranaga and for himself. Toranaga describes the *Anjin-san*, or Pilot, the Japanese name for Blackthorne, as "wild and dangerous and unpredictable, always an unknown quantity, unique, unlike any man I've ever known" (1139), but he tames him as he would a falcon and sets him loose on his enemies at will. In an effective shift, Clavell moves the focus from Blackthorne, who has dominated most of the book, to a final focus on Toranaga, and in doing so, shifts the perspective of *Shogun* from a Western view to an Eastern one. Blackthorne has grown as a man and has accomplished much as a hero, but in the final analysis, he is but a pawn, a puppet, a tame falcon in the hands of Toranaga, the master gamesplayer, puppeteer, and falconer. He has broadened his perceptions, but his eye is still limited by his personal interests and personal goals; he lacks the broader vision that would enable him to understand his place in the overall historical pattern. Toranaga has diminished him. The film version's inability to capture this shift in perspective is a measure of how masterful Clavell's novel is.

The portrait of Lady Mariko helps readers make this perceptual shift. We learn at the beginning of the novel about her father's disloyalty and her whole family's betrayal of their feudal allegiances, a betrayal that has alienated her from her husband and made her seek release in *seppuko*. However, Toranaga has forbidden her that course of action and has instead placed on her the burden of taming the captured barbarian, Blackthorne. Mariko is able and infinitely patient, the perfect teacher. She controls her revulsion at barbarian manners and smells, and maintains a polite, understanding manner as she translates and teaches. Because she is a Christian, her translation and interpretations are conveyed in a way Blackthorne can understand. Though Clavell does not explain where she learned her magnificent English, her impact as a character is impressive, and she helps both Blackthorne and readers understand and appreciate the Japanese way of life.

As is appropriate in Japanese literary conventions, Mariko's romantic interlude with Blackthorne is a fleeting moment, for her destiny is already written. She serves Blackthorne well and, in so doing, serves Toranaga better. Her reward is an opportunity to redeem the honor of her family as Toranaga's falcon, sent against his prey and released to an honorable death for unswerving loyalty. Thus, on his instructions, she whispers the secrets that Toranaga gives her to Father Alvito and to the Christian Lord Kiyama and defies the regents in general and Ishido in particular to buy Toranaga time and to win him allies. She does so knowing that her death is inevitable, and when the chance for an honorable end comes, she takes it. Her sacrifice makes her a Christian martyr, wins Toranaga time and sympathetic allies, and restores honor to her family name and to her husband. It also frees Blackthorne to be a better servant to Toranaga, with no interfering private loyalties.

The priest Dell'Aqua rightly calls Toranaga "as clever as a Machiavelli and as ruthless as Attila the Hun" (306). Toranaga is first presented as a distant figure, powerful, awesome, but incomprehensible, his motives and character unclear. Lady Mariko explains his situation to Blackthorne, and thus provides insights that personalize him and that reveal his astute political acumen. Scenes of him drinking and dancing (reminiscent of the musical comedy *The King and I*) make him seem jovial, and his arranging his subjects' lives for their good suggests benevolence. However, Book Six reveals how calculated Toranaga's public image is. Blackthorne never sees through this personable persona, but readers share Toranaga's final monologue and thereby gain insights into his being that are veiled from Blackthorne.

Despite his denials, Toranaga's driving goal is to be shogun, to unite Japan under one ruler, himself, and to eliminate the corrupting influence of foreign traders and priests. He engineers all of his vassals and his tamed Christian to help him achieve these ends. Godlike, he knows their strengths and their weaknesses and uses both. He understands Yabu's disloyalty and makes it as much a part of his strategy as Mariko's loyalty and her need for honor. He says of Mariko, "In the chess game for power I sacrificed my queen but Ishido's lost two castles" (1134), and dismisses her loss with the consolation that she will live forever in legend. His subjects marvel at his ability to predict Blackthorne's behavior, but he attributes his skill to his having taken time to study him. After emphasizing the importance of taking time to study men, especially important men, whether friends or enemies, he predicts exactly how and why Blackthorne responds to Father Alvito. In the tradition of Ryunosuke Akutagawa's short story "Rashomon" (1915), Toranaga's interior monologues in Book Six reinterpret the events of the first five books, revealing that even Lady Mariko's final letter to Blackthorne, which helped Blackthorne accept her death and honor it, which gave his life new direction, and which most readers would respond to as a touching lover's farewell, has, in effect, been dictated by Toranaga as part of his long-range strategy. In a like manner, Toranaga tells Buntaro that he offered Mariko a chance to divorce Buntaro and she refused, but doesn't explain the complicated set of circumstances that affect the interpretation of her act, because his goal is to give Buntaro face and to end his dangerous competition with Blackthorne.

Toranaga rejects as flattery Father Alvito's analysis that "We're all clay on the potter's wheel you spin" (1151), but confirms the truth of that assertion in his repeated use of falcon and hawk imagery to distinguish between his subjects and to describe how he uses them. His falconer calls him "the greatest falconer in the realm" (1208), and he is, both literally and metaphorically. As he surveys his falcons and hawks for the day's hunt, he also surveys his subjects, evaluating their functions in falcon imagery, describing one as "a falcon that you feed from your fist, to fly at a prey and call back with a lure" (1195). He calls Blackthorne "a short-winged hawk" (1207), and Mariko, a nobler bird, a "peregrine" (1207). When Toranaga releases his favorite peregrine, he imagines it his gift to Mariko and to her spirit, though his assistant realistically sees it as the practical move of an experienced falconer, just as his release of Mariko to death was a practical move (1207). Such imagery was common in medieval literature and is appropriate for Toranaga as a feudal lord, but it also sums up Toranaga as a manipulator, writing his "legacy" to future generations and changing his nation's history by installing a dynasty that would bring about a golden age.

Blackthorne, as a favorite falcon, is set apart from Toranaga's usual hunters because Toranaga, who is usually among predictable people, craves the intellectual challenge of unpredictability. Unpredictability is his forte as a leader, and it is Blackthorne's greatest gift to Toranaga. Toranaga uses Blackthorne, a barbarian outsider, as his window on the West; however, this window reveals the secrets necessary to shut out the West.

Through the character of Toranaga, Clavell provides a dual vision of reality. One view is a tolerant appreciation of Japanese virtues. Toranaga is a wise leader, doing what he sees as best long-term for those under his protection and as best for Japan. He is forgiving of human weaknesses that do not threaten his rule, and he involves himself in every area of his subjects' lives to promote harmony at every level—in the family as well as in the nation—harmony being the most prized Japanese ideal. However, this is only a part of the total view, for Toranaga is also a ruthless, murderous tyrant, indifferent to individual life, who callously sacrifices his subjects to achieve power and who manipulates a barbarian to defeat barbarians. Which is the real man? Which is the real Japan? These are questions Clavell leaves to his readers to answer.

GENRE CONVENTIONS

As historical fiction, *Shogun* must meet two sets of standards: those of historical accuracy and those of fictive narrative. As a history, *Shogun* creates a well-rounded and credible portrait of seventeenth-century Japan, of its art and architecture, its gardens, weapons, and poetry, its social hierarchies, political policies, and strategies, its traditions and values. Clavell spent four years researching and writing *Shogun*, assuring authenticity and accuracy by traveling to Japan, a country whose people he had no reason to admire after his experiences at Changi. He read the sixteenth- and seventeenth-century accounts of Europeans in Japan, and drew particularly on the letters of the Jesuit Father Joao Rodrigues, though the records of others, like Cosme de Torres, S.J., St. Francis Xavier, S.J., Francesco Carletti, Rodrigo de Vivero y Velasco, and Alessandro Valignano, S.J., also point to Clavell's accuracy and his careful research. Carletti, for example, asserted, "There is no nation in the world which fears death less" (Cooper 1974: 42), while Valignano emphasized the patience of the Japanese, their willingness and training to endure "hunger, cold and all sorts of human discomforts and hardships" (44), perceptions echoed in the book. Valignano's emphasis on the Japanese custom of not transacting important or difficult business face to face but to depend instead on the intercession of a third person might have given Clavell his idea for Blackthorne's objection to Ishido handing a message to Kiritsubo (Toranaga in disguise). Clavell's fictive Rodrigues echoes the real Joao Rodrigues's descriptions of the Japanese, and in his warnings about Japanese duplicity (*Shogun*: 193), he paraphrases Joao Rodrigues's statement that the Japanese are "so crafty in their hearts that nobody can understand them," for which reason they are said to have "three hearts: a false one in their mouths for all the world to see, another within their breasts only for their friends, and the third in the depths of their hearts, reserved for themselves alone and never manifested to anybody" (Cooper 1974: 45). Friar Domingo's report on the Jesuits' request to the Pope to keep other Catholic religious orders out of Japan so as not to confuse a mission that required a cautious, concerted effort is confirmed by church records (Laures 1954: 124).

The historical Englishman Will Adams (whom Clavell first encountered in his daughter's history book) was, like Clavell's fictive hero, a pilot-major of a Dutch fleet of five ships who set out to sail around the world like Magellan and who ended up in Japan. There Ieyasu Tokugawa, a powerful political figure, realized Adams's value to his own ambitions and burned Adams's ship to keep him in Japan so he could use him in his dealings with the Portuguese and the Jesuits. Johannes Laures, S.J., in *The Catholic Church in Japan*, provides a valuable description of Clavell's historical model:

> Perhaps the greatest of all dangers which threatened Christianity was the appearance of the Dutch and the English on the scene. In 1600 the Dutch ship *De Liefde* was driven aground on the coast of Bungo. Among the few survivors of the stranded ship was the pilot, William Adams, an Englishman. The entire crew was interned, and the Portuguese, greatly alarmed at the appearance of prospective rivals for the profitable trade monopoly they had enjoyed for so many years, urged Ieyasu to punish the newcomers as pirates. (Laures 1954: 149)

Laures notes that "this cruel advice had some semblance of justice," since the Dutch ship carried guns and ammunition but little merchandise, but that "Ieyasu not only did not comply with the request of the Portuguese but treated the unfortunate survivors with kindness and consideration." Laures goes on to report that William Adams was "a good pilot" and "a capable shipbuilder and mathematician" and "very soon succeeded in winning Ieyasu's favor," much to the consternation of the Catholic missionaries, who realized "the danger of the presence of this staunch Protestant near the real ruler of Japan" and who "tried by every possible means to neutralize his influence" (149). Tokugawa later became Japan's first shogun and united clashing factions under his rule, while Adams became the "only foreigner ever to become a Japanese samurai" (*The Making of Shogun*: 17). Adams, like Blackthorne, received permission to build a new ship, but Tokugawa gave it to the governor general of the Philippines, though he did allow Adams to travel to Siam and even China on business for him, and through Adams engaged in some trade with the Dutch. Adams, says Laures, told Tokugawa that the Spaniards and Portuguese robbed the foreign countries they dealt with and intended to conquer Japan through their Christian missions (Laures 1954: 149). In fact, Catholic writers blame Adams directly for the persecution of the church under Tokugawa. Adams continued as advisor to Tokugawa, and then to his successor until his own death in 1620, four years after the death of Tokugawa. The Japanese erected a monument in his honor, and the log of Adams's journeys and five of his letters home reside in the British Museum (*The Making of Shogun*: 23).

Because Clavell is writing fiction rather than history, he makes changes. Thus, Will Adams becomes Clavell's John Blackthorne, but Blackthorne is not like Adams in all respects. Clavell's Lord Toranaga corresponds in some degree to the real shogun, Ieyasu Tokugawa, and Clavell's Nakamura corresponds directly to the Taiko, or head ruler, Hideyoshi Toyotomi, father of Tokugawa's ward, the heir apparent. A real Jesuit priest, Joao Rodrigues (1561–1633), who was the most influential European in Japan and served as confidant to Hideyoshi and Tokugawa, provided the name of Clavell's Portuguese pilot Rodrigues, and was the model for Father Alvito and other Jesuits in the novel (*The Making of Shogun*: 20). Clavell says he reworked historical reports for dramatic effect. For instance, the real Tokugawa and Hideyoshi sealed a bargain by urinating together and mixing their urine; Clavell heightens reality by relocating the scene at the top of a castle, changing the details of the bargain to fit his plot, inventing the thoughts of the two men, and giving them new names. The descriptions of the Jesuits writing Japanese-Latin and Japanese-Portuguese dictionaries and the first Japanese grammar book, of their function as translators and interpreters, and of their active involvement in the silk trade between China and Japan correspond to the historical record. Father Rodrigues, in fact, personally sought Tokugawa's assistance in reducing anti-Christian activities, and shortly before Tokugawa had himself invested as shogun, he actually encouraged Father Rodrigues to extend his missions.

Clavell has been criticized for not using the historical names, but his explanation for his changes is that though he is a writer of historical fiction, he is not writing history per se. Instead, he is a novelist, using an interesting historical situation as a basis for creating fiction. He argues that all historical accounts are merely someone's version of what happened and that he is providing an intuitive version, founded on a solid historical base, but that he is ultimately creating an imaginative synthesis of what may or may not have been a reality. His goal is to infuse his fictive version with people who seem real so that the historical period, conflicts, and personalities take on a life of their own and so that those events and the clashes of cultures and ideas they represent will suggest modern parallels. This is why Clavell carefully says that, "*Shogun* is not the story of Will Adams. It is the story of an Englishman who went to Japan and became a samurai" (*The Making of Shogun*: 23). It is this interweaving of fact and fiction that characterizes the historical fiction genre, and it is the mass of detail, the interlocking of different plot threads, the scale and significance of the conflicts, and the focus on a forceful, towering figure of legendary proportions, Lord Toranaga—a strategist, a Machiavellian master of intrigue—that suggest the epic potential of the novel.

ALTERNATIVE READING: DECONSTRUCTION

Shogun lends itself readily to deconstruction, an inventive critical approach. Deconstruction, a theory about language and literature developed in the 1970s by the French critic Jacques Derrida, is based on the assertion that every text contains nonverbal conventions and codes that make meaning indeterminate and that literary interpretations, then, are really arbitrary reflections of particular cultural and/or social perspectives. Consequently, a shift in perception can provide new insights into a literary work. Deconstruction postulates the idea of multiple possible readings of a single text, and even seemingly contradictory readings derived from polarities or opposing perspectives. For every yin, argue deconstructionists, there must be a yang, for every light, a dark. Sometimes this argument presupposes no single truth, only multiple interpretations, with meaning discovered through opposition or contradiction. To deconstruct a text, one need only find an antonym for every descriptive word employed, and then find evidence for that antonym in the text. For example, a love story, by the very fact of its focus on love, in effect, also makes a statement about its opposite, hate or an absence of love.

There is a rebellious quality to deconstruction, an undermining of existing hierarchies, a questioning of received values. However, there is also an impulse to dismiss the author's intentions as irrelevant to the reality of the text, to counter thesis with antithesis, and to give both equal weight. Thus, deconstruction has been regularly attacked as nihilistic, relativistic, subjective, and overly skeptical. Nonetheless, a deconstructionist view of *Shogun* can provide some insights into the book.

Since Clavell argues that writing *Shogun* and reevaluating Japan and the Japanese was his way of coming to terms with his wartime experiences, a deconstructionist might argue that Clavell reflects the Stockholm syndrome, identifies with his captors, and goes too far in giving the devil his due. Although the novel begins with Blackthorne's anger at samurai who torture noncombatants, much as their World War II descendants did, as Clavell captures Blackthorne's gradual conversion to a Japanese perspective, he ends up lionizing cruelty in the service of Spartan military medieval values. The first sign of Blackthorne's changed attitude is his open admiration for the bravery various Japanese display in the fulfillment of duty: for kamikaze suicides; for samurai he knows battling seemingly impossible odds; for Mariko, sword in hand, standing firm for Toranaga and later ordering hundreds of samurai to die in defense of her right to leave Osaka Castle. By the end of the novel, the sadism portrayed in the first two books of *Shogun* has been transformed into an almost admirable existential angst, a philosophical stance that allows the Japanese to face physical discomfort—cold, wetness, hunger, injury—with studied indifference and to have contempt for those who fail to share their sense of honor, obligation, and sacrifice. In other words, the reality of Japanese military behavior has not changed from Clavell's experiences in the Changi prison camp and his descriptions in *King Rat*, but the interpretation or perception of that reality has. In fact, this shift in perception is an underlying feature of the novel that helps raise it above the general run of historical fiction and to transform it into a powerful story that captures the imagination. From Blackthorne's point of view, Toranaga's initial treatment of him—his imprisonment, then rescue—seems inexplicable, but readers learn that Toranaga accepts Blackthorne's suffering as the price of Blackthorne's education and that Toranaga has had his men watching, protecting, and guiding Blackthorne as he gathers information and gains understanding, until Toranaga can use him once again in one of his power plays.

In terms of historical events, if Clavell is to depict Blackthorne as allied with Toranaga, then he must emphasize their shared dislike for Jesuits and the Jesuit mission because Toranaga's historical counterpart, Ieyasu Tokugawa, was personally responsible for the restoration of the Edict of Exile that expelled Christian missionaries from Japan and for the martyrdoms which followed. Ironically, Toranaga-Tokugawa's anticlerical stance and retreat into isolation run counter to Clavell's usual argument that a clash of cultures, and particularly a meeting through trade, is of long-term good for both cultures. By this standard, Toranaga, instead of being the hero he seems in the novel, is a xenophobic isolationist and hence a villain, and Blackthorne, as his friend and supporter, is a traitor to his European heritage. The Jesuits, in contrast, are simply fulfilling the European mission Clavell supported in *Tai-Pan*: to go among the heathen, to learn their ways, to teach them ours to mutual benefit, and to use trade as the tool to accomplish this end. In other words, Clavell is, in fact, condemning the Jesuits for what he has praised elsewhere.

Father Alvito is a representative case. He meets all of Clavell's requirements for a Western, capitalist hero. From his youth, he has lived among the Japanese and studied their language and culture and has made it his own, so much so that he has learned to think like a Japanese and to anticipate their logic and political moves. Alvito is struck, as are all Clavell's Western travelers, by the huge population of Japan, which was twenty million at a time when the population of all of England, including Wales and Scotland, was barely three million, and is convinced that the hundreds of thousands of converts already made can influence the temper of all Japan. Alvito has used trade to make himself and his associates an indispensable part of the Japanese economy, and he has helped establish schools to facilitate cultural interaction and understanding. He and his fellow Jesuits have helped transform the southern island by converting many there to Roman Catholicism, but they have walked a tight line between interference and assistance, maintaining a balance that is Japanese in its subtlety. Father Alvito is in direct contrast to Captain Ferriera, the Portuguese entrepreneur for whom dealings with the Japanese are purely commercial ventures to be exploited for personal advantage and personal profit. Ferriera is a thorough villain, but Blackthorne's plans for what he would do if he could get his ship and crew back are no different from Ferriera's—to plunder the Black Ship and sail for home. A further irony is that Blackthorne, convinced he has attained some influence over Toranaga, has played directly into his hands and has provided him the excuse and the supporting evidence to justify closing Japan to the West, as the historical Tokugawa did so effectively that Europeans did not again make inroads into Japan until the nineteenth century, the setting for Clavell's other Japanese novel, *Gai-Jin*.

In other words, reversing polarities broadens reader perspective and provides insights into the psychology that makes *Shogun*, in many ways, an anomaly in Clavell's canon: it is pro-Japanese and pro-isolationism, and it values cultural conversion instead of cultural sharing and blending, and group loyalties over individual loyalties.

6

Noble House: A Novel of Contemporary Hong Kong
(1981)

Hong Kong is but a dot on the map of China; and yet it is a place of world-wide importance because of its ocean-borne commerce.

Sir Cecil Clementi, governor of Hong Kong, 1935

The mighty spirit of free trade . . . fused the interests of European and Chinese merchants into indissoluble unity.

E. J. Eitel, *Europe in China: The History of Hong Kong*

Noble House is what Americans call a "blockbuster" and the French "a river novel," one as long and with as many separate stories as a river. Critics have praised it as "a sprawling Chinese banquet of a book" (*People*), "rich with possibilities" (Christopher Lehmann-Haupt, *The New York Times*), "seamless," "epic," and "steep[ed] in fascinating lore and history" (*The Cincinnati Enquirer*). Despite its need for judicious pruning (in other hands, it would have been several novels), *Noble House* skillfully interlocks thirty separate plot lines. With its main themes of human diversity and complexity, *Noble House* is both diverse and complex.

PLOT DEVELOPMENT

Ian Dunross, a direct descendant of *tai-pan* Dirk Struan, holds center stage and deals with the transformations wrought by the long-term meet-

ing of East and West. Dunross juggles international concerns for profit
and protects free enterprise from the Soviets and the British Labour
Party. He supports dependents, friends, and relatives, assures "Old
Friends" status with the mainland Chinese, and fulfills obligations as-
sumed by Noble House a century before.

The basic plot is as follows. In a time of crisis, Dunross takes over
Noble House, a private banking house and international shipping firm,
and sells public stock in the firm to prevent the bankruptcy pending from
an uninsured billion-dollar cargo lost at sea. The action revolves around
an economic war for control of Noble House, a war involving shifting
alliances, sexual liaisons, lush parties, kidnapping, murder, swindles,
racetrack bets, and espionage.

Dunross's "comprador" or head Chinese business advisor, Phillip
Chen, has secretly copied all Noble House confidential papers to insure
his indispensability. His American-educated son, John Chen, has sold
copies of these copies to the head of Par-Con Corporation, Lincoln (Linc)
"Raider" Bartlett, to facilitate Bartlett's attempt to take over Noble
House, and has also stolen one of the coin halves given to Jin-qua in *Tai-
Pan* and obtained for the Chen family by their illustrious ancestor Gordon Chen in the same novel. However, before he can pass on the coin
half, John Chen is kidnapped for ransom by a gang called "the Were-
wolves." Phillip Chen meets the kidnappers' demands, but at the same
time hires smuggling chieftain Four Fingers Wu and his thugs to track
the kidnappers, since regaining the missing coin is vital to the survival
of the house of Chen. Wu's men find John dead, but torture his kidnappers to get the coin half for Wu, who plans to use it to force Dunross to
invest Noble House funds and power in narcotics.

The plot twists and turns like the back streets of Hong Kong and like
Dunross's Byzantine mind, but even the narrowest lane leads back to
Dunross. Dunross's key rival is Quillan Gornt, a descendant of Tyler
Brock. Gornt initiates a bank run to demonstrate his power to "Linc"
Bartlett, with whom he forms an alliance to undercut Dunross by manipulating the Hong Kong stock market. As these ruthless entrepreneurs
sacrifice anyone to attain their ends, Dunross strives to save family, company, Hong Kong, China, and personal "face." Dunross plays by Asian
rules, anticipates Chinese indirection, and copes with industrial espionage. Aided by Casey Tcholok, the American business representative
of Par-Con, he overcomes the business trap Linc Bartlett, John Chen,
and Quillan Gornt have set for him, wields his influence to assure mainland Chinese business backing for Noble House, and wins Noble House

a contract to ship South American minerals to China. By the time a Hong Kong mudslide kills Bartlett, Dunross has already undermined Bartlett's attempted raid of Noble House and turned the stock market in his own favor; Gornt has lost a fortune; Wu's son Paul Choy has taken over the family business and used the stolen Chen half-coin to negotiate a favorable and legal business connection with Noble House; and the connections between China and Noble House have tightened.

These high-level capitalistic business ventures dominate the foreground, but in the background, various spy organizations compete for information and control, and Communist agents, in particular, seek a toehold in Hong Kong. A deep-cover spy from the People's Republic of China (PRC), Brian Kwok, is exposed and undergoes chemical debriefing before Dunross negotiates his freedom, while a devious triple agent, Roger Crosse, betrays Americans, British, and Soviets for personal advantage. KGB Captain George Suslev, who is in charge of a well-equipped spy "trawler," engages in blackmail, electronic espionage, and cat-and-mouse games with MI-6, the CIA, and the Hong Kong CID or Criminal Investigation Department, headed by Robert Armstrong. At the same time, the U.S. Mafia engages in gun running, and the Macao gold traders join in behind-the-scenes power plays and vie for the most advantageous alliances.

STRUCTURE

Except for a prologue set on June 8, 1960, the day Ian Dunross assumes the title of *tai-pan* of Noble House, the novel covers ten days in August 1963, starting on Sunday, August 18, 1963, and ending on Tuesday, August 27, 1963. The time caption headings for each chapter (for example, 8:30 a.m., 12:30 p.m., 3:45 p.m.) suggest urgency: a countdown to a crisis deadline, a time bomb ticking, ready to explode unless competent action is taken immediately. The *Noble House* countdown parallels the Hong Kong countdown as the expiration date of the British lease with China approaches. The initial day establishes the problem; every day thereafter records the mounting dilemmas with which Dunross must deal, until on Sunday, August 25, Dunross makes his secret deal with China. On August 26, Linc Bartlett dies. On August 27, the final threads are tied.

Except for the initial prologue, the entire action is framed by the heroine, Casey Tcholok, the American business representative of Par-Con.

Her arrival in Hong Kong initiates the major conflicts, and her departure marks a return to normality. Clavell's patterns of contrasting characters and ideologies and his reliance on Dunross as narrative center unite disparate story lines and lend unity of subject and direction to the novel.

GENRE CONVENTIONS

Noble House is a mix of cinematic and literary genre conventions. Like the movie *Wall Street*, it depicts the detailed moves and countermoves of a business raid and of insider trading. Like *Earthquake* or *Condominium*, it paints a harrowing picture of a disaster, a Hong Kong mudslide that collapses towering buildings and buries their occupants. Like *Backdraft*, it looks closely at a major fire, in a crowded restaurant with only one exit. As in Len Deighton's *Ipcress File*, John LeCarre's *Tinker, Tailor, Soldier, Spy*, and many other spy novels, the CID, CIA, MI-5, MI-6, KGB, and Hong Kong Special Intelligence (SI) play Cold War espionage games that include Kim Philby–like moles deep in the system, double and triple agents, modern chemical and psychological techniques for quickly emptying an agent of information, and the liquidation of opposition agents. Like Dashiell Hammett's *The Glass Key*, *Noble House* exposes behind-the-scenes big-city politics and politicians who betray public trust for private gain. Like F. Scott Fitzgerald's *The Great Gatsby*, it reveals the lives of the rich and famous as different from our own. Like a Dick Francis mystery, it captures the shenanigans behind horse racing, and the injuries suffered by both horses and riders.

Noble House is also a crime novel, telling of Mafia chieftains pushing their way into legitimate businesses and of street gangs and triads robbing and terrorizing. It tells of the narcotics trade, of gunrunning, and of police corruption. But it also includes Horatio Alger rags-to-riches stories, and threatens riches-to-rags reversals of fortune. Anne Collins, a reviewer for *Maclean's*, finds it a "nineteenth-century Trollope-style chronicle of the manners, mores, business and politics of the embattled British ruling class of Hong Kong" (Collins 1981: 61). *Noble House* is also a reminiscence of a wartime romance and of the daily dangers of being a World War II pilot, a cross-cultural romance, a story of father-son and father-daughter relationships, the story of a family dynasty, and finally a feminist tale of an American businesswoman successfully outwitting male competition.

This mix of genres creates a fully rounded portrait of Hong Kong. Such a mix lends greater depth than would be possible within a single genre.

NARRATIVE VOICE

Typical of Clavell's novels, the narrative shifts perspectives through the literary device of a third-person omniscient narrator who describes action and setting, records dialogue, and listens in on the fears and worries, hopes and dreams, reactions and strategies of a huge cast of characters. At times, interior dialogues are wooden, simply imparting information important to the plot; at times, they are simply "onstage whisperings" (Lehmann-Haupt 1981: 317) that suggest matters of importance. There are no real rapid-fire exchanges in Clavell, despite deep rivalries and antagonisms between characters. Sometimes Clavell tells us what characters think before they speak and contrasts what they say with what they think, or with other people's interpretations of, or speculation about, what is said. Characters speak for themselves and are judged by their words and deeds, as in a play or film. *Noble House* includes words in Mandarin and Cantonese Chinese (as well as dialects like Hoklo and the pidgin of Macao), Japanese, Portuguese, French, and Russian.

The thoughts of Dunross dominate the book, followed by those of American businesswoman Casey Tcholok. The tension comes from the reader sharing Dunross's thoughts, plans for action, motivations, internal struggles, plots and counterplots while observing his cool, controlled public image from the perspective of those around him. The public performances of both Dunross and Tcholok are tightly controlled, even when they are seemingly casual, but beneath their smiling fronts simmer volatile private emotions.

THEMATIC DEVELOPMENT

As its almost 1,400 page length suggests, *Noble House* has many themes. Perhaps its most striking theme has to do with Hong Kong. Clavell argues that the city is a unique experiment in capitalistic venture and cross-cultural relationships. It epitomizes the good that can result from the peaceful meeting of East and West. Another theme is that organic, interlocking cause-effect chains tie past to present and future. Knowing the long-term responses caused by present actions is a cornerstone of business and civilization. A recurring theme given more weight in *Noble House* than in Clavell's other books is a warning against Soviet expansionism. Two of Clavell's other recurring themes, cultural differences and gender differences, have a changed focus in this book. The dominating cultural differences are between the English and the Americans, with the Chinese sharing the English reaction to Americans, while the gender theme suggests that though a woman should suit her strategy to her nature, a hard-working, competent woman can not only compete with males but give them a good run for their money.

Hong Kong as a Unique Experiment

Noble House is a tribute to a fascinating city that has become an international definition of successful interface between East and West. Hong Kong has always had one of the highest population densities in the world—as of 1994, it had 14,005 persons per square mile (London has 11,075, New York 22,811). Clavell notes that the percentage of Chinese to Westerners has remained quite constant from the founding of the city to the present day. In 1990, about 98 percent of the population of 5,812,000 was Chinese, most of whom had their family origins in Kwangtung province, and there were 60,000 Europeans and Americans, 57,000 Filipinos (mostly domestic servants), and 30,000 Indians and Pakistanis. Clavell tries to do the impossible, to capture in one book the essence of so complex a city. At the novel's close, one feels that the story is just beginning, that the expiration of China's lease of the New Territories (including Hong Kong) to Britain on July 1, 1997 will begin an even more complex relationship between East and West, and that the amalgam that is Hong Kong is forged steel, a metal stronger than any one of its components.

Clavell's spokesman, journalist and novelist Peter Marlowe, a survivor of the Changi death camp and a friend of Dunross, calls Asia "the center of the world," Hong Kong "the nucleus," and the people of Hong Kong "the cream" of China (*Noble House*: 1129). As a writer, Marlowe voices his (and, by extension, Clavell's) difficulties in dealing with the city. He says that each one of the millions of Chinese and thousands of Europeans in Hong Kong has "a vast heritage, marvelous secrets, and fantastic stories to tell." He knows that no matter how much he tries, he'll never really know much about Hong Kong Chinese or Hong Kong. He has tried to uncover the private stories of only a few of the freebooters, *tai-*

pans, and pirates, of the accountants, shopkeepers, and governmental officials, millionaires, opium dealers, and coolies who make up the city, and doing so has made him understand the hopelessness of his mission. Hong Kong is a "potpourri" with too many stories to be told, try as he might. In a clear parallel, Clavell too has tried as he might in *Noble House*, giving us the stories of cleaning ladies and jockeys, policemen and criminals, smugglers and military officers, cooks and bankers, and, like Marlowe, leaves readers with the sense that he has only scratched the surface.

Two interlocked characteristics of Hong Kong that Clavell illustrates again and again are its inhabitants' willingness to gamble—to gamble their lives, to gamble on life and, especially, to gamble on business odds—and their lust for money and for power. In *Noble House*, the governor of Hong Kong sums up this perception as follows: "greed pride lust avarice jealousy gluttony anger [*sic*] and the bigger lust for power or money ruled people [of Hong Kong] and would rule them forever" (803). Moreover, Hong Kong's motto is *moh ching, moh meng* (no money, no life). When newcomers step off the plane in Hong Kong and ask about the smell, they are told it is the smell of Hong Kong—the smell of money. Historically, Hong Kong began as two gambles: a British gamble that a good port could be the key to China and that 155 years would give them time to open a gateway that could never be closed, and a Chinese gamble that long-term contact with the West at this control point could benefit but not undermine them. The Hong Kong police force, with its intentional mix of Chinese and Europeans, has been a gamble on intercultural relationships, and the Hong Kong stock market and businesses are a continuous gamble. The people of Hong Kong are gambling on that city's future when the British lease with China expires in 1997.

Clavell captures this gambling spirit and makes it the essential ingredient of his most successful entrepreneurs: they ultimately win out because of some combination of skill, daring, and *joss*. Moreover, nearly every character in the novel, major and minor, gambles in some way: on business, on politics, on family, on love, or on the competence or incompetence of others. Clavell's dynastic Noble House and its *tai-pans* gamble that China will need Hong Kong's door to the West, and they see the destiny of the Noble House as Asian, not Western.

Clavell uses a horse race as the climactic crux of his novel, the event at which antagonisms are worked out, revelations made, and finances reversed for the stock market, the threatened banks, and Noble House. It seems as if all Hong Kong has bet on the races, from the lowliest beggars and toilet maids to the highest city officials. At the track, Dunross plays on the greed of Bartlett, the American business raider, and persuades him to make a side deal to hedge his bets; Dunross then transforms that side deal into the confirmation of an upswing that turns the financial tide in his favor. Millions are made, and millions lost, and life goes on. Given Clavell's thesis that Hong Kong was founded on a gamble and continues to be a giant gamble and that its citizens gamble on its economy daily, the structural placement of the horse race is an intentional part of his message and of his portrait of the city. The racetrack was one of the earliest businesses established in Hong Kong and is symbolic for many of the British colonialists of a little part of England they keep with them. However, Hong Kong has made this track its own, so its private seats are indicative of the city's class structure, but its wide-open gambling appeals to all classes. Hong Kong functions on Chinese *joss*, and bets on horse-racing become indicators of personal *joss* in other areas of one's life. It is like the Chinese belief that the luck experienced on the first day of the new year foreshadows the luck of the entire year, so New Year's Day is the time to gamble wildly and hope for *joss*. Thus, from a Chinese perspective, gigantic gambles even on a horse race provide an appropriate metaphor for the way life is conducted in this exotic, foreign, yet so capitalistic a city.

History as Organic

Clavell does not think of time and history as separate units, locked off from the present, but instead as part of an organic whole in which past and present intertwine. He emphasizes this theme by tightly interlocking *Noble House* with past events in other novels and by anticipating concerns of novels set or written after 1960.

First is the family history. The characters of *Tai-Pan* are the illustrious ancestors of *Noble House*, their portraits hung on the wall and shown off to special guests, their lives now legends, and their deeds and motivations a matter of myth, part truth, part guesswork, part total fantasy. Even Stride Orlov, Dirk Struan's chief captain, has a place of pride in the family gallery. Gossip throughout the book is signalled by phrases like "rumor has it," "legend is," "legend says," and "there's a story that." Details that the readers of *Tai-Pan* know as facts are slightly distorted or given a different interpretation in the modern legend, and parts of the story that were left incomplete in *Tai-Pan* are filled out in more detail in *Noble House*. Legend has it that Dirk Struan beat Gorth Tyler to death with a Chinese fighting iron and that Tess "Hag" Struan, after destroying her father financially, slashed a portrait of him, buried the knife in his oil-painted heart so hard that it impaled the picture to the wall, and then ordered it left that way to remind future generations of their heritage of hate. There are stories of Tess's lovers, both European and Chinese, male and female, and of her incredible wheeling and dealing behind the scenes of Hong Kong for three-quarters of a century. In the Chens, the Eurasian branch of the family, the legends are the family secrets passed on from father to son to strengthen their understanding of their ties to and holds over Noble House. For instance, Tess Struan ordered that her fabulously expensive emerald necklace be buried with her body, but the Chens have hidden it away in the family vault instead.

The family ties connect past and present. At a dinner party at which Dunross shows off the portraits, guests are struck by the physical similarities between Struan and Dunross, the piercing eyes, firm jaw line, and taunting, "half-devilish smile" that challenges and dares (304). The Struans say that British pride in ancestry comes from family continuity. Struan could face any crisis; so, too, can Dunross. Alastair Struan has inherited a weakness of will from the Robb Struan branch of the family. Likewise, Tyler Brock had a streak of cruelty and a lack of concern for the consequences of his acts, and his descendant Quillan Gornt is cruel beneath his urbane manner and totally unconcerned when he starts a run on the Ho-Pak bank, ruining some of its investors and depositors.

The Struan legacy has a Chinese sense of family continuity and of family commitment to China that is reinforced by family ritual such as the passing of power from *tai-pan* to *tai-pan* following Struan rules and the reading of the first *tai-pan*'s letter confirming blood ties to China through the T'Chung and Chen families. It also entails obligations, including the Jin-qua coins and a sworn commitment to the destruction of the family nemesis, the Brocks.

Clavell works in reminders of the continuance of other family lines. For instance, Aristotle Quance, the womanizing painter of *Tai-Pan*, has fathered four separate branches of prominent Eurasian families, and his paintings, which were in such demand in *Tai-Pan*, have become valuable heirlooms in modern-day *Noble House*. The Wu family of *Tai-Pan* continues its illegal smuggling activities in *Noble House*, and the descendants of Jin-qua still watch over the house of Struan.

In addition to family heritage, however, Clavell finds other ways in which past histories affect present actions. His two key characters from *King Rat*, Peter Marlowe and Robin Grey, reappear here and are still very much products of their prison camp experiences. Grey, the brother of Penelope Dunross, is so driven by hatred and class consciousness that he has become a rabid spokesman for labor and a spy for the Soviets. Marlowe, in contrast, has been tempered by the experience and has learned tolerance, acceptance of differences, and discretion. He is devoted to his family, haunted by the past, and committed to better understanding his world and to improving it through communication. Like Clavell, he has written screenplays and novels about East-West relations, including a novel much like *King Rat*, which he calls *Changi*. The contrast between Marlowe and Grey is a lesson about the ways in which different natures respond to adversity.

With *Noble House*, Clavell paves the way for *Whirlwind*. Near the end of *Noble House*, taking the advice of his friend and top-level information source Alan Medford Grant (Gresserhof), Dunross investigates the possibility of oil under the North Sea and sends as his representative to Scotland his cousin David MacStruan. MacStruan's orders are to move into a Scottish community and to begin making Noble House an important Scottish presence. He is to make contact with the descendants of Jamie McFay, a character who appears in *Gai-Jin*, and, in a joint venture, set the stage for a Noble House expansion based on North Sea oil.

Thus *Noble House* depicts a city and a culture that are products of the past presented in *Tai-Pan*, *Gai-Jin*, and *King Rat*, and contains actions that prepare the way for future events in *Whirlwind*. Clavell's spokesman, Peter Marlowe, says, "Chinese believe the past controls the future and explains the present" (*Noble House*: 277). Clavell's entire canon is a working out of this world view.

A Warning about the Soviet Threat

The warnings about the Soviet desire for world domination, which are also expressed in *Tai-Pan* and exemplified in *Whirlwind* and *Gai-Jin*, receive full treatment here. A Soviet ship docks in Hong Kong, its key officers KGB members, its goal espionage. Equipped with the latest spy equipment, it gets photographs of and information from the new American carrier in port. One officer buys a microfilm of classified information from an American sailor. Another officer tries to blackmail a former Russian aristocrat, Dunross's head horse trainer. A third, Robert Crosse, is the triple agent responsible for "turning" Kim Philby, the real and infamous British traitor, that is, causing him to change sides. Crosse is the most dangerous spy of all: he has a pivotal position in the British service, works hand-in-hand with the Hong Kong police at the highest level, and feeds information and sources to the Soviets, but hedges his bets with the British and possibly the Americans. With the Vietnam War soon to begin, this Soviet connection at the heart of the Hong Kong establishment has dire consequences, especially given the Americans' innocence about Asia, their naivete about the corruptibility of their representatives, and their confident assertions that they will not be "sucked into the abyss" of Vietnam (610).

Contrasting Cultural Attitudes: American Directness versus English and Chinese Obliqueness

A theme important in *King Rat* and vital to *Noble House* is the contrast between the British and the Americans, a contrast Clavell, who has lived in both worlds, relishes. His British colonials are proud of their roots and take pride in family heritage and family continuity, while the American Bartlett brags that he has never even seen a photograph of his grandparents, much less his great-great-grandparents and that what he has made of himself is far more significant than who his ancestors were. Dunross notes that the English play the game of life with different rules than Americans. The entire novel illustrates, to some degree, these differences.

Clavell dramatizes American directness, informality, and business-first mentality grating on both Chinese and British formality and propriety, and his British finding common cause with Chinese associates against the Americans. The body language and conversational ploys of Clavell's Americans are open and direct, the values Americans often assume are universal. However, his Chinese and British characters find such behavior unnerving and indicative of bad breeding. After a morning of business, the British and Americans meet for lunch. To an American, this would mean a business lunch during which negotiations would continue, but informally. Casey Tcholok's suggestion that the Bartlett/Struan officials follow the American habit of sending out for sandwiches and working through lunch is rejected as an appalling custom, and her offer to update Dunross on the proposal ironed out leads him to think, "How American to come out with it like that—no finesse! Doesn't she know business is for after lunch, not before" (134). And, of course, she doesn't, and further pushing simply allows Dunross to make a subtle Chinese-style modification that will partially undercut her efforts. Later in the story, she creates more antagonism with her habit of interrupting conversations that do not include her, though part of the antagonism is not simply because she is American, but because she is an American woman.

When, during lunch, the American tycoon Linc Bartlett automatically calls the *tai-pan* by his first name, "Ian," something his long-time British associates still dare not do, the entire British and Chinese contingent gasps in horror. Clavell cleverly records both what is said on the surface ("No need to stand on ceremony. Is there?") and what is thought behind the social mask ("we prefer to work up to these things around here—it's one of the few ways you tell your friends from your acquaintances . . . first names are . . . private . . ." (136). From the British perspective, the British businessman Andrew Gavallan's decision to still call Bartlett "Mr. Bartlett" instead of "Linc" is a very neat way of putting Bartlett down, "a loss of face," says Clavell, "that neither of the Americans would ever understand" (136). Using first names with business associates is simply not done in much of the world. It is as gauche as a student calling a professor by his or her first name. When the discourtesy continues, the *tai-pan*'s expression does not change, but his eyes grow cold. Everyone else knows that the Americans have been so offensive that retaliation will occur.

The British-American conflict parallels the Chinese-American conflict. High-ranking SI officer Brian Kwok believes that Americans talk too much and too loudly, that their directness must be a sign of stupidity, and that they cannot be trusted with secrets. Four Fingers Wu, who is very proud of his son Paul's Harvard education and American business sense, nevertheless calls his son a "barbarian" because he speaks what is on his mind rather than disguising it in innuendo and obliqueness as a Chinese would do. Paul prides himself on being American, but his father frets that his seventh son has been trained by barbarians to be a barbarian and to do business the way barbarians do. The prediction that Dirk Struan made about Western educational systems transforming the perspectives of Chinese youngsters and making them representatives of a Western rather than an Eastern value system seems to be coming true in this book. In a like manner, the colonial families who have stayed in the Far East for generations have moved closer to adopting Asian perspectives.

Contrasting Attitudes toward Male-Female Roles: Chinese and British Chauvinism versus American Feminism

In *Tai-Pan* and *Gai-Jin*, which are both set in the nineteenth century, Clavell shows women trapped by biological necessity, social pressure, and cultural expectations that limit their development. They must struggle to attain their hopes and dreams, yet must maintain respectability if they are to have any force in the world or place in society. In *Noble House*, the Chinese women of twentieth-century Hong Kong are still trapped in nineteenth-century patterns. The birth control pill has given British women greater freedom and wider choices, but, in general, they, like their Chinese counterparts, accept Hong Kong as a man's world in which women are limited to traditional roles. However, Casey Tcholok, Linc Bartlett's business partner and Clavell's representative American woman, has been raised to think of herself as equal to men and has a view of her self-worth, competence, and potential that shocks and challenges both the Asians and the British. Clavell respects the successful American woman and feels she has much to teach other women, but he also suggests that what she could learn from the Asian and British women would lend her greater power.

Early in the book Clavell sets up an interesting confrontation between Casey and Struan's officials. Despite critical attacks on Clavell as a chauvinist, here he clearly depicts a highly competent American businesswoman giving chauvinist British and Chinese males their comeuppance. Casey is tall, big-boned, and beautiful. Her family owned a small import-export company, and she and her sister grew up around "haggling, negotiating and the problem of profit" (145). From an early age, she was treated as an equal. She worked her way through school and even took courses at the Harvard Business School. Hard work, intelligence, and perspicacity have made her what she is—indispensable to the Par-Con Corporation as treasurer and executive vice-president. Moreover, as she points out to skeptical British listeners, she thinks of her job as a job, not as a man's job, and her seven-year contract requires that she be treated as an equal.

The Chinese and British shock at having to deal with a woman begins with John Chen, who is stunned by Par-Con sending a female representative to Hong Kong. The Struan board members, who expect the top-level executive of a major company to be male, are equally stunned, and their assumptions throw them off their stride and cause them to arrogantly assume that they can manipulate Casey Tcholok because she is a woman. At first, they try to make small talk, pat her hand, call her "my dear," offer her coffee or tea, and compliment her beauty, but when she insists they judge her on her ability and proceeds with her presentation and negotiation agenda in an organized, informed, impressive fashion, they turn hostile.

Bartlett has anticipated their chauvinism and has turned over full power to Casey, not simply because he trusts her professionalism and competence but also because he understands that his opponents will underestimate her—as they do. She fogs their thinking with rapid mathematical calculations and then, playing to their negative assumptions about her skill, baits a trap. When they insultingly assume that any offer she might negotiate must be confirmed by Bartlett to have validity, she sweetly brags that she has clearance to commit up to twenty million dollars on the deal. As she had expected, they think she has given away the game and are so delighted with the figure and their own cleverness that they do not think the agreement through in a hard-headed way. Dunross, informed about the negotiations, suspects a flaw, but even he is lulled by his subordinates' report that Casey's weak spot is impatience and that "her Achilles' heel" is her desperate desire to be accepted "in a man's world" (126). As a result of their underestimating her ability, the deal goes through at a much more profitable price than Bartlett had expected. Casey makes a large commission, and Noble House is placed in a more precarious situation than need be.

Later, Casey's American values are once more assaulted at a private dinner party where, British-style, the women leave the room to let the men talk business. When the ladies get up to leave, she makes no move to join them. Finally, Lady Joanna explains the custom of the ladies leaving the men alone with port and cigars. Casey is dumbfounded. What her hostess and fellow guests see as good manners, she sees as sexism. She points out that in the States that custom went out before the Civil War, but the ladies insist that Hong Kong is a part of England and that English rules apply. When she appeals to Dunross, he insists that she comply; when told that she can't fight city hall, she retorts that she has been doing so all her life. Clavell's portrait is sympathetic, and though he has the British explain their view, Casey, the heroine of the book, sees an injustice those around her are blind to.

The contrast between Casey's view and that of English ladies is based on very different perceptions of self and function. Casey sees herself as an equal to men. Dunross's wife, Penelope, provides the British perspective. She sees herself as mother and wife, ready to pick up the pieces when allowed to. She loves her husband very much, but she understands that his business dealings are off limits, that he probably has a young and beautiful Chinese mistress (he does), and that she can never be a part of those areas of his life that mean the most to him. She is disturbed at a woman talking business, yet understands that the world is changing and that her daughter might one day be independent like Casey. Like the ladies in her circle, Penelope knows that Hong Kong is an exciting place for a man but is threatening to British women, who must grow old gracefully while nubile young Chinese women compete for their husbands' attention.

Despite the blatantly sexist attitudes of his males, Clavell respects competence, and when Casey proves competent, she earns the right to demand acceptance. Casey demonstrates her professionalism and her personal competence time after time. Her performance under pressure in manipulating the Noble House board of directors is professional. Furthermore, she does not lose her head in times of crisis. When people leap to escape fire aboard a floating restaurant, Casey does what no other woman and few men in the novel do: she dives into the filthy harbor waters to pull victim after victim out—coolly, efficiently, effectively. Later, when mudslides topple apartment buildings and bury many alive, she unhesitatingly plunges into the chaos to pull a child to safety before the walls collapse. A surprising plot twist is that Noble House would probably have gone under if not for Casey's innovative financing and her confirmation of the contract Bartlett planned to renege on.

Despite her competence, Dunross and Gornt argue that she still has much to learn from the East about how to use her female power effectively. They conclude that she should employ her sexuality as a tool and as a weapon. Gornt purposely challenges her desire to be one of the boys by inviting her aboard his ship for a "men's night out" gathering of business associates. Casey had been offended that she had not been invited to Taipei as Bartlett had been, but she is equally offended at being invited when the men have brought their Chinese mistresses. Gornt calls attention to her contradictory attitudes by emphasizing the trust placed in her by such an invitation. However, he also makes her aware of her physical vulnerability by assaulting her in his cabin and then roaring with laughter once she understands how helpless she is. They return amicably to shore, but though she laughs at her fears, she has had a harsh lesson about female vulnerability. Dunross's lessons are gentle; he calls attention to the lovely Orlanda Ramos's feminine attractions, and he warns Casey that the only way a woman can have power in a man's world is the way his ancestress Tess "Hag" Struan had power: by manipulating men and events so that she ended up with the purse strings, and then by working through men to achieve her own ends. However, privately, Dunross tells David MacStruan, the future *tai-pan*, that with the right training, Casey has the potential to be as good a business-woman, as powerful a competitor, and as effective a head of a dynasty as Hag Struan.

As is typical of Clavell's technique, the strongest lesson grows out of competition between two contrasting characters and cultures: the forth-right American, Casey Tcholok, and the artful Eurasian, Orlanda Ramos. Although Casey is dubious about what Gornt and Dunross try to teach her, she learns the value of their perspective through her competition with Orlanda. Bartlett and Casey have taken a very businesslike ap-proach to their relationship, have confessed their love for each other, but have put off sex and marriage for seven years while they build their business and hone their skills. For Casey, marriage to Bartlett depends on career fulfillment more than love. Orlanda, in contrast, decides that Bartlett can help her escape the financial, social, and racial limits of her life in Hong Kong, and she resolves to use all of her wiles to reel him in: a big, rich, American fish. Although Orlanda at first seems to be a gold digger, readers come to understand what drives her and to believe that contact with Bartlett transforms what began as her calculated plan into a genuine love affair.

Orlanda's impoverished parents sold her to Gornt when she was a child, and she has depended on him ever since. He trained her to please him, and now she uses what he taught her to win security. She uses clothing, perfume, and body language to ravish Bartlett's senses and make him desire her, but she also makes him see her as a vulnerable person, worthy of love, rather than as a one-night stand. She seems open and honest, revealing herself a little at a time, and then demonstrating her love by offering him freedom. Casey at first feels cheated, for she truly loves Bartlett, but she realizes that she drove him into Orlanda's arms.

At the novel's close, extremes meet. Casey, the competent business-woman, has come to appreciate Orlanda's very different approach and to learn from it. She doesn't know whether Bartlett's final words to Dun-ross about marriage refer to marriage to her or marriage to Orlanda, but she suspects Bartlett meant Orlanda. Casey knows that the mudslide has left Orlanda penniless, and so she arranges for Bartlett's profit to go to Orlanda. She also volunteers to get Orlanda started in business. In doing so, she has recognized in Orlanda a vulnerability which Gornt and Dunross have made her see in herself. Her final lines indicate that she is open to challenges and is willing to commit herself to daring action and high goals—to one day be *tai-pan* of the Noble House, like Tess Struan.

Clavell uses contrasting characters very effectively to emphasize cultural differences, the strength of custom, and the power of the individual—whether male or female—to win respect through competence.

CHARACTER DEVELOPMENT: CONTRASTING CHARACTERS

Noble House carefully balances contrasting characters and contrasting cultural attitudes. The contrast between fathers and sons, so important in *Tai-Pan*, takes on deeper significance here because the sons are separated from their fathers not only by generations but by cultural outlook. The cultural contrasts between East and West have become less striking as the melding of cultures creates Chinese with Western values and ambitions, and Westerners with a Chinese sense of time and strategy. Clavell's new focus is a contrast of British and Americans and a dramatization of changing male-female relationships. Contrasts in perspectives, attitudes, and relationships provide an underlying structural unity of matched pairs of dramatic opposites that unify diverse plot lines.

Contrasting Parental Relationships

In *Tai-Pan*, Clavell focused on generational conflicts that seem a part of Western life patterns as sons strive for maturity independent of parental values and perspectives and seek to discover themselves. Because part of his grand plan in *Noble House* is to demonstrate the effects of 150 years of Western contact on Asians, Clavell depicts tumultuous Asian father-son relationships in which Chinese fathers are amazed at their sons' Western-style challenges to their authority.

In *Tai-Pan*, the relationship between Gordon Chen and his father was Chinese: the son, trained to serve his father and his family well, kept his distance and was respectful, grateful, and most of all obedient. In *Noble House*, this is the kind of relationship Brian Kwok had with his father, a strong Maoist who instilled in his son a patriotic mission to study Western ways and to become a security systems expert but to remain forever loyal to China. Thanks to his father's planning, Brian, despite his Western education, always had a strong, loyal Chinese male model nearby to advise and influence him, a friendly "uncle" to guide his interpretation of events and relationships. Partly because of his training and partly because of his father's death when Brian was a child, Brian retains an idealistic image of his father and a strong sense of his duty to his memory (though a British mentor, his superior and friend Robert Armstrong, has gradually become a counter–father figure). Two other Chinese sons in *Noble House*, John Chen and Paul Choy, violate this traditional Asian father-son relationship. The contrast between constructive and destructive patterns illustrates the dual potential of Western influence.

The greatest violation of the Asian father-son relationship is that of Phillip Chen's rebellious, treacherous son John, for whom self-interest outweighs family obligation. Given eight days to become dutiful or be cut out of the family line forever, a terrifying threat for a Chinese son, John joins Western rebellion with Chinese secretiveness and betrays his father, family, and Noble House. His father learns the full extent of his treachery slowly, piece by piece, including his having provided the heads of Par-Con Corporation information about how to neutralize his father. If Phillip Chen is ever connected to his son's underhanded deal with Par-Con, the Chen family will be destroyed, financially and socially. But John does not care.

Not content with destroying his British relatives, the Struans, and endangering his father and family, John has also stolen from his father's secret hiding place a Jin-qua half-coin given to the family a century and a half before as a guarantee of future Noble House obligation. In stealing this coin, John not only betrays his present family, but also his ancestors and the future generations of his family. His revenge against a father who demands the devotion and subservience expected of a Chinese son is an act of self-destruction, for, from a Chinese perspective, it destroys his own future. Ironically, the family connections he seeks to escape actually do destroy him. Thugs who hope his wealthy father will pay a large ransom kidnap and kill him. John's betrayals temper his father's enthusiasm for rescue; Phillip Chen will do what is proper and will pay millions of Hong Kong dollars, but John is dead to his family long before they learn of his death. Though John Chen appears in only a small part of the book, the repercussions of his acts affect relationships and activities throughout the novel. Like Gornt, John represents Western free enterprise untempered by the generosity and responsibility of a Dunross or a Tcholok. His violent death seems deserved.

The hidden conflict between Phillip and John Chen is echoed in the conflict between Four Finger Wu and his son Paul Choy (born Wu Fang Choi), whom Wu, on Dunross's advice, pretends is his nephew. Wu, a notorious smuggler, taught his son to follow his instructions unquestioningly, for the family good. When he sent him to the States to study, he carefully instructed him to outwardly conform to the ways of the "foreign devils" but to never forget their inferiority to the civilized Chinese. Nevertheless, Paul, like John, has been changed by his American education and thinks of himself as American. He has a *sansei* girlfriend, a third-generation Japanese-American, a relationship his father would never understand because of the centuries-old Chinese hatred of Japan.

Superficially, Paul is the perfect Chinese son, dutiful and willing, loyal to father and family. His balance of aggression and restraint helps him win the support of both Dunross and Gornt; he ingratiates himself to Dunross by getting a job with Gornt, then makes himself invaluable to both, while using his position to profit his family. Paul's American training makes him want to shout angrily when his father threatens to ostracize him if he fails to follow instructions precisely. However, unlike John Chen, Paul admits that he is not truly American, but Chinese, and must obey his father. Paul is torn between gratitude to his father for the opportunities he has provided and deep distress at the illegal activities his father forces him to engage in.

Thanks to his Harvard training, Paul understands the intricacies of high finance as his father never can. The insider knowledge he gleaned at Gornt's allows him to invest heavily in the stock market. He understands the significance of Hong Kong's lax regulations and the potential for a Chinese-run stock market separate from the British-run market. Again and again, Paul's American-style tendency to act without consulting his father frustrates and angers Wu, who is used to instilling fear in his sons and in demanding complete submission from them. But this Westernized son doesn't respond to such ploys. Wu believes that sons are a father's wealth, but concludes that they could also be a father's death if he is fool enough to completely trust them (577). Consequently, to ensure Paul's silence, he forces him to engage in a drug-smuggling pickup at sea and the drowning of a Werewolf kidnapper.

When Wu dies in the mudslide that destroys the Rose Court apartments and Paul finds the Struan half-coin hidden on his father's body, he acts immediately to achieve his dream of starting his own empire. First, as a good Chinese son, he takes care of family matters. He offers his brother, Wu's successor, his business expertise and a large percentage of his stock market profits. He persuades him to abandon the narcotics business and modernize the remaining businesses, and then negotiates for himself a position equivalent to a Mafia *consigliere* or top business advisor. His superior Western education—the evidence of which is the millions he has made on the stock market—confirms his right to such a position. His next step is to negotiate respectfully but firmly with Dunross for business rights that will move him into legal, high-level finance (pharmaceuticals, gambling, and a Chinese stock exchange) and high-level social status (membership on the board of Noble House and a much coveted stewardship of the Turf Club). Unlike Gornt and John Chen, "Profitable" Choy represents Western free enterprise tempered by moral responsibility and obligation to family and community. Paul has his faults, but he is the type of Westernized Asian Dirk Struan had dreamed Hong Kong would produce.

The relationship of Dunross to his son is not explored in any depth, but his relationship to his daughter in some ways parallels the Chinese father-son conflicts. Because the birth control pill has totally changed the status and potential of women, the role of fathers must also change. Dunross's daughter, Adryon, is nineteen, attractive, precocious, and a great worry to her father, who has a hard time believing she is old enough to date, have sex, or even marry. It is her mother, with whom Adryon shares secrets, who recognizes her daughter's need to be treated as a modern young lady and who lectures Dunross on his fossilized conceptions of fatherhood. Dunross threatens suitors to behave or be dealt with "without mercy" (445), but is as powerless to control his daughter's future as the Chinese fathers are to control their sons' futures. Fathers can threaten and cajole, but they cannot prevent the changes in thinking time brings.

Contrasting Main Characters: Responsible Entrepreneur versus Irresponsible Robber Baron

The tribute that *Noble House* makes to free-wheeling capitalism is qualified. Its successful entrepreneurs are clever, daring, and capable, but Clavell presents their successes not simply in terms of profit but in terms of their effect on the community. Dunross is Clavell's prototype of the responsible capitalist, Gornt his prototype of the irresponsible exploiter.

The difference lies in their sense of obligation; what they do has repercussions up and down the social scale, but Dunross carefully considers the effects of his financial actions, while Gornt does not.

The differences are pronounced in every area of their lives. Gornt is a single, predatory male; Dunross is a happily married family man with children whom he adores and whose futures he worries about. Gornt views women as possessions and purchased Orlanda Ramos from her family to train her to meet his needs, and though he treats her well, he views her as a tool to be used. He supports her financially and buys her gifts, but only in return for favors that require her to submit her interests to his. At one point, he hires a prostitute to put Orlanda in her place. As Orlanda says, Gornt makes her know where her "rice bowl" rests. Dunross, on the other hand, is a gentleman, chivalrous and protective. He loves his wife, is proud of his son, and worries about his daughter. He feels protective of the widowed Riko Gressenhof, smooths the way for medical treatment of Kathy Gavallan, who has multiple sclerosis, and provides financial support for family members injured in an automobile accident in Europe. He bears on his shoulders the burdens of his entire extended family and of the people who depend on them.

Both men are very much a part of the Hong Kong establishment, but Gornt has no compassion for the Chinese, while Dunross finds his roots in China, and his relationship with many individual Chinese is that of "old friends." Gornt's ruthless financial maneuvers dramatize his indifference to community obligations. More important to him is a demonstration of his power and a chance to injure his rival. Dunross, in contrast, is hard-nosed, but responsible. He acts with honor, using wealth and position to build community and to support not only his immediate family, but numerous relatives dependent on the family business, as well as other long-term employees, including large numbers of Chinese. Gornt's motivations are ambition, lust for power and prestige, and revenge. Dunross is not driven only by ambition; he enjoys the risks of big business, but his ultimate ends are respectable. He is the representative of a dynasty committed to bringing Western concepts of justice to China, and he takes this commitment seriously.

CHARACTER DEVELOPMENT: IAN DUNROSS

Noble House is Hong Kong's story, but it is also Ian Dunross's story, for it is men like him who make Hong Kong great. Most historians recounting the stories of the founding fathers of Hong Kong note the num-

ber of people on the fringes of society who, through sheer effort and a
little luck, rose to prominence. Dunross comes from a line of middle-
class merchants who have proven their worth to China and to Hong
Kong. Dirk Struan fought his way out of poverty, and the rules he set
down for choosing the *tai-pan* do not follow the English pattern of pri-
mogeniture. Instead, the rules combine the American concept of meri-
tocracy and the Chinese view of family autonomy in which family
specialists perform such necessary functions as banker, lawyer, tax authority, and so forth.

Under Struan's rules, the choice of *tai-pan* is limited to the family, but
to an extended family with members on several continents. An individual within that family must first prove his worth through hard work and
successes that make his family accept him as a responsible leader. When
he is finally chosen *tai-pan*, he becomes the business head and accepts
all the family burdens (the skeletons in the closet, the secret obligations,
the responsibilities to unknown people in distant places) that this entails.
Dunross has accepted this burden, and his virtue lies in his being a mid-
dle-class man whose competence, hard work, and fierce determination
have placed him in a position of responsibility.

Clavell identifies with Dunross and guides readers to understand, appreciate, and root for him, and for the values and concepts he represents.
Summed up in Dunross are the values that Clavell's novels teach: the
liberating power of free enterprise that rewards industry and ingenuity
and allows people with drive, competence, and skill to overcome social
barriers; the strengthening of perception that comes not only from experiencing other cultures firsthand but also from becoming part of them;
and the importance of commitment to community and to family. It is the
quality of its members that makes Noble House envied and respected,
that makes it a truly noble house, a model of success, but also a model
of commitment.

ALTERNATIVE READING: A NOVEL OF IDEAS

Noble House can be read as a novel of ideas instead of as simply a
family dynasty/business novel. Normally, a realistic novel seeks to re-
create everyday experience so as to convince readers that the world it
depicts is an accurate representation of everyday life. Thus, details of
place, character, and action are judged on the basis of their verisimilitude
or approximation to the real world. In a novel of ideas, however, the

action is subordinate to the philosophical foundation behind that action. Concepts are more important than characters, and many key characters represent values, ideas, points of view, or ideologies. The novel becomes a vehicle for speculating on significant questions or for promulgating social, philosophical, or economic beliefs. In doing so, it reminds the reader that the world of the novel is not the real world, but a representation of ideas in conflict. This different sense of representation moves the novel away from the realistic and toward the allegorical. The plot loses the arbitrariness of "real life" and instead serves the working out of an idea or ideas. Characters also serve ideas, becoming representations of types, perspectives, or concepts without the contradictions and quirkiness that provide a sense of reality. Their natures result less from individual personalities or particularized traits than from the need of the novelist to have them act out certain patterns which suggest ideas. Theme dominates. A good example of the novel of ideas is Ayn Rand's *Anthem* (1946), in which individual characters are less important than the assertion that individualism and rational self-interest are desirable.

Although *Noble House* is far more realistic than Ayn Rand's novel, and contains individualized characters and interesting twists of plot that create the illusion of reality, like *King Rat*, the philosophical base of *Noble House* is a struggle between capitalistic free enterprise and Communism, between the individual and the group. This philosophical struggle takes precedence over plot and character as Clavell plays off characters and nations to demonstrate the value of capitalism. Clavell sets his novel during the Cold War, the period of great competition between the Communist and capitalist powers, when every political and social occurrence, no matter how trivial, was thought of as an ideological battle. This time period—the Cold War, the beginnings of American involvement in Vietnam—makes the novel an appropriate arena for such a confrontation of ideas. The Hong Kong setting is equally important, since the city is an experiment in free-wheeling capitalism on the doorstep of two gigantic experiments with Communism: Red China and, by extension, the Soviet Union. This battle of competing economic systems infuses the book with a spirit of ideological urgency, since the struggles taking place here are more than just personal and financial: Clavell sees them as struggles for the heart and soul of the world, with Hong Kong as the battlefield.

Capitalistic enterprise and ideology are represented by Ian Dunross, Quillan Gornt, Linc Bartlett, Casey Tcholok, and Paul Choy, while members of the Communist team, including ship's captain and KGB agent

George Suslev and triple agent Robert Crosse, remain shadowy figures dealing in blackmail, treason, and terror. For readers, the choice should be easy: it is a choice between highly individualized and humanized characters and bland, dehumanized ones, between men and women engaged in life for its own sake and those committed to the abstract ideology of Communism that treats individuals with contempt. For Clavell, the greatest enemies are the British representatives of the Labour Party who advocate bland socialistic conformity and the restriction of individual freedoms, particularly the freedom to engage in free trade. Clavell attributes the rise of a middle class and of a democratic view of government to free trade, and argues that free trade guarantees greater wealth for many and improved living conditions for all. He sees men and women like Dunross, Bartlett, Tcholok, and Choy as creating wealth, which, through trickle-down economics, can improve conditions for even the lowliest laborer.

In other words, Clavell interlocks political and business struggles. Hong Kong is the showplace of capitalism, with the competing socialist model never far away. Fortunes are made and lost in the ten days of the novel, and lives are totally transformed. Human mettle is tested, and personal values challenged and altered before the final action is complete. The stakes are high, and personal disaster is possible. Nonetheless, all the participants compete, using intellect and wit, expertise and planning. Thus, the novel is a tribute to the ingenuity, cleverness, and daring of capitalistic entrepreneurs.

Against this wildly exciting business contest is set the disapproval of British socialists, representatives of the Labour Party who find the individualistic flavor of Hong Kong an insult to their view of bland group control. It is fitting that the key spokesman for controlling, limiting, and containing the capitalistic energies and activities of Hong Kong was once the officer in charge of enforcing Japanese prison regulations on British and American prisoners of war, whose underground, capitalistic, black-market activities helped them survive the horrors of "socialistic" military controls.

However, Clavell's treatment of this meeting of economic and political philosophies is not totally black and white. The rivalry between Gornt and Dunross comes to represent the negative and positive potentials of free enterprise: grasping capitalism untempered by any sense of responsibility, as opposed to capitalism as a means to support and protect home and kin, a capitalism based on obligation and duty. Clavell reinforces this point in his contrast of Wu and his son Paul, the former responsible only to himself, the latter enjoying playing the stock market but also feeling responsible to his extended family.

In keeping with Clavell's view that contact with different ideologies, values, and methodologies inevitably transforms both cultures, the novel illustrates how far China has come since the China of *Tai-Pan* in its movement toward Western values. Basically, Clavell argues that China's brand of Communism cannot hold out against the inroads of capitalism because capitalistic enterprise can help solve many of China's present problems. China expert Kevin Lane, finds "Hong Kong's growth and prosperity as a British colony alongside a strongly anti-imperialist China ...paradoxical" (Lane 1990: 6) and agrees with Clavell that Hong Kong, against all odds, is China's door on the world. In *Noble House*, Clavell argues that, though still an alien culture, with a focus on communal rather than individual values, China cannot close its doors to the West. It has become dependent on Hong Kong as a population outlet in times of trouble and as a source of income and goods; illegal and legal traffic flows in and out of Hong Kong and back and forth between Hong Kong and the mainland. In the novel, the degree to which China has come to depend on the West is clear from China's willingness to bail Hong Kong banks out of a potential collapse and to save Noble House from financial ruin. That is all part of the interactive bargaining that Clavell finds so vital to national and international health.

The fact is that in this novel the interests of Hong Kong and of mainland China and the interests of the Chinese immigrants to Hong Kong and of the Hong Kong *yan* (Europeans who have become natives of Hong Kong) have become so intertwined, the Westerners so Chinese and the Chinese so Western, that the rigid separation and alienation that was a part of *Tai-Pan* is no longer true. Western education, Western technology, and Western business have, as Dirk Struan had hoped, transformed China and the Chinese. Hong Kong has provided safe haven for political and economic refugees from China and has been a protected staging ground for all sorts of mainland political activities: it has also brought huge economic benefits as Western capital has been channeled to the mainland in the form of bilateral trade, investments, loans, and gifts. Clavell depicts Hong Kong as central to involving China in the West and to providing a gateway to carry into the Chinese heartland Western ideas about economics, culture, and justice.

Many long-time British residents of Hong Kong have acquired Chinese perspectives despite their very proper British manners and accents. Dunross looks British, but he is a new breed, a Hong Konger. He values

British individualism and British justice, but he speaks Chinese like a native, thinks with the obliqueness and complexities of the Chinese mind, hires a Chinese architectural expert to make sure his business buildings meet the requirements of *feng shui* (an ancient Chinese system for positioning buildings to ward off evil spirits and negative influences), and feels committed to China. He calls the relationship between mainland China and Noble House one of "old friends," and the quiet, understated, top mainland Chinese government official with whom he deals agrees. Clavell may well think of Dunross as a man of the future, a future no longer divided by national, racial, and ethnic borders, but rather a world in which people become blends of their mixed heritages. (This is not quite the same as the changes predicted by the head of McDonald's in Japan, Den Fujita, in *McDonald's: Behind the Arches*, wherein he affirms that Japanese who eat McDonald's hamburgers and potatoes for 1,000 years instead of the fish and rice of their historic heritage can expect to be physically transformed: "we will become taller, our skin become white and our hair blond.")

The result of the interaction of the two conflicting ideologies and contrasting cultures is a complexity of relationships that acquire a certain strangeness and unpredictability. To emphasize the deep-rooted ties between mainland China and Hong Kong, Clavell makes Dr. Sun Yat-sen (a graduate of the Hong Kong College of Medicine and the founder of the Republic of China) dependent on Noble House for his education and protection, and indeed historians like Lo Hsiang-lin and Jung-fang Tsai confirm that the influence of foreigners on Hong Kong Chinese may have contributed to the overthrow of the monarchical Manchu government in China and the founding in 1949 of the Peoples's Republic of China (283). Even Brian Kwok, who feeds secret information about Russian activities to mainland relatives, thinks of himself as a real citizen of Hong Kong, acting in the best interests of that city and rooting for its success against outsiders. Tiptop, the Red Chinese official whose handshake loan saves Noble House, is supposedly a committed ideologue, dedicated to Maoist principles and to the *Little Red Book* in which they are enunciated, yet he is committed to a safe and stable Hong Kong, and so are the behind-the-scenes political heads from whom he takes orders. The Bank of China, a Communist toehold in the West, invests and loans as actively as any capitalist bank.

In other words, in *Noble House*, Clavell depicts his larger economic and cultural theories at work. Free enterprise is infectious. It changes people. It improves their quality of life. It promotes independence. Prolonged contact with it demonstrates its superiority to socialistic or Communistic group efforts, in which motivation to achieve is undercut by the absence of personal benefit. Clavell postulates that trade with China over a long period will transform Chinese thinking, and that the Chinese cannot stop those changes; however, it will also affect Western thinking, and Westerners cannot stop those changes either. But whichever way the influences flow, it is capitalism that will promote social and personal advances.

Whirlwind
(1986)

"... the Islamic revolution in Iran is a cataclysm as significant and as unprecedented in world history as the French revolution of 1789 and the Russian revolution of 1917.... [It] forces us to reassess the balance of progressive and reactionary ..., of traditionalism and modernism, in all revolutions."

Said Amir Arjomand, *The Turban for the Crown*

In *Whirlwind*, Westerners caught up in the reforms of post-Shah Iran, which is led by the reactionary Moslem Shi'ite sect, find the familiar transformed beyond recognition, and past friends and lovers, now wrapped in their cloaks of Islamic revolution, incomprehensible. This novel depicts the contradictions, irrationality, emotionalism, and fanaticism of reactionary Iranian factions, as Western husbands find Iranian wives adopting with enthusiasm the *chador* (the long black robe that covers the body from head to toe) and joining rioters in the streets, and businessmen are shocked by the vehement anti-Western stance of their long-time business associates and by the brutality of Iranian Islamic "justice" with its kangaroo courts and on-the-spot executions.

Clavell had visited Iran frequently during the Shah's reign and had good friends who showed him an insider's view of the country, but he also read extensively about Iran and Iranians. It took him three years to write *Whirlwind*, which he sold at auction. The publisher, William Morrow and Company, reportedly paid Clavell the highest price ever for a novel: five million dollars. The novel was a huge financial success, selling four million paperback copies in the United States alone.

PLOT DEVELOPMENT

Whirlwind continues the sagas begun in Clavell's earlier novels, bringing together representatives of the Hong Kong–based Noble House, who are struggling to control helicopter concessions in war-torn Iran, and the descendants of the Japanese house of Toranaga, representing the Toda shipping company, who are striving to gain oil and gas concessions in the Persian Gulf. At the end of *Noble House*, tai-pan Ian Dunross instructs his nephew Andrew Gavallan to establish a Scotland-based helicopter company. In *Whirlwind*, Andrew Gavallan is now head of S-G Helicopters. This company has operated in Iran during the Shah's reign and has helped the Shah of Iran's forces develop and supply rich Iranian oil centers. The novel is set at a crucial time in history: the fall of the Shah and the rise of the Ayatollah Khomeini and the reactionary, militant Islamic forces which support him. Westerners find the Islamic revolution unexpected since Iran had been an independent monarchy for more than 2,500 years. Gavallan and his man-on-the-spot, Duncan McIver, must decide whether to stay and hope for a new contract with the revolutionary government or to get out with the least loss of men and capital. In the meantime, mullahs (religious leaders), Communists, fleeing officers, and local chieftains all commandeer company helicopters for revolution, for escape, or just for joyrides. S-G's American competitor, Guerney, has already left, abandoning its helicopters. Khomeini's antitechnology, anti-Western message, and his fanatical followers' destructive application of his message, combined with the uncontrollable and dangerous competing factions that the end of the Shah's dominance has now freed, constitute the "whirlwind" that makes the decision to leave inevitable. Also, the Iranian Moslems describe Khomeini as God's whirlwind; the Shah had sown the wind, they say, and consequently reaps the whirlwind.

The novel is a countdown from February 9, 1979, when the crisis begins, to March 2, 1979, when the escape plan kicks in, to March 4, 1979, when all personnel and the larger "212" helicopters and support equipment have left. The mission's code name is also "Whirlwind," a combination of the Moslem associations and the English slang for helicopter, "whirlybird." During the mission, the scattered S-G personnel and equipment must be organized, the local Iranian partners kept in the dark, and secrecy maintained. The main suspense of the book is whether or not the Western businessmen can be secretive enough and clever enough to leave the country safely, with all their key property intact. The main action is the nearly simultaneous departure of helicopters loaded with materials and men for a hazardous flight over the Persian Gulf to safety, and the care and planning involved in insuring the safety of the helicopters and their contents once they land in another Moslem country, which includes changing the Iranian identification numbers on leased helicopters to British numbers upon landing. The threat of an avalanche delays the closing of the Zagros Three oil rig station; some group members disappear, are imprisoned, or are injured; mullah-led Shi'ites overrun bases; and conflicts with formerly friendly nomads complicate the mission. One pilot has a heart attack during the final flight and another lands his helicopter on a supertanker, but all who make it into the air survive. Even Erikki Yokkonen, who is kidnapped by Azerbaijani nomads, reaches Turkey. The most exciting part of the novel is the final escape countdown, and that section could easily stand on its own as a suspenseful adventure story.

STRUCTURE

Because of the size of *Whirlwind* (the paperback edition is 1,270 pages long), Clavell must use a number of organizing structures, the most obvious of which is chronological order. The novel begins on Friday, February 9, 1979, and continues to Sunday, March 4, 1979. The large structural units, which Clavell calls "Books," each focus on a key day during this time period, on February 9, 11, 12, 13, 17, 18, 20, 23, 24, 26, and 28, and March 2, 3, and 4. The last two units are the shortest ones. The novel moves step by step from the recognition of a crisis to the consideration of potential solutions and then to a final decision about an escape strategy. The next stage involves working out logistics and communicating these logistics clearly to all participants. Friday, March 2, opens with the evacuation plan in progress, and Sunday, March 4, sees the mission accomplished and the final narrative threads tied together.

The second overall organizing pattern is spatial. Each time unit is subdivided into chapters which focus upon geographic areas, like the island of Siri in the Persian Gulf or the Iranian cities of Bandar Delam, Dez Dam, Isfahan, Longeh, and Qazvin. The helicopter bases and personnel are scattered throughout Iran, their location marked with bold black circles on a small map at the beginning of each chapter. Key locations anchor central plot elements; the base of outside operations is at Al Shargaz, near the United Arab Emirates, and the base of inside operations is at Kowiss, but there are helicopters at the oil rig Rosa and at Zagros Three. Teheran and Tabriz are the centers of family confrontations, and Mount Salaban and the Zagros mountains are the centers of armed confrontations. Within chapters, the geographic region is further broken down by introductory headings to orient the reader: "Near Tabriz One, at the Village of Abu Mard: 6:17 A.M.," "At Lochart's Apartment: 2:37 P.M.," and so on. The combination of place and date suggests urgency and emphasizes the difficult logistics of the mission. Such place and time labels are conventions of adventure film narratives.

A third organizing structure is a symbolic frame that begins and ends with the same character, Hussain Kowissi, a symbol of confrontation and of Iranian hatred of the West. The novel begins with Kowissi musing on the image of the Shah having sown the wind, and reaping the "whirlwind" of Khomeini and of the Islamic revolution. Kowissi is on his way to join the Shi'ite forces and to seek martyrdom. When the S-G helicopter of Andrew Gavallan's son Scot flies over, Kowissi fires his Soviet AK-47 assault rifle at the Western "demons," wounding Scot and nearly bringing down the helicopter. This is the first visible act of civil war and anti-Western frenzy. The rest of the book traces the growth and spread of that revolutionary fervor, the conversion or execution of nonbelievers, and the expulsion of foreigners. Kowissi reappears throughout the book, leading ragged mobs in a take-over of a helicopter base, preaching Shi'ite values, and even trying to convert one Westerner, Conroe Starke, whom he believes has been touched by God. Kowissi is sincere in his obsessions, and it is his superstitious belief that Starke, though an infidel, has in some way been the tool of Allah that leads Kowissi to allow Starke and his crew to leave, while pretending the flight is an ordinary one. As the book closes, when the Westerners have left and the Khomeini regime is in place, Kowissi has the final say: an Eastern judgment on the limitations of Westerners and a fanatical resolve to carry the revolution beyond Iran. This frame helps the reader face the realities of Iran's revolution. Iran has become a closed circle, a medieval fortress from which Westerners have been driven and whose gates have resoundingly closed against them. However, the goal of the Shi'ites is to enclose more and more territory as a direct challenge to the West's influence.

A fourth underlying structural pattern is a division into sections alternating between Iranian nationals and Western outsiders, between the strategies of high financiers, expatriate pilots, lovers, and revolutionaries, and between the single and the married. The main logic of the novel's internal structure involves contrasting cultures and contrasting personalities.

The general cultural contrast is, of course, between East and West, with Clavell illustrating differences in attitudes toward technology, religion, justice, politeness, marriage, family, and the roles and rights of women. Such contrasts are at times superficial. Iranian merchants are better bargainers than Chinese merchants, say the Japanese. Iranians, like other Asians, never point the bottom of their foot toward someone unless intentionally giving insult, and they never use their left hands (their "toilet" hands) to eat or drink. Westerners prefer beds to sleep on; Iranians prefer carpets. Westerners like complex indoor plumbing; Iranians are accustomed to a hole in the floor. However, many of the contrasts are highly significant and affect action and attitudes throughout the book.

A key contrast involves attitudes toward technology. Westerners value technology and see it as a tool that can better life. Iranians have difficulty understanding its nature; they respond to it as an alien concept imposed on them and therefore as something to be cursed and destroyed. Whereas the Westerner prohibits fire near an open gas or oil line, the Iranian shrugs and smokes a cigarette. A Westerner says a work accident results from preventable stupidity, but his Iranian coworkers say "Insha' Allah" ("In the hands of Allah"), in other words, "What will be, will be. It is the will of God."

The contrasts continue throughout the book. Westerners consider religion a private matter, between man and God; the Iranians consider it a public matter, demonstrated by self-flagellation in the streets, public protestations of faith, and the wearing of the *chador* for women. The systems of justice and punishment differ, too. Azerbaijani Abdollah Khan tells his Nordic son-in-law Erikki Yokkonen, "We are an Oriental People, not Western, who understand violence and torture" and, "Life and death are not judged [here] by your standards" (224). The execution of large numbers of rich and poor, many of them sincere Moslems, makes this point most forcefully, as does Khomeini's first speech upon returning to Iran, in which he says, "I pray God to cut off the hands of all foreigners," describing the Moslem punishment for theft (218). The British, a people Clavell in earlier novels characterized as inscrutable, are, by Iranian standards, forthright and direct. Clavell's Iranians esteem indirection, obfuscation, and circumlocution as good manners: one should never be blunt or direct. Persiaphile Tom Lockhart points out that the Farsi language reflects the attitudes of its speakers and is designed for indirection. He also notes the Iranian custom of always having a ready answer, even about things the speaker doesn't know anything about.

Perhaps the most striking difference is the contrast in attitudes toward family. Whereas the Westerner focuses on the individual as central, the Iranian regards the family as all-important. Family comes first, family dominates, family decides, and family looks after family. Naturally, the attitudes toward family affect the attitudes toward women, who are servants and tools of the family; they must obey the head of the household. The family of Sharazad, Tom Lockhart's wife, decides she should divorce and remarry, and she has no say in the matter. The Khan decides his daughter, Azadeh, will serve his purposes better if she is allied with a Soviet rather than with a Finn, and his word is law. Readers may ask why Azadeh or Sharazad don't simply leave and why they take family commands as unbreakable laws. Clavell's answer is that they cannot do otherwise; family dominance is so firmly a part of their cultural identity that women are doomed to destructive patterns. Whereas a Western woman might rebel, defy her family, and defend her husband against her father, the Iranian woman, in the novel, submits to her father or seeks escape in death.

Contrasts like the above, between Western and Iranian perceptions and patterns of behavior, dominate *Whirlwind* and are vital to its characters and themes.

Throughout *Whirlwind*, Clavell relies on short vignettes or powerful images to convey insights that define the broader picture. One example is a description of two Moslem groups fighting, one a local faction, the other representing the central government. Both act in the name of Allah for a righteous cause. The ayatollah leader of one faction is wounded and then executed, but he dies smiling, with "the Name of God on his lips," while opponents and supporters alike weep openly, "envying him Paradise" (336). In another case, an S-G pilot, Charlie Pettikin, looking out the window of his Teheran apartment, sees fires spring up from where the Green Bands of Shi'ite Moslem fundamentalists are fighting. Then, the fighting stops as battlers on both sides hear the religious cry of the muezzins "from minarets everywhere" calling all Moslem believers to afternoon prayer, and Pettikin is filled with dread at this incomprehensible unity of feuding factions. A large shark near an off-shore oil rig becomes a recurring symbol of what Iran has become for Westerners: destructive, predatory, alien, swallowing them and leaving little trace.

CHARACTER DEVELOPMENT

Despite its fascinating topic and Clavell's careful research and accurate portraits, *Whirlwind* fails initially to grip the imagination as forcefully as his other novels do. This is partly because Clavell does not counter the book's broad scope with a focus on a single individual to whom the readers can relate and with whom they can identify, and whose personal experiences could provide a basis for interpreting the whole. Instead, the action is diffuse, and readers follow the fate of a company rather than the fate of a single individual. Because the structural pattern shifts from location to location and group to group, character development initially seems sketchy, relying on stereotypes developed through contrasts with other characters. Only well into the book do characters become individualized. Even characters like Duncan McIver, Erikki Yokkonen, and Tom Lockhart, who receive more attention than the others, do not control their own destiny, but are instead caught up in the momentum of events, and are in danger of being destroyed by those events. The key women around whom events revolve, Azadeh Yokkonen and Sharazad Lockhart, are more important as representatives of cultural attitudes than as individuals, and this will be discussed later.

Characters who manipulate events behind the scenes remain shadowy, and readers must depend on their knowledge of those characters from Clavell's earlier books. Though Andrew Gavallan and Ian Dunross are well known to those who have read *Noble House*, in *Whirlwind* they are stick figures necessitated by plot. Gavallan is needed to coordinate the action from a neutral area. Clavell humanizes him in two ways: by portraying his worries about his injured son Scot, whose escape depends on Gavallan's plan, and by contrasting his relationship with his son Scot with Kowissi's relationship with his young son and the Soviet spy Petyr Mzytryk's relationship with his son Igor. In the background is Sir Ian Dunross, whose information network helps Gavallan anticipate events and save his company. However, Dunross never comes on stage. He remains a background figure whose advice guides Gavallan and prepares readers for action on the Iranian front.

Initially, most of the helicopter pilots merge in the reader's mind, separated only by national identity or characterized by a single action or by a striking personal detail or trait. One is French, another Canadian; one is married, another not; one is older and more experienced than his trainee. However, as readers see them in action, they become more individualized, and their individuality is lent depth by contrasts. For example, Jean-Luc is a stereotypical French playboy who enjoys sexual conquest but is too egotistical to ever love anyone but himself. He is a daring pilot, but nonchalant and careless about people. While his helicopter team works hard to keep the Iranian helicopter personnel from recognizing that their escape flight is anything more than a regular trip, he arrives with stacks of luggage, chatting about departure. However, he has already betrayed his friends' plan to a paramour who is a Palestinian Liberation Front (PLO) spy. His womanizing contrasts with the hesitant but sincere romancing of Pettikin, an older man who falls genuinely in love with a flight attendant named Paula. Jean-Luc's attitudes and behavior also contrast with those of Conroe Starke, a former Vietnam helicopter squadron commander, whose reminiscences about Vietnam provide insights into his character, and whose attractive and loyal wife, Manuela, helps personalize him. Starke protects the men under him as ''People of the Book,'' and Kowissi's fascination with his knowledge of the Koran and Islam buys the team time. When Starke takes a bullet meant for Kowissi, he saves his whole crew.

Another pilot, Scragger, nicknamed ''Scrag,'' is humanized when he teaches his neophyte copilot Ed Vossi to fly blind. Helping injured Iranians in emergencies wins their allegiance, and one man he saved, Turik Abdollah, risks his life to warn Scragger of danger. When sabotage threatens disaster, Scragger's skill saves his chopper and the representatives of Toda Shipping. Scragger's World War II experiences in the Pacific and the stories of his ex-partner, the first American to enter Changi prison camp at the end of the war, have fueled his anti-Japanese prejudices. Clavell provides character development by having Scragger fly Yoshi Kasigi, of Toda Shipping around the region and by having him confront Kasigi's regrets for the war and yet his willingness to torture modern Iranian terrorists to find hidden bombs aboard a Toda ship. Kasigi, a descendant of Yabu Kasigi, who in *Shogun* was a strong supporter and then betrayer of Yoshi Toranaga, accepts American and British hatred as justified by Japan's wartime atrocities. The reader's interest in Kasigi's character comes more from the confrontation of cultures, experiences, and prejudices than from the character himself. We know him through the reactions of others and through his thoughts about how to deal with such reactions.

Duncan McIver, the Iran-based coordinator of the escape, is humanized through his relationship with his wife, Genny, who defiantly sticks by his side. In her conversations, she recalls family and friends, past times, and past pleasures. McIver is also humanized by his wife and friends' concerns about his required company physical, his doctor's warnings about heart problems, and his flying solo, all of which heighten tension as the countdown proceeds.

A great deal of action revolves around two other main characters. Erikki Yokkonen and Tom Lockhart, both of whom are married to Iranians, are knowledgeable about Iranian culture, but are puppets manipulated by Iranian relatives and historical events. Erikki is a large, physically strong Finn, a fierce fighter who can skillfully use his traditional Finnish knife, the *pukoh,* and who explodes violently, "like an avenging warrior," when his wife is threatened (401). He blames the Americans and the English for giving Finnish lands to the Russians in 1945, and he hates Russians passionately. He won the Khan's permission to marry his wife, Azadeh, by swiftly and bloodily killing the Khan's would-be assassins, but he and the Khan have an uneasy truce. Erikki seems to have a penchant for being in the wrong place at the wrong time and is frequently stirred to bloodlust. His antagonism to the Khan, his jealousy of his wife's former lover John Ross, and his fears for his wife's safety motivate his actions, but at the end he and Azadeh depend on the whim of a Turkish policeman for protection against the Khan's murderous representatives and for release from jail without charges for theft and kidnapping.

Tom Lockhart is a devil-may-care Canadian flyboy, but he is not credibly individualized. He has married a rich, beautiful Iranian, Sharazad, and is dependent on her family to support him and his wife in the lifestyle to which she is accustomed—they live in an expensive, richly furnished Teheran apartment. He has studied Islam and wants to share his wife's culture, but we never enter his mind deeply enough to find out what motivates him. He has learned Farsi and describes it as a language of love and of innuendo, and he has a greater sympathy for Iranians than do the other members of his team. He deals most effectively with Nitchak Khan, the proud *kalandar* (village head) at Zagros Three, and plays the Persian conversational game with him according to ancient custom and traditional patterns. These include quoting from the *Rubaiyat* and the Koran, alluding to history, and winning the women's hearts with his praise of their magical powers. However, he is so tossed about by events that our main image of him is of a man on the run, shuttling between business and family.

Clavell has tried to use Lockhart to provide a sense of balance. Here is a man who appreciates Persian culture and who chooses to stay with his wife rather than flee, but even so, Sharazad's family treats him with contempt. The contrast between Erikki and Lockhart is one of realist and idealist: Lockhart hopes for the best even at his moment of death, and Erikki expects the worst and meets it headlong. For Erikki, the attacking mobs are "the real face of Iran" and the forcing of the *chador* is a rape of his wife's soul (265).

Of the spies, KGB captain Igor Mzytryk, the son of Petyr Mzytryk (who appeared under the alias "Captain Suslek" in *Noble House*), stands out. He is "a professor of terrorism" who foments revolution, spreads disinformation, and leads various assaults in the Soviet interest. He is variously disguised as an Iranian Marxist named Tudeh Fedor Rakoczi, as a Kurd from the Soviet border named Ali bin Hassan Karakose, as "Smith" when dealing with the British, and as Dimitri Yazernov, a Soviet representative to the Tudeh Central Committee. The Soviets have "a country to possess," he thinks, and sets about possessing it (269). He describes himself metaphorically as a farmer who plants seeds, nurturing and guarding the plants until harvest, working round the clock in all seasons, patiently enduring good years and bad. His farm is Iran, and his goal is to make that country Soviet soil. He leads the famous attack on the American embassy in order to empty the CIA safe of documents and cipher books.

The Iranians are more sketchily drawn than the Europeans and British, and they just remain types. There is the ace flier Yusuf Kyabi, who trained at Texas A & M and who has become totally Westernized. He attacks mullahs as "impoverished, dull-witted peasants" who are "easy prey for trained insurgents" (140), and he calls Khomeini "a narrow-minded fanatic" who wants to return Iran and its people, particularly the women, back to "the Dark Ages" (149). He is summarily executed because of his convictions. There is an Iranian named Wazari, who after spying on the helicopter crews and figuring out they are leaving the country, ingratiates himself to them by taking a beating but not betraying them. He gets out on one of the helicopters and gets a British passport as well. There is also Karim Peshadi, who is Sharazad's cousin and who has been in love with her since childhood. He helps Lockhart by destroying documents that would reveal Lockhart's involvement in a helicopter hijacking, but is caught in the act and killed.

Although they are not sympathetic to Khomeini, Captain Hushang Abassi and his brother Ali Abassi become Khomeini supporters so they can do what they love most—fly an F-47 with their elite military force. The Moslem Tudehs (Communists) Ali and Bijan compare themselves to

Robert Jordan in *For Whom the Bell Tolls* as they set up explosives to sabotage oil lines. General Valik, who is one of Lockhart's in-laws and a supporter of the Shah, insults Lockhart as a kept man and then tempts him with an offer of twelve million rials, the Iranian currency, to fly family members and high-ranking fellow officers out of the country. That Lockhart might be arrested and imprisoned for hijacking and that he cannot return to Iran if he does so does not interest Valik. After Lockhart has flown to, but will not cross, the border, Valik tries to kill him. Lockhart is "family" when he is needed but an outsider when he is not, and only Valik's wife's sense of obligation saves him. Valik, who owns houses in London, Surrey, and California, and has bank accounts in Switzerland and the Bahamas, sums up the corruption under the Shah.

Even more negative portraits abound: the perverse and cruel Azerbaijani Khan and his conniving son; the rich pederast who buys a bride to demonstrate his wealth; the officers who are on one side one day and then have convincing proof of their loyalty to the other side the very next day; the mullah who can be bribed with new eyeglasses and free air travel. Esvandiary, the new Iranian head of the Kowiss base, is so malicious and hate filled that one pilot tries to drop heavy equipment on him. Large, faceless mobs of Iranian fundamentalists—"roaring, senseless, mindless" (73)—rampage through the novel, beating women not completely covered in *chadors*, chanting calls to destruction, and executing all in their path. Clavell's image of these Iranian masses, who take on a power and a character of their own, could have been taken straight from one of Sir Richard Burton's books, for, according to Burton, "Iranians are a violent people, death seekers" in the service of Allah (Burne 1985: 198).

Clavell does a good job of capturing an alien mentality, but he does not help readers appreciate it. He explains why individual Iranians are doomed, but he doesn't make us like them as individuals.

THEMATIC ISSUES

Whirlwind provides a portrait of the dual impulses that have wrenched modern Iran, the conflict between order and impulsiveness, between Western logic and Eastern mysticism, between a thrust toward a technological future and a fear of modernization. It depicts a people who want video cassette recorders and transistor radios but who also want to be medieval Moslems. It captures the hypocrisy, cruelty, and fanaticism of Islamic revolutionary factions bent on dominating their rivals at any cost, but tearing their country apart in the process.

Rejection of the West

Just as Clavell's other novels have opened up the Asian cultures of China and Japan to Western eyes, so *Whirlwind* opens up Iran (in southwest Asia) to Western examination. In almost every case, Clavell's books have focused on periods when the East has tried to reject the West: the Japanese rejecting Westerners in *King Rat*, *Shogun*, and *Gai-Jin*; the Chinese rejecting Westerners in *Tai-Pan* and being forced only by war to grant them inroads, and the Chinese looking forward to Hong Kong being returned to China in *Noble House*. *Whirlwind* is similar: it records a revolution in which the East rejects the West and which moves a nation backwards instead of forwards. Clavell's Iranians pride themselves on Iran being Asian, an Oriental country. Clavell depicts Iran as a country where West has met East and has seemed to have made vast inroads into the psyches of the people, only to have been totally rejected. A governing thesis for Clavell, throughout his canon, is that contact between East and West can change both Easterners and Westerners. However, in *Whirlwind*, few are changed, and most of those Iranians who have been Westernized are eliminated from the equation by execution. Others respond as Esvandiary does. For years, Esvandiary served as an affable, friendly assistant and betrayed no sign of anti-British feeling, but suddenly he sheds his pro-Western guise and angrily denounces the British for what he calls 150 years of colonial exploitation. Villagers enthusiastically return to their ancient traditions of stoning adulterers and cutting off the hands and sexual parts of accused rapists. Even Clavell's Westernized Iranian heroine, Sharazad, who has married a foreigner and who loves to shop in Paris, enthusiastically dons the *chador*, joins what she calls "our Glorious Freedom Fighters," marches in the streets with them against the Shah's elite force, the "Immortals," and accepts that the only way to defy her family is to seek religious martyrdom (135).

Western Sympathies

From a Western point of view, Iran under the Pahlavis, the Shah's family, had made major strides toward modernization and toward twentieth century attitudes, strides Clavell praises throughout *Whirlwind*. Muhammad Reza Pahlavi took power in 1941, at age twenty-two and was driven out by Muhammad Mosaddeq in the early 1950s, but then returned with strong backing from Western powers. In the 1960s and 1970s, the Shah became a powerful ruler, determined to modernize Iran, with an iron fist if necessary. Clavell argues that the Shah saw Iran under his leadership as "the real arbiter of East and West," partly because of what he saw as the "inherent superiority of Iranians," with their three thousand years of civilization, partly because of his close ties with the United States (79).

Anwar Sadat's wife, Jehan Sadat, in her book *A Woman of Egypt*, confirms this self-image of the Shah and is highly sympathetic to his vision of Iran as a psychological and cultural crossroads of civilizations, as it had been a caravan crossroads for four thousand years. The Shah began a series of ambitious reform programs, known as the White Revolution, which included rapid industrialization, land reform, and the emancipation of women. Tens of thousands of Iranian students studied in the United States and Germany during his regime and learned Western values and Western ways, and pilots and soldiers were trained on American bases and adopted American military-style organization and attitudes. Westernized Iranians pushed for even faster, greater changes, while Moslem conservatives disapproved. The Shah's elite secret police, SAVAK, who were reportedly CIA and FBI trained, became notorious for their brutal treatment of the Shah's critics, particularly the mullahs or Moslem clergy, and the power of the conservative mullahs was further undercut by a concerted effort to upgrade living conditions in even the most isolated of villages. Western technological goods poured into the country, and Iranian soldiers found themselves stationed in backward villages teaching modern concepts of hygiene, waste disposal, basic preventative medicine, and medical care. Villagers drafted into the military were taught new ways and given more nutritious food and better clothing than they had ever had. The Shah's bill of rights for women gave them new rights, rights that their fellow Moslems in other countries did not have: the right to appear in public without the veil or traditional dress, the right to choose their own husbands, the right to divorce, the right to an education, and even the right to vote. Women exchanged their medieval *chadors* for Parisian fashions and used Western cosmetics. Western dress came into vogue, and Western films, dubbed into Farsi, gained popularity; in fact, John Wayne's Farsi voice was so well known that when Iranians heard the real voice of John Wayne, they rejected it as fake. The Shah built modern hospitals and schools and established kindergartens. He tried to develop a middle class to lessen the dichotomy between the traditional pattern of a few very rich amid a large majority of very poor. He built roads and railways that were engineering wonders. During his reign, Iran had more warplanes than Britain and more tanks than Germany and was the biggest military power in the Middle and Near East, says Clavell (363). That Iran could fall back into medievalism seemed beyond belief.

From a Western perspective, these changes helped move Iran from a backward, superstitious, medieval culture to a modern, technological one. Clavell demonstrates how superficial these recent changes were in the light of a thousand years of tradition and Islam, how quickly the changes were eliminated, and how suddenly Iran plunged back into the Dark Ages of a fanatically reactionary, Khomeini-driven, Moslem state. Widespread dislocation and government corruption created a general unrest that led to an outbreak of riots in 1977 and 1978. Sudden and dramatic wealth created by oil revenues increased the divisions between urban and rural, Westernized and traditional, and the technologically literate and illiterate. The opposition was strengthened by support from numerous factions, all united in their hatred of the Shah's methods. The opposition disapproved of the Shah changing the calendar from the sacred Islamic one to a newly invented one counting back to Cyrus the Great; they disapproved of rights for women; they disapproved of SAVAK's attacks on mullahs; and they disapproved of the close alliance with the United States. By November of 1978, the Shah had placed Iran under military rule, but the Islamic fundamentalist Ayatollah Ruhollah Khomeini spurred the opposition from his exile in Paris. Finally, on January 6, 1979, the Shah lifted military rule and not many days later left the country. Khomeini entered Iran on February 1, welcomed by ecstatic Moslems chanting his praises as their country's religious savior, and by February 12, 1979, Iran was proclaimed an Islamic republic.

Clavell sets his novel in this tumultuous period of political, social and religious change, his action beginning eight days after Khomeini had returned and ending three weeks later. His dominant theme is a lament for what is lost and a fear of what is to come.

The Dangers of Isolationism

Whirlwind provides insights into an Iranian perspective and into the richness of Iranian culture, but also into the dangers of Iran's limited perspective. Whereas Western maps show a world in which the Americas, Europe, and Africa are centrally placed, with the Middle East comparatively small, the Iranian world map is Irano-centric. That is, Iranians see Iran as the center of the world, with other countries secondary to it; the Americas, for example, are split down the middle and consigned to the edges of the map. Clavell's characters learn the effects of this Irano-centric vision. The Moslem fundamentalists that Clavell depicts are not at all concerned about world opinion. To them, Westerners are outsiders, and although Americans in particular are instruments of the "Great Satan" America, anyone vaguely Western is probably the cause of something bad, so French, Scandinavian, British, and even Japanese (Westernized by their values, modernity, and lifestyle) find themselves the objects of hate, insults, and physical threats.

Fanaticism

The fanaticism of Shi'ite Moslems is, then, another key theme. Abdollah Khan rages against what he calls America's "foul policies, foul arrogance, foul manners, foul jeans, foul music, foul food, and foul democracy," as well as "their disgusting pornography" and "their evil antagonism to Islam" (226), and throughout the novel anyone accused of being an American or an American sympathizer is in danger of losing his life. The "Great Satan" America is to blame for all ills. Clavell describes Moslem courts as making hundreds of judgments a day and ordering confiscation of property and immediate execution by firing squad, without evidence or a real trial. Emir Paknouri, Sharazad's first husband, an elder of the bazaar and chief of the league of goldsmiths who donated millions to Khomeini's cause, is accused of money lending by a jealous bricklayer and is executed along with Colonel Peshadi, the hero of Dhofar, where he smashed Marxist aggressors in southern Oman. Also executed is a respected journalist named Turlak, who is a courageous critic of the Shah's regime. Sharazad's father, Jared Bakravan, is brought in under armed guard for questioning about people accused of betraying Moslem values under the Shah. Bakravan is exonerated, but a fanatical guard has him executed anyway. The swiftness and extreme nature of Iranian Shi'ite justice leaves no room for rectifying mistakes. Execution occurs, with or without evidence of guilt.

Clavell finds the Iranian militants dangerous and fears the threat they pose because of their pivotal position in the Middle East. Over 60 percent of the free world's oil passes through the Strait of Hormuz. Although he doesn't mention it directly, Clavell is disturbed at the idea of so fanatical a religious group controlling so much oil, and of the West yielding to its threats out of fear of repercussions. At the end of the novel, Clavell shows the Japanese poised to take advantage of the Iranian oil market, their eyes closed to human abuses. The American refusal to give their old ally the Shah U.S. sanctuary happened too late for inclusion within Clavell's time frame. (Khomeini used the fifty Americans taken hostage in the American Embassy in Teheran in November of 1979 to pressure the U.S. government to eject the Shah.) Nonetheless, Clavell sets the stage for readers to understand the disturbing possibilities created when fanatics control so much oil.

Hussain Kowissi, the devout, sincere mullah whose activities Clavell follows throughout the book, has the final say. He is a hard man, deeply committed to extremist values. His wife dead from childbirth, his small son at his side, he wears the black robes of his religious calling and has a Kalashnikov rifle slung on his back as he rides forth to spread the radical Islamic message of *jihad* or "holy war" against the West. He tells his son, "Now we are soldiers of God," and explains to him the difference between Islamic and Western views:

> They believe the life of an individual is priceless, any individual. We know all life comes from God, belongs to God, returns to God, and any life only has value doing God's work. . . . We are neither Eastern, nor Western, only Moslem. (1269–70)

The final words of the book are the ritual chanting of the Moslem protestation of faith: "God is Great. . . . There is no other God but God" (1270). Clavell's British have left Iran, and the country is left in the hands of fanatical Moslem extremists who, in a matter of days, destroy what took years to build. They are content with poverty and with dying for a religious cause. Their women are slaves and their children illiterate and impoverished, but God speaks to the men through their mullahs and ayatollahs and Paradise awaits their souls, so death as a martyr is welcome to them.

Factionalism

Another of Clavell's themes is Iranian factionalism. Iran's population is ethnically complex; it is predominantly Aryan (Farsi is an Indo-

European, not a Middle Eastern Semitic language), but one-third of the population is made up of Turks and Arabs, and Armenians and Jews complete the picture. Each group speaks a different language or dialect so there are at least ten different languages in a country of approximately a million and a half square miles and sixty million people. The largest demographic group is descended from migratory Aryan tribes from Central Asia. Of these, the Persians, or Farsi, make up well over half of the total population and dominate the central plateau area, including the major cities, Teheran and Isfahan. The Gilani and Mazandarani live to the north and around the Caspian sea; Kurds, Bakhtiari, Lurs, Baluchi, and Azerbaijanis are nomadic tribespeople. These nomads are mainly herdsmen, who have strongly resisted cultural changes and have even demanded separate nation status. Clavell's British soldier John Ross and his Gurkhas move among such nomads, particularly among Kurds from the Zagros Mountains. Azadeh's father, Abdollah Khan, who lives in Tabriz, is the tribal leader of the Azerbaijanis. He bears the hereditary title "khan," opposes both the Shah and the Shi'ite extremists, and at times finds common cause with the Soviets in his political gamesmanship to keep the Azerbaijani land under his control.

Clavell believes in the value of diversity, and he provides a sense of the very different ethnic groups that were brought together and protected under the Shah. However, he also makes very clear how the drastically different lifestyles, local government organization, and family and group patterns would make it easy to promote dissent and division. Clavell shows the divisions within the divisions and the conflicts within tribes, as well as between tribes, that only a strong central government or a powerful unifying idea could control.

Clavell draws parallels between demographic factionalism and religious factional divisions. Under the Shah, a number of minority religions thrived. There were practitioners of the ancient Persian religion, Zoroastrianism, as well as Jews, Christians (particularly those from an old Eastern sect, the Nestorian Church), and practitioners of Baha'i, a modern religion that emphasizes spiritual unity, peace, universal education, and equality of the sexes and whose followers Moslem fanatics severely persecuted. Of the Moslems, most are Shi'ites, and only a minority, particularly the members of ethnic minorities, are Sunnis. Under Khomeini, Shi'ite Islam was made the official state religion and Iran became the world center of Shi'ite Islam. The Sunni Moslems are moderates, recognizing the equality of all Moslems under God; Shi'ite Moslems believe in a medieval hierarchical world in which Islamic scholars are superior

to ordinary people and deserve the highest spiritual and political positions. Consequently, the Shi'ite Moslems accept the word of ayatollahs,
high-level spiritual leaders analogous to Christian archbishops or the
Pope, as law. As a result, Khomeini's dictates, whether religious or otherwise, were accorded a respect and obedience simply unthinkable for a
Western leader.

Clavell portrays a period of transition during which secular Iranians
were forced to become Shi'ites, flee the country, or face certain death.
Particularly disturbing for Westerners is Clavell's depiction of the shal-
low, empty-headed Sharazad, who, like her namesake Sheherazade in
the *Rubaiyat*, is beautiful and exotic, fascinating and sexually alluring.
However, she is swept up in the enthusiasm for Khomeini, and naively
assumes that a rekindling of Moslem faith is a good thing, without ever
understanding that she will lose all her rights, be subjected to cruel,
jealous male relatives, and be reduced to a male possession. Also disturbing is the sudden and unprepared-for mystical conversion of Lockhart to Islam, and his leap of faith shortly before a needless death. This
may be Clavell's attempt to balance the account by showing a positive
side to Islam, but given the many instances of fanaticism, the conversion
is unpersuasive.

Horrors of Civil War

Related to the theme of factionalism is that of civil war, with its ironies,
conflicting loyalties, confusions, and horrors. The short tale of two brothers, Hushang and Ali Abassi, is particularly touching. Students together,
soldiers together, they served missions as pilots together and plotted
strategies for dealing with the changes wrought by revolution together.
However, Hushang shoots down an escaping helicopter, not knowing
that his brother is the pilot and that former military friends are aboard.
The irony is heightened for readers when he proudly brags that he blew
the craft out of the sky.

Iran's Ancient Heritage

In contrast to what the Shi'ite extremists destroy, Clavell provides a
taste of Iran's ancient heritage. Ancient Iran, called Persia, was once a
great world power, a center of civilization, trade, and culture. *The Ru-*

baiyat of Omar Khayyam, a long narrative poem, is considered one of the world's greatest pieces of literature, and its influence on Western writers has been widespread. Medieval Iranian love poetry set the world's standards for exploring the theme of love. For example, the pattern of describing women in exaggerated terms derives from a venerable Persian/Arab tradition. Therein, women's eyes burn with passion like suns, their teeth sparkle like stars, the roses in their cheeks are as red as cherries, and a curl of hair on their forehead might represent a deadly scorpion that pierces the heart of the lover and whose sting only a kiss can cure. Another common Iranian poetic image is to describe women as deer, their large doe eyes soft and brown, their flight from would-be lovers fleet. These ancient poetic conventions for describing women influenced French, Italian, and English love poetry of the medieval and Renaissance periods (Shakespeare parodies in his sonnet #130, "My Mistress' Eyes"). In *Whirlwind*, Sharazad has taught her Western husband, Tom Lockhart, the Farsi language of love, with its poetic exaggerations and poetic conventions. Clavell tries to capture in English the literary quality of this traditional and ancient speech.

Political Blinkers

Another theme throughout the book is human blindness to political and social realities, a blindness shared by both Westerners and Iranians. An Iranian intelligence officer discussing the future of his country with Westerners cannot believe that, in the midst of a revolution, they still "misunderstand the explosive forces ripping Iran apart," especially given the hundreds of alarm signals and intelligence reports, the years of warnings made to politicians, generals, and intelligence agents at home and abroad (752). Clavell shows this high-level blindness in ordinary citizens. Sharazad and Azadeh optimistically dismiss villagers as harmless, uneducated, and simple, mullahs as parasites on the backs of the villagers, and their husbands' predictions that Khomeini will lead Iran backward into medievalism as misinformed. Sharazad quotes her father, saying that without foreign generals and the evil Shah everything will be better, that they will possess their land and oil and selves and "all live happily ever after" (395). Her father is equally convinced that with foreign banks closed, local business will prosper and all will be well.

Warnings about Soviets

Clavell ties this theme of blindness to his warnings about the Soviets. These cautions have recurred throughout his canon, but are particularly significant in *Whirlwind*. Because of its strategic location, its 1,976 mile-long coastline, its command of navigation through the narrow Strait of Hormuz, and its rich oil fields, Iran would be a rich plum for the Soviets. Clavell depicts Soviet flights over northern sections of Iran, Soviet infiltrators fomenting riots and manipulating events to increase the power of the Communist-Moslem alliance, and master spies like Petyr Mzytryk dealing secretly with local chieftains to strengthen Soviet influence in the area. Within a year of Khomeini's takeover, the Azerbaijan region of Iran became a Soviet satellite. Clavell further warns that the Soviets owe Western banks over eighty billion dollars for loans that have financed their purchase of sophisticated American spy equipment through Asian and European dealers; they brag that someday the entire Middle East will be theirs.

Nationalization versus Privatization

A final theme concerns the rights of private businesses versus nationalization. Clavell asks whether a nation should have the right to confiscate the private property of foreign investors and, as a capitalist on the side of free enterprise, answers with a resounding "No!" The nationalists who take over the oil rigs and air bases are portrayed as illiterate, corrupt, greedy, and destructive. The Shah's government still owes Gavallan's helicopter company for past services, and the Khomeini government expects the company to carry mullahs and Moslem revolutionaries for free—at gunpoint if necessary. Because of the Iranian government's failure to pay, the helicopters still legally retain their British registration, so when the copters land outside Iran, employees paint on the British codes.

GENRE CONVENTIONS

As he usually does, Clavell draws on a number of generic conventions. These include the Frederick Forsyth–style suspense drama in which a number of separate groups, couples, or individuals, at first seemingly distant, are drawn tighter and tighter into a web that, in the final stages of the action, brings them all together, for good or for ill. The pattern is to introduce characters in different locations and to shift between them with shorter and shorter units of exposition as they come closer and closer to the explosive final encounter. Because Clavell's book is not primarily a suspense novel, some of the encounters occur before the final denouement, though all of the main Western characters who survive reach their destination: the tiny Arabian Gulf coast emirate of Al Shargaz. As in the Forsyth-style suspense pattern, there is a final countdown to the climax, and a summing up of the fates of the survivors.

Another pattern on which Clavell builds is the British adventure story of derring-do in faraway colonial places. Clavell's main figure of this type is Captain John Ross ("Johnny Brighteyes"), the youthful sweetheart of Azadeh; he is a Sandhurst graduate who is now a British officer, a paratroop captain trained for combat and survival. He is the third generation of a family of Katmandu colonials who befriended Indian Gurkhas in the British Army, and he, like his father and grandfather, is in line to bear the Gurkhali title of "Sheng'Khan" ("Lord of the Mountain") for bringing honor to his regiment. (A Sheng'Khan must scale a worthy Nepalese peak alone, use the *kukri* blade with skill, and save the life of a Gurkha.) With his bright blue eyes, his reticent manner, and his two loyal Gurkha soldiers (his silent teachers and close comrades, Sergeant Tenzing and Corporal Gueng), Ross is like a mythic figure out of the pages of colonial legend. He rescues Pettikin from angry Moslem troops, tosses grenades with dexterity, destroys British intelligence secrets in the Zagros Mountains seconds ahead of the Soviets, and howls like a banshee when he beheads a foe. The image of a British officer disguised as a native nomad, marching over long distances on foot, speaking strange tongues, living off the land, and feeling more at ease with tough Gurkhas than with fellow British, is straight out of nineteenth-century adventure books. So is the description of his rescue of Azadeh and, despite his injury, their flight across harsh lands, disguised as local natives, fighting off attackers and outwitting border guards.

If this were just an adventure story, Ross's death from a terrorist bomb would have been a tragedy. However, amid so many stories of death and destruction, Ross's sacrifice is lost, his body "left like a carcass" (1100). And Iran at the time of this novel is littered with nameless carcasses. Clavell's point depends on the contrast between the plight of the individual and the fate of large masses of people, the personal concern against the group concern, which divides Western from Eastern thought.

There is also in *Whirlwind* another kind of British adventure story; it resembles the stories of native uprisings like the siege of Khartoum in the Sudan, the attack on British troops by the Watusi in Central Africa, or the Sepoy Rebellion in India. There are terrifying scenes of angry Moslems, whipped to a frenzy by hate-filled mullahs, rioting in the streets, attacking Westerners indiscriminately: "Sullen faces, people out of the Dark Ages. Ugly . . . a silent brooding dread" (234). In one scene, Erikki and Azadeh are trapped in slow-moving traffic when villagers recognize them as outsiders and become outraged that Azadeh is not wearing a *chador*. They surround and rock the car, shouting hate-filled slogans and curses. Their numbers and the ferocity of their attack overpower even the large, strong Erikki, and he and Azadeh would have been stoned to death if not for their sudden rescue, ironically by a Soviet who wants Erikki's aid. In a later scene, Sharazad, dressed in a *chador* which billows out behind her "like a great black wing," joins in a religious protest march in the hopes of dying with God's name on her lips so she can go to Paradise. However, as she marches forward with the conservative Green Bands, shouting "Allah-u Akbar" (God is Great"), she begins to realize the "satanic revolutionaries" on whom they march are students her age fighting bravely for women's rights. The mindless surge crushes her and carries her forward. When her *chador* and scarf are ripped from her in the heat of confrontation, the group she is with, "the mob beast," turns against her and threatens to kill her. Although Lockhart comes to her rescue, the two are soon caught up again in the riotous frenzy, and die when the pin of Sharazad's own protective grenade is accidentally jarred out of place and the grenade explodes (1187–1194). These scenes, like others throughout the novel, depict enraged masses of native peoples stirred to violent action by xenophobic hatred of all things Western, mindlessly destroying whatever they touch.

Whirlwind is also a story of espionage. The American CIA officer Vien Rosemont, who is half Vietnamese–half American, dies alongside Ross early in the book, but throughout the novel, British intelligence officers like Robert Armstrong (a friend of Brian Kwok in *Noble House*) compete with Soviet intelligence officers like Petyr Mzytryk and his son Igor for control of Iran. Armstrong works for MI–6, and is on loan from the British as chief advisor to the Iranian Department of Inner Intelligence. His assignment as intelligence expert is to watch and report, but through him we see chaos and revolution; intelligence officers form alliances, make deals, set up underground networks, and battle for secret control of key people and key areas. The torture and debriefing of Igor Mzytryk reveals British and Iranian traitors, including Lord Robin Grey (of *King Rat* and *Noble House*) and other operatives working in the top levels of the British Labour party, Abrim Pahmudi (the head of the Iranian secret police, SAVAMA), and Roger Crosse (a triple agent from *Noble House*), whom the KGB assassinate to protect their secrets. Azerbaijani Abdollah Khan has secret meetings with the ship commander, Gregor Suslev (the old Soviet spy from *Noble House*), whose real name is Petyr Mzytryk and whose true role is KGB First Directorate deputy controller for Asia. However, Armstrong turns the Khan against his Soviet ally by revealing a plot to tempt the Khan to Tblisi and then hold him hostage while having him denounced at home for fleeing the country. Later Armstrong black-mails McIver into transporting him and his vital reports out of the country.

Most dangerous of all the spies is the Persian intelligence master Hash-emi Fazir. Hashemi carefully manipulates others so he can squash "several scorpions with one stone" (928). He sees himself as an "avenger" killing Jews and infidels on God's orders. His men blackmail the beautiful PLO spy Sayada Bertolin into acting as their double agent, and they joyfully torture captives like Mzytryk with unnecessary cruelty. Hashemi envisions himself as a modern Hasan ibn al-Sabbah, the head of an eleventh-century fanatical band of hashish-taking zealots, the Hashshashins, who terrorized the Middle East (the word "assassin" comes from this group). Hashemi plans to use psychedelic drugs to get simple-minded zealots to do the same: carry out a campaign of assassination and terror.

Sections of *Whirlwind* follow the patterns of romance fiction. One pattern is that of the tragic young couple in love (Lockhart and Sharazad), thwarted by misunderstandings and family opposition, caught up in trying times that separate them because of nationality, and finally discovering the strength of their love, as they die in each other's arms at a moment of discovery and happiness. Another romantic pattern is that of the happily married woman (Azadeh), in time of great need, suddenly rescued by a former lover (John Ross), who for years had been only a bittersweet memory of an unfulfilled youthful romance; he finds her still attractive and still the true love of his life. However, her loyalty to her husband (Erikki) and her former lover's sense of honor prevent a new relationship; he saves her life when her husband cannot and dies soon thereafter. Erikki is a stereotypical romantic hero, but he is also sensitive to his wife's culture, her sense of self, and her rights as an individual.

Nonetheless, in *Whirlwind*, all love interests pale beside the larger questions of life and death.

ALTERNATIVE READING: A FEMINIST VIEW

Feminist critics judge literary works on the basis of their handling of gender. They ask whether the works depict men and women as equal in talent and potential, or whether they adhere to the old-fashioned gender divisions of males as active and females as passive, of males as hunters and builders and females as child-bearers and keepers of the hearth. Feminist critics are interested in the female experience as distinct from that of the male and with women's struggles to battle and undercut male dominance. They may believe in a feminist mystique that makes women unique and special and separate from males, but at the same time, they argue for equality in the home, the workplace, and government. They point out that gender differences have historically been used to oppress women and to deny them fundamental rights, and they are critical of traditional role separations based on gender, of women as housewives and males as providers. They value literary works in which there are strong women, performing competently. Some feminist works focus on women bettering males, and joining in a wise, intuitive sisterhood against what they see as brawny, self-righteous men, who trust logic over intuition and who are more comfortable in a male pack than in mixed company. They resent stereotyped portraits of women as physically limited or as childlike and in need of protection, as narcissistically preoccupied with age, weight, and physical beauty, as jealous and unpredictable, as fuzzy thinkers, or as driven by biology and sexual drives. Their critical approach tends to be subjective rather than objective, intuitive and personal rather than analytical. They see themselves as righting historical wrongs. However, they alternate between images of women as victims and images of women as powerful. Susan Brownmiller, in "Sisterhood is Powerful," captures the attitudes that dominate some feminist criticism when she argues that "women as a class have never subjugated another group," "have never marched off to wars of conquest in the name of the fatherland," and "have never been involved in a decision to annex the territory of a neighboring country, or to fight for foreign markets on distant shores." She asserts: "Those are the games men play, not us. We see it differently. We want to be neither oppressor nor oppressed. The women's revolution is the final revolution of them all" (Brownmiller 1970: 134). Clavell's Iranian and Arab women contradict Brownmiller's assertions: they participate in their own subjugation and in the subjugation of religious groups they oppose; they march in protests and do battle in the streets; they become political tools in the hands of male extremists and prove willing to physically battle foreign infidels or even Moslems with a different perspective; they oppress their fellow women and are themselves oppressed; they play complex games within the family circle; and their attempts at revolution are befuddled and ineffectual. Because Clavell's position on women's issues is complex and at times contradictory, feminist critics might find *Whirlwind* difficult to categorize.

A standard criticism of Clavell is that he depicts a man's world in which women are mainly secretaries, receptionists, wives, lovers, mistresses, and prostitutes, and only in rare cases does he portray businesswomen equal to their male counterparts. Clavell argues the importance of gender differences and encourages women to use their femininity as a tool for success. Some of his Western males are clearly playboys who respond to women as sexual objects, and his Iranians, in the main, consider women possessions to be protected as one would protect valuable property, but also to be disciplined like children or pets, and to be traded commercially for family gain. Even his more enlightened males see themselves as protectors and providers and their wives or lovers as needing their assistance and guidance. On the other hand, Clavell is quite obviously in favor of the rapid strides forward that the Shah made for women's rights and is appalled at the sudden and total loss of those rights under Khomeini, a reaction feminists should share. He respects women who prove themselves to be equal partners, willing to share the family burdens, and his portraits of male playboys and tyrants are clearly intended to be negative.

Clavell sympathizes with Iranian women, depicting their daily struggle to feed, clothe, clean, and care for growing numbers of children, their husbands' demands for the birth of a child (preferably a male) a year, and the heartache of seeing daughters sold to much older men to lead lives of servitude. Under Moslem law, Sharazad must obey her father totally, and when he dies, she must obey her older brother, who takes on the patriarchal role. The males of the family decide whether or not she will divorce her husband and whom she will marry thereafter. A disturbing sequence describes the family pleasure at selling her in marriage to a very rich pedophile who wants Sharazad only because of her family and business connections and as proof of the power of his wealth.

Another disturbing image is that of Azadeh's father treating her with cruelty and disdain to exorcise his lust for her. Clavell purposefully calls attention to the plight of these subjugated women.

The Iranian women are contrasted with the main British woman in the story, Genny McIver. She is happily married, a mother and a house-wife, and pleased to be such. Her husband is her life. They are a devoted couple, and she accompanies him on all his overseas assignments, de-termined to share his life. By feminist standards, she is a dinosaur, living a life women should seek to escape. By Clavell's standards, she is a model of virtue. Her attitude is in contrast to most of the other European wives of the story, who prefer the safety and comfort of a familiar culture and are unwilling to give it up simply to be near their husbands, espe-cially when the husbands are often away on oil rigs or helicopter flights anyway. McIver shares his secrets and the secrets of the company with Genny, and she helps him plot strategy, interpret character, anticipate responses, and cope with conflict. She acts subservient when it helps her achieve her purposes, but she is a hard-headed, determined woman who absolutely refuses to follow her husband's orders when they would leave him to fight battles alone. When she sees a role in which she can con-tribute, she does her part, for instance, carrying a detailed escape plan to Gavallan. She initiates the escape plan and helps the men refine it, and she uses her femininity and modesty to overcome Iranian interfer-ence. She is Clavell's image of an ideal wife. A feminist would describe her as having submerged her personal interests for the sake of a socially imposed role; Clavell would say she is a happy woman who has chosen to support and assist her husband.

While Clavell and feminists part company in their attitudes toward the role of women in Western society, they are in agreement in their opposition to the role imposed on women in Eastern societies. The ex-periences of Sharazad and Azadeh demonstrate the dichotomy between Eastern and Western attitudes toward women. On the street, without a *chador*, they are prey to the fantasies of the sexually repressed: men fol-low them, shouting obscenities and openly displaying their sexual parts in insulting invitations. Clavell portrays a society so sick that it can only view women in two categories, as submissive, dutiful wives or as pros-titutes who deserve rape and stoning. Women in ski suits, pantsuits, or even short dresses (that is, above the ankle) are to be abused and at-tacked. Male repressions and obsessions force women to hide indoors or to totally cover themselves when outdoors as defense against the unbri-dled emotions and impulsive acts society condones. Feminist Kate Millett's response to arriving in Tehran confirms Clavell's description. Millett sees the women as "like black birds, like death" (Millett 1982: 49–50), "a sea of chadori, the long terrible veil, ... ancient, powerful, annihilating." The women are "prisoners in it," bitter, driven, enraged, and "closed utterly," and the "small" Iranian men swagger about in "absolute control," their "oppressive" military weapons oversized, intimidating. Whether on the left or on the right politically, their threat to women is the same, says Millett: "the same obdurate male stance," the convinced assurance that their women are happy because, "They do what we want" (54).

The Shah's Marriage Protection Act and Family Act protected women against summary divorce, against polygamy, and against confiscation of property. It gave them the right of divorce and the right to vote. Among Khomeini's first proclamations was a denunciation and abolition of the Shah's legislation for women. Coeducation was abolished, wearing of the *chador* enforced, and women exhorted to do their "God-ordained duty to bear and bring up children and look after their Masters [husbands]" (*Whirlwind*: 680). Clavell captures the enthusiasm and commitment of the women who marched in protest in all the major Iranian cities, but were beaten by frenzied, self-righteous males—among them their brothers, sons, husbands, and fathers.

Clavell shows Iranian men and women to be as divided as if they were separate races. The women, as a result, lead thwarted lives. The males interpret Sharazad's flightiness as a need to have children, and the mullahs suggest a child a year fulfills a wifely duty. Clavell depicts Iranian women behind the veil forced to cultivate a sweet exterior behind which they are subtle, secretive, and vengeful, like Azadeh's stepmother. He also suggests resultant sexual patterns that differ from those of the West. Azadeh and Sharazad, both happily married women, bathe together, sleep together, and touch each other sexually—without guilt—and they do the same with the women servants who have cared for them for years. Azadeh's brother and father both find her sexually attractive, and exorcise their lust by dominating her life. Her father sees her as a bargaining chip to be used in his negotiations with Petyr Mzytryk, just as Sharazad's brother sees Sharazad as a bargaining chip to strengthen his business ties and increase his business opportunities. Clavell finds all this appalling and writes to appall readers as well. Despite his theories about the primacy of business and politics, his story makes the plight of Iranian women—their loss of human rights and of human dignity—the greatest tragedy. In other words, superficially, Clavell might seem to epitomize the male chauvinist, but his major theme in *Whirlwind*, a protest against the abuse, ill treatment, and victimization of Iranian women, should win feminist approval.

Another interpretation might explore Michel Foucault or Edward Said's criticisms of the constructs that have shaped Western knowledge of Middle Eastern societies. Just as feminists deplore male stereotypes of women, so Foucault and Said deplore Western stereotypes of Easterners. The stereotypical image of Orientalism is one of a "vast, homogeneous culture infused with irrational religiosity and mysticism, exotic yet penetrable femininity, irrepressible emotion, voracious sexual appetite, and a brute will to especially savage political despotism" (Scullion 1995: 17). This is the image of Iran Clavell cultivates in *Whirlwind*, but because Clavell's image is tempered with sympathy and a genuine regard for the past achievements and the lost potential of Iran and Iranians, such an interpretation would founder on Clavell's well-rounded portrait of the nation's agony.

8

Gai-Jin
(1993)

The policy of seclusion was beneficial to Japan. . . . The Japanese were able to absorb . . . only the good points of Western scientific culture, and . . . avoid . . . the spiritual culture which may not have been agreeable to the spirit of Japan
    Izuru Shimmura, *Western Influences on Japanese History and Culture*

Reviewers have enthusiastically praised *Gai-Jin* as "absorbing," "artful," "compelling," "dynamic," "engrossing," "entertaining," "epic," "exciting," "exhilarating," and "exotic." It has been described as being "as colorful as an ancient Kabuki play" (*People*); as providing "grand historical perspective," "rich characters," and "complicated action" (*The New York Times*); and as being "a feast of intrigue, romance, blackmail, plot and counterplot . . . in a century and culture . . . distant . . . yet oddly familiar," with motivations that "cut across time and place" (*The West Coast Review of Books*). A reviewer for the *Christian Science Monitor* has compared *Gai-Jin* to a Japanese *jubako*, a set of fine lacquered boxes fitted within each other, for Clavell's careful plotting neatly interlocks opposing sets of characters and cultures. A reviewer for the *Washington Post* has described *Gai-Jin* as "Clavell . . . at his best."

Indeed *Gai-Jin* (Foreigners) has all the ingredients readers expect from a Clavell novel: an exotic setting (the Japan of 1862); a turbulent moment of history accurately depicted (the burning of Yokohama and the Japanese awakening to the political implications of foreign trade); financial double-dealings and political and industrial double crosses; blackmail and murder; cross-cultural negotiations (between Japanese, British, French, Russian, and Chinese); and the complex relationships and intrigues that occur in a monarchic, feudal society in which a variety of forces vie for dominance. Clavell explores not only dark human motivations (ambition, greed, lust, fear, hatred, revenge, survival) and alienating differences (race, culture, religion, and ethnic identity), but also binding universals (duty, obligation, love, friendship). The story is exciting, the action captivating, and the delineation of differences between Japanese and Western attitudes, philosophies, and patterns of thought worthy of interest; the female characters are especially well drawn.

PLOT DEVELOPMENT

Gai-Jin begins with the Brocks, the Struans' rivals in *Tai-Pan*, poised to snatch key trade from Noble House. The present Noble House *tai-pan*, Culum Struan, has never lived up to his legendary and unscrupulous father, Dirk Struan. His wife, Tess, the daughter of Tyler Brock, rules behind the scenes. When Culum dies ignominiously, Tess refuses to install her son Malcolm as *tai-pan* until he gives up his French fiancée and returns to Hong Kong from Japan.

Gai-Jin begins with an effective cinematic scene, highly visual and distanced. A panic-stricken girl in a long gown gallops sidesaddle toward the coast; the spires of two churches and the sails of British warships are in the distance, and behind her is a bloody scene of massacre. Identically clad samurai warriors, their banners flying, stand in protective formation around a black-lacquered palanquin; a decapitated Englishman lies in pieces before them, his head to one side—West and East meeting in a defining moment. Clavell paints a broad canvas with sweeping implications captured in the tiny personal moment. Like the rest of his canon, *Gai-Jin* depends on confrontational dialogue (of Frenchman advising Englishman, of Englishman questioning Japanese, of Scottish lass confronting wayward Scottish lad) and on interior monologues; the third-person distancing of the narrator at times assumes a first-person directness (particularly in the case of Angelique Richaud and of the Japanese concubine Koshi).

The main story line of the European characters is simple; the novel is not. The young, inexperienced heir to the Noble House, Malcolm Struan, is handling family business in Japan when, on a horseride with friends, he is stabbed in the belly by a samurai warrior who is angered by the *gai-jins'* failure to bow to his lord. Other members of his party are chopped to pieces. Malcolm's wound never heals properly, and eventually it kills him on his wedding night. Before his death, he defies his mother's demands that he return immediately to Hong Kong and that he break off his engagement to Angelique Richaud, a beautiful French girl with bad family connections and little hope of a good marriage elsewhere. Instead, he plots with a revenge-motivated Edward Gornt (the illegitimate son of Morgan Brock) to defeat the Struans' traditional foes, the Brocks, and to establish a strong Struan foothold in Japan; he also intends to marry Angelique despite his mother's objections. Angelique must deal with rape, pregnancy, abortion, blackmail, her husband's death on their wedding night, rejection by her fearsome mother-in-law, and then courtship by Edward Gornt.

In the business subplot, the Brocks attempt to bankrupt Noble House. Underwritten by the Victoria Bank of Hong Kong, in which they have part interest, the Brocks have speculated heavily on an ingenious scheme to underbid Struan sugar contracts, corner the Hawaiian sugar market, and barter sugar for Southern cotton (the American Civil War is in progress). This cotton, presold to French interests, will be shipped legally from France to Geneva and on to Lancashire cotton mills that are desperate for raw materials. However, using their company as collateral leaves the Brocks vulnerable. Gornt's access to the Brocks' business papers and stationery and to the official Brock "chop" (the company seal) allows him to create a paper trail that, when revealed to the U.S. government in Washington, will thwart the Brocks' dealings with the South. The loss of the American market will be a major financial blow. The Struans' and Gornt's influence on two key Victoria Bank board members, and two fictitious, backdated letters spelling out the Brock's financial maneuvers, confirmed by the private seal of the now dead Brock representative to Yokohama, allow for a double cross that will crush the Brocks' financially and will restore Noble House to financial stability.

The plot of the Japanese characters is far more complex. Clavell delineates the tension between Shogun and Emperor as ambitious warlords compete for control. Toranaga Yoshi, the descendant of the sixteenth-century Lord Toranaga Yoshi, plots to undercut the weak teenaged Emperor and his consort, to overcome the reactionary Sanjuro forces, and to help move Japan into the modern age. Yoshi reminisces about events that took place in *Shogun*, about how his ancestor used the English sailor

"Anjin-san" to help break the power of the Portuguese Jesuit priests and the Christian daimyos. In *Shogun*, Toranaga breached Osaka castle with *gai-jin* cannon; in *Gai-Jin*, his descendant balances his fear of colonial subjugation with his need for European technology and seeks foreign weapons because they are crucial to power. Ironically, the antiforeigner Sanjuro forces entangle Japan with Westerners, through the diplomatically controversial attack on unarmed British, through the rape of Angelique, through Europeans emotionally bound to the Yokohama Floating World, and through the scheming and final escape of Hiraga and Akimoto. The plot dramatizes the Western push to engage the Japanese, and Japan's evasion of Western controls.

HISTORICAL FOUNDATIONS: FACT AND FICTION

Clavell's historical fiction has a factual base and reflects the political realities of nineteenth-century Japan. Once Shogun Tokugawa Ieyasu (Clavell's Toranaga) had defeated his rivals at Sekigahara and united Japan under a single rulership, he drove out the Portuguese Jesuits and began a policy of total seclusion except for a single contact point at Nagasaki, where Dutch and Chinese trade representatives did limited business from segregated quarters on Deshima Island. Under law, farmers were forbidden to use the wheel, only samurai could carry weapons, housing restrictions and hostage holding limited the power of the daimyos (middle-level feudal lords), and careful land distribution insured shogun control of economic centers and strategic military points.

Gai-Jin is set in a period of peasant uprisings, samurai unrest, and power struggles between daimyos. The arrival of Commodore Perry's fleet in 1853 had forced the shogun to lose face by seeking the advice of the daimyos. The shogun's action drew the Imperial House, which for centuries had been totally excluded from policy making, into the controversy. The signing of a disadvantageous commercial treaty in 1858 led to further questioning of the shogun's leadership and to samurai attacks on foreigners in the Yokohama area. Yokohama had been a small, unimportant fishing village in the early 1800s, but under the Perry Treaty of Kanagawa in 1854, it had become a foreign trade center and the doorway to Tokyo (then called Edo or Yedo) and hence to all Japan. A thriving European community grew there, jostling for trading power, and businesses, warehouses, and a red-light district sprang up too.

Clavell begins his story in 1862, with a fictionalized version of the historical murder of an Englishman named Richardson (Clavell's Mr.

Canterbury), who was cut down by samurai in the retinue of the rebellious prince of Satsuma, on the Tokaido national highway between Yedo and Yokohama. The British demanded an indemnity and punishment of the offending samurai, but Prince Shimazu, who was responsible for the region, refused. The novel ends with the 1863 British retaliatory bombardment and partial destruction of Satsuma's capital, Kagoshima. Most historians agree with Clavell's interpretation that the Japanese reaction to this murder and their refusal to give satisfaction resulted from traditional samurai arrogance and an unwillingness to recognize outsiders as having any status.

The same year, two sentries were killed in an attack on the British legation, and a number of Europeans were attacked in Yokohama. Later, the daimyo of Choshu, a far western province of Honshu, having acquired firepower with European help, fired on Dutch, French, and American ships in the Straits of Shimonoseki. An allied fleet, mainly British, then bombarded Choshu. Also in 1862, a power play led to the marriage of the young shogun to the emperor's sister, and a strong movement to drive barbarians off Japan's sacred soil seized the popular imagination with the stirring call to arms of *sonno-joi* ("Revere the Sovereign and Expel the Barbarians"). In 1890 (close to fifty years after the action of *Gai-Jin*), foreign trade rights were again rescinded.

Clavell's fiction fleshes out the events behind these facts of history. His fictional characters move through historical times, amid real rulers or places at actual historic turning points, with episodes and characters from the early days of Yokohama only thinly disguised. Lord Toranaga Yoshi, Lord Sanjiro, Shogun Nobusada, Princess Yazu, the *shishi* samurai, and the shipwrecked fisherman turned interpreter correspond to historical figures whose lives are documented by historians. As for the Europeans, John Canterbury is the murdered Charles Richardson; Sir William Aylesbury is Sir Rutherford Alcock, British Minister to the Japans; Jamie McFay is Ernest Satow; Dr. George Babcott is Dr. William Willis; and so on. Although the Struans or the Brocks have no exact historical counterparts, they are modeled on the conniving European entrepreneurs who opened trade to Japan. Some critics wish Clavell had retained real names, but fiction gives Clavell the flexibility to explore conflicts, emotions, and motivations and to thereby create a sense of sharing in the "true" story behind the bare bones of history.

A case in point is that of Clavell's fisherman turned samurai, translator, and cultural advisor. There are historical references to a real-life Japanese fisherboy named Manjiro who, at fourteen, was shipwrecked on a deserted Pacific island (Blumberg 1985: 57–59; Kareko 1956: 107–108). Rescued by an American whaler, he was taken to Massachusetts as "John Mung" and educated. When Manjiro returned to Japan, he faced possible execution under Japan's Exclusion Edict, which demanded that "He shall be executed who went to a foreign country and later returned home" (Blumberg: 58). Manjiro proved his Japaneseness by stamping on a cross to prove he wasn't a Christian and by standing trial eighteen times; in fact, his knowledge of the West made him too valuable to kill, and he was designated a samurai. When Commodore Perry's "giant dragons puffing smoke" steamed into Edo Bay in 1853, the Shogun called on Manjiro to translate both language and culture: he was the only person in Japan with firsthand knowledge of the United States. Later, he wrote *A Short Cut to English Conversation* and recorded his observations of Westerners, including such "strange" American customs as marriages without go-betweens, sightseeing honeymoon trips, public kissing, men removing their hats indoors, the absence of bowing, the use of chairs, the reading of books in the toilet, the piercing of ears for jewelry, not using rouge, powder, and the like, and giving babies cow's milk as a substitute for mother's milk. Clavell's version of Manjiro, Misamoto, is much like his historic counterpart.

Thus, Clavell builds on history, but features the personal themes and goals of characters to provide a dramatic view of history in the making.

STRUCTURE

Gai-Jin consists of a chronology of events from September 14, 1862, when samurai warriors attack Malcolm and Angelique, to January 13, 1863, when Edward Gornt sets sail to confront Tess Struan in Hong Kong, followed by a brief Afterword about the British bombardment of Kagoshima seven days later and the resultant shift in power that complicated Japanese internal politics for years thereafter. This five-month period was historically crucial to the relationship between Japan and the West, and the activities engaged in by both Japanese and European characters typify the period and define national characteristics.

Gai-Jin is divided into five books which trace key events within each of the five months. Book One (chapters 1–17) treats three days (September 14, 16, and 29). It introduces the main characters and sets the stage for East-West conflict, beginning with murder and ending with rape. Book Two (chapters 18–31) deals with October 13–16, October 19, and

November 6, 7, 9, 16, and 21. It explores the diplomatic and personal ramifications of the two offenses perpetrated in Book One. Book Three (chapters 32–41), which focuses on November 29, December 1–4, and December 6 and 8, provides the Japanese perspective and shows the cultural interaction between the two sides as public and private negotiations begin. Book Four (chapters 42–50) describes the events of December 9–14, beginning with a secret marriage at sea and ending with a secret burial at sea. Book Five (chapters 51–62) begins with January 1–3, moves forward to January 11, 13, and 14, and ends with a summary of the events throughout the rest of the month and shortly thereafter. It bears witness to the burning of Yokohama, then ties up the disparate actions, and interlocks final events. A brief Afterword sums up the events of the next seven days and key events thereafter.

An alternating spatial arrangement, related to a contrast of Japanese and Europeans, also unites *Gai-Jin*. The scenes shift from Yokohama, where the Westerners reside, to wherever the Japanese are: Yedo (where the emperor resides); the Shogunate Palace; Kanagawa and Hodogaya (both towns on the Tokaido road); the distant province of Choshu; the villages of Sakonoshita and Hamamatu, and the cities of Kagoshima, Osaka, and Kyoto. Except for a few stray Cornish miners and the British military force at the end, the main European characters are confined to Yokohama. East meets West for pleasure in the "floating world" brothels of Yokohama and for diplomacy at nearby Kanagawa. The action in all the other locations is solely Japanese.

Despite these structural patterns, *Gai-Jin* lacks a unified focus. The difficulty could be diffuse plot threads involving almost fifty characters with complex relationships and motivations. However, Clavell has juggled as many characters before without a breakdown in unity. The difficulty could be digression; however, some digressions provide needed background information (the history of the Toranaga Shogunate and of Noble House) and others broaden the scope of the novel (the strategies taught in Sun Tzu's *The Art of War* and British diplomat Phillip Tyrer's paean to Western technological progress). Perhaps the difficulty lies in the patterns contrasting cultural, gender, and generational perspectives. Although structural contrast has been Clavell's major organizing and thematic device throughout his canon, *Gai-Jin* departs from Clavell's usual pattern in several ways.

First, instead of the Western mind set against the Eastern in clear-cut ways, minor differences within major groups (for instance, French versus English versus Russian) complicate the larger categories and undercut the defining distinctions necessary for dramatic play between opposing views. Furthermore, Clavell opts for delineating cultural differences through assertions more often than through dramatic evidence or action. Although these assertions are voiced by characters (a Japanese wonders at Western naiveté; a Westerner warns about the horrible surprises in Chinese cuisine), without demonstration they sometimes sound like stereotyped generalizations: the British are pompous, priggish *puka sahibs*; the French are devious, vulgar, unscrupulous connivers; the Chinese are devious, vulgar, unscrupulous double-dealers, but are loyal to family and clan; the Japanese are xenophobic, cruel, manipulating, arrogant racists and liars, but they are dutiful. The cultural depictions may be accurate or may represent a true view of cultural bias, but they are more convincing when the characteristics delineated grow out of a situation or a confrontation and are thus elicited from the reader rather than being stated by a character or by a third-person narrator. Nonetheless, when the contrasts work, they are highly effective. In *Gai-Jin*, Clavell's most effective handling of such cultural differences is through his characterizations of Tyrer and Hiraga, as they study each other's language and culture and together share shock, horror, outrage, intrigue, and a confirmation of personal goals. Furthermore, Clavell's contrasting portraits of Japanese and Western women are sympathetically drawn.

Second, whereas the male perspective dominated *Tai-Pan* and male-female perspectives were balanced in *Noble House*, the female perspective dominates *Gai-Jin*. In this novel, the men hurry about, busily engaged in diplomacy, trade, and chicanery, but the main emotional thrust of the book consists of the worries, fears, plans, defeats, and successes of the women characters behind the scenes. Moreover, these women are not strong and modern, with control of their own destinies; they are totally dependent on males and on their own ability to disguise their cunning and intelligence and to manipulate those around them.

Third, instead, of father-son relationships, a mother-son relationship dominates. The mother is a powerful background figure, and the son is weak and wayward. He is defiant at long distance, but fearful of his mother's strong hold over his future. Fourth, Clavell's usual pattern of two strong rival males is missing. The Brocks and the Struans are still competitive, but Malcolm's injury necessitates others acting for him, so little space is given to rivalry. Instead, his main opponents are his mother and his own injured body.

As he has in his other novels, Clavell has used multiple characters, contrasting cultures, and digressive material effectively. These are not what make *Gai-Jin* seem diffuse and unfocused. The main difficulty is the absence of a strong central character to provide psychological unity and to speak for Clavell as Marlowe does in *King Rat*, Dirk Struan in *Tai-Pan*, John Blackthorne in *Shogun*, and Ian Dunross in *Noble House*. Malcolm Struan is too young and too ill to dominate, and his fears that his mother can reduce his power and command his underlings reduces the reader's respect for his opinions and for his interpretation of events. Angelique is too self-serving, too helpless, too bound by the strictures of her age. The result is that, despite the novel's limited time period and its organizing patterns, without a strong central character to dominate the materials and to give them a unity that derives from a single, consistent perspective, *Gai-Jin*'s great length works against it. As a result, it is a structurally weaker, less unified novel than Clavell's other works.

CHARACTERIZATION

Despite the novel's many characters, four stand out as significant: Malcolm Struan, Edward Gornt, Angelique Richaud, and Jamie McFay.

The main male character is Malcolm Struan. Normally this would be his coming of age story, as he learns to break the chains by which his mother holds him under her sway, or achieves some great coup, and proves his ability and right to rule Noble House. But however brave his attempts to take charge of Noble House, to live up to his responsibilities, and to make command decisions, he is weak-willed, and his physical wound weakens him more. His blindness to Angelique's limitations and strategies make him seem even weaker.

The man destined to take Malcolm's place in Angelique's arms seems much stronger by contrast. He is Edward Gornt, a Shanghai trader from Virginia with a chip on his shoulder and revenge for his mother's ill-treatment by both Brocks and Struans on his mind. Appealing but perhaps untrustworthy, Gornt blames the Coopers, the Brocks, and the Struans for the chain of disasters that ruined his mother, lost him his inheritance, and created his present insecure situation, and he has vowed to destroy his father, Morgan Brock, and to exact payment from the Struans for Dirk Struan's purposeful ruin of the Tillman family finances. His deep-seated hatred makes him willing to plot long-range strategies to achieve his ends rather than to hotheadedly seek immediate satisfaction. First, reasoning that sons must pay for the sins of their fathers, he seeks revenge against the Struans in order to gain his "proper" place in life, as a *tai-pan* of his own business dynasty. From his initial contact with young Malcolm Struan and his fiancée, Angelique, Edward Gornt works toward entangling Struan money in his Japanese investments and winning a Struan bride. He enlists Malcolm Struan's support in achieving his other goal: revenge on the Brocks for the seduction and then rejection of his mother. His hatred for the Brocks, who have destroyed his mother, burns deep. He is determined to break his father Morgan Brock, to pursue him into bankruptcy or prison and, out of the wreckage of his fall, to finance his own business (696–97, 1088). As with all of Clavell's upwardly mobile, ambitious, and driven entrepreneurs, Gornt has done his homework and learned backroom trading secrets that, in the right hands, could indeed ruin the Brocks financially. However, Gornt's role is limited to the second half of the book, and his involvement with Angelique to Book Five.

The most interesting and best developed character in *Gai-Jin* is Angelique Richaud, who is irritating, scheming, at times charming, at times petulant and naive, yet a woman of the world. Angelique is potentially another Tess Struan, a strong woman who stands behind her man but who artfully directs his actions. She has used her beauty and wiles to win the most eligible bachelor in the Far East, to hide her rape and pregnancy, and to win a new love, a man with the strength of will and cleverness to challenge her intellect. She muses on the naivete of men, "with their stupidities of patience and mendacity and wrong priorities," and asks herself, "what do they know?" (1088). Her physical passion for her Japanese attacker makes her reexamine her relationship with Malcolm Struan, but she is enough of a realist to destroy the Japanese when the opportunity to do so arises, locking him on her balcony and calling to the guards to shoot him. She manages Malcolm Struan well, though her insistence on chastity almost loses her his affections; despite the seeming helplessness of her situation, she acts with strength, fortitude, and an instinct for survival. Her letter to Tess Struan earns her Gornt's respect, especially because of the way she agrees to Tess's stipulations and yet still holds the sword of Damocles over her. Her plan to yield her personal political power so as to increase Gornt's, if he marries her, stuns him even more. He knows that she is devious and that he will need great vigilance "to tame this filly" (1196). He proves a fit match when he guesses her conditions for marriage and emphasizes "joint performance" for mutual success. However, she answers his promise that she'll get what she wants with her unspoken confirmation, "Yes, I will" (1200). Any future battle between the sexes will involve both giving and getting, loving and manipulating.

Angelique's final lines close the European plot of *Gai-Jin* and set the stage for a future battle between Tess Struan, the Woman of Hong Kong, and herself, the Woman of Yokohama. Angelique dreams of founding a dynasty and enacting revenge on Tess Struan "for all the anguish she caused." She has recovered her losses and her reputation. She has found a strong man to provide respectability and the means of revenge. She attains a maturity lacking in Clavell's young males in this book, for beneath surface accommodations she has become her own woman, determining her own destiny—by cunning and by force of will.

As Malcolm Struan's right-hand man, Jamie McFay, the loyal manager of Struan's in Japan, facilitates the plot by aiding the Malcolm-Gornt scheme against the Brocks, helping Tyrer's Japanese friends escape from Yokohama, directing firefighting, and so forth. He is torn publicly between his obligations to Tess Struan as acting *tai-pan* and to her son Malcolm as heir apparent to the title, and privately between his accommodating, satisfying Japanese lover, Nemi, and his demanding Scottish fiancée of many years, Maureen. Maureen's intercession has won him the blessing of Tess Struan and the financial backing necessary to establish his own firm in Yokohama. However, the strong bonds of friendship, experience, and commitment he and Maureen form with Gornt and Angelique presage a future conflict of loyalties and the need for strength and integrity to steer his new firm through troubled waters.

THEMATIC ISSUES

Gai-Jin is not a single-theme novel. It moves in several directions and teaches many lessons: (1) about cultural differences that affect intercultural relationships, and about the Japanese in particular; (2) about Japanese attitudes that could lead to future conflicts; (3) about the Asian nature of Russians; (4) about the absurdity of an isolationist policy in a technological world; (5) about the nature of time; and (6) about the restrictions historically placed on women. Each of these themes will be discussed in this section, except for the restrictions placed on women, which will be discussed in the section entitled "Alternative Reading: Feminist Perspectives."

Cultural Differences

Gai-Jin, a truly multicultural novel, makes no concessions to political correctness. Its central theme is that culture defines attitudes and values, and that when different cultures meet, the clash of values and attitudes usually creates a negative initial impression, with each side assuming its own superiority. A second key idea is that with time and proximity, different cultures adjust to each other and individuals learn to respond on a personal level that helps them overlook divisive cultural differences, though these may never be totally overcome. In working out this thesis, *Gai-Jin* depicts the interactions of Chinese, French, Russians, Dutch, and Americans, as well as the British (English, Scots, Irish) and Japanese. It builds on contrasts in attitudes, values, and actions, and involves clashes of perspectives and goals. It provides a taste of both Japanese and European daily life, and portrays characters from one culture becoming intimate with characters from another.

Although it depicts regional and ethnic differences, its broader sweep contrasts the perspectives, values, strategies, and goals of Easterners and Westerners. Clavell explores both moments of true communication and failures of understanding between cultures. While helping Westerners understand the Eastern mind and perhaps vice versa, and while giving readers a sense of the human spirit at work in different cultures, Clavell never stoops to the cliché that "all people are alike." Experience has taught him otherwise, and it is the differences that historically have so often resulted in misunderstandings and strife. Clavell believes that East should learn from West and West from East, to mutual benefit. Thus, one major goal of *Gai-Jin*, and of Clavell's entire canon, is to help Westerners see with Asian eyes.

In *Gai-Jin*, the breakdown in communications between Japanese and Europeans begins with violence. The Japanese retainers encountering the British party had expected a traditional bow to their lord, with heads touching the ground and rumps in the air, a sign of complete submission to authority. The Englishmen, who considered themselves equal to any lord, had raised their hats and given cheers—a royal salute—from atop their mounts, to show their respect. But their height above the lord and their shouting were direct insults—disrespectful, brazen, even insolent—by Japanese standards. The Japanese conclude that *gai-jin* are "vermin without manners" and that whatever they say "doesn't matter" (97) so they attack with drawn swords, chop one Englishman to pieces, and slash another.

Members of the English community are shocked by what seems like an unwarranted, murderous attack on unarmed civilians by a military contingent, and fear other such assaults. The negotiations about compensation for the murders reflect even deeper differences. The Europeans blame the individual samurai who performed the deed and want them punished. They believe that demands for compensation from the lord whom the killers served will act as a deterrent. The Japanese assume that the death of a few underlings, the actual killers, is irrelevant, but that loss of face, both immediate and potential, is the real subject of diplomacy. By this standard, the European loss of face in not being able to understand the Japanese chain of command and in not being able to retaliate immediately gives the Japanese an edge of superiority in any negotiations, but the style of negotiations could result in a Japanese loss of face. Thus, the negotiations about the attack and retribution are really about broader political concerns like territory, weapons, authority, and long-term power. Clavell shows how easily misunderstandings can occur, and how ignorance about the etiquette of another culture can produce unexpected confrontations and irreversible disasters.

Toranaga Yoshi notes that Westerners respond emotionally and act on impulse during negotiations whereas every Japanese action, even the seemingly whimsical or quirky, is, in fact, carefully calculated and carefully orchestrated. The Europeans openly announce titles and relationships. The Japanese use fake names and titles and hide who is what. The person with real power always seems to be a nonentity. At one point, the Europeans totally misinterpret relationships, assuming that a lowly translator is an important lord and that the shogun, who sits near him, is a nobody. Japanese indirection keeps Europeans confused about the lines of power and unsure about who has the central authority.

The Japanese, in turn, judging Western behavior by their own, find *gai-jin* totally unpredictable. The English, in particular, pride themselves on their honesty; the Japanese are shocked by such naivete for they consider lying natural and necessary, a standard way of dealing with the complexities of life. Hiraga, in his initial encounter with Tyrer, cannot quite believe that anyone could be so naive as to ask a question of an enemy or believe his answer. "Surely he cannot be that stupid?" he asks, and wonders what gods he is being asked to swear by since in his opinion there are none (314–15). This contrast in openness takes physical as well as verbal form. Westerners show a range of real emotions; their faces are open books. The Japanese, in turn, are closed books with brown paper covers; all emotion is hidden by a blank mask, inscrutable to Western eyes. Clavell describes the end of a day of negotiations: "By five o'clock European tempers were frayed, the Japanese still polite, smiling, outwardly imperturbable . . . so sorry, not this month, perhaps next, but no, so sorry we do not have authority" (146).

By switching from one perspective to another, Clavell helps readers understand and, to some degree, sympathize with, or at least appreciate, very different interpretations of the same behavior. From the perspective of a people who bathe regularly and often and for whom cleanliness is indeed next to godliness, the nineteenth-century Europeans' personal habits seem repulsive, their body odor unbearable. For a people who value skill and tradition and social distinctions, even the differences in weapons are telling. At one point, Toranaga Yoshi feels shamed by the necessity of carrying a gun and blesses the wisdom of his predecessors in outlawing their manufacture and importation; for him, the outlawing of guns has helped ensure Japanese peace for 250 years. His attitude is like that of the rogue samurai played by Toshiro Mifune in the classic Kurosawa film *Yojimbo*. Yoshi considers guns vile and cowardly, "worthy only of stinking gai-jin" (491), because guns can kill at a thousand paces and the shooter may not even see who he kills and the killed may not know who has inflicted the deadly wound. What bothers him the most about guns is that "any simpleton, low person, maniac, filthy robber, man or woman" can use such weapons against anyone, "even the highest lord" or the "most perfectly schooled swordsman" (491). Later, he contemplates the beauty of suicide in the traditional way, with a "clean sword . . . the minute and the hour and the day chosen with god-like power." Where the Westerner sees a sin against nature and against God, the Japanese sees the beauty and power of choice and control: "to choose your own death time made you a god: from nothing into nothing. No more sorrow grinding you to petals of pain" (1009). Ironically, while disdainfully rejecting the gun as too Western, that is, a direct, democratic leveler, Yoshi agrees that slow poisons are effective and useful. Poisoning was an ancient art in Japan, which appealed to the Japanese for the same reasons it appealed to Neapolitans: its subtlety, secrecy, and deviousness. Japan is a rigidly regulated, highly organized, law-centered society requiring people to carry travel papers to move from village to village, limiting the residential areas and travel plans of even top-level officials and authorities, restricting weapons possession to trained samurai, forbidding beggars, and expecting a formalistic, polite pattern of speech with gradations of respect for different levels of authority. Westerners, in contrast to Japanese, often seem chaotic and ill-governed: loose cannons, potentially destructive and dangerous. One character asks, "who knows what mischief they [gai-jin] can invent?" (39).

Clavell describes some East-West differences that are exotic and interesting, but not vital to understanding, for example, the blackened teeth and ritual attire of upper-class Japanese: "small black lacquered hats set square on their shaven pates and tied elaborately under their chins, the vast shouldered overgarments, multicolored ceremonial silk kimonos, voluminous pantaloons, thong sandals and shoe socks split between the toes—*tabi*—fans in their belts and the inevitable two swords" (146). He provides a sense of the complexity of the Japanese language, with its special court language reserved for conversing with the emperor, and its different vocabulary and rhythms for men and women. In fact, because most of the Europeans have learned Japanese from dalliances with courtesans, they speak female Japanese instead of male Japanese, and the Japanese males with whom they deal puzzle over whether they are homosexuals who speak this way because of their hidden sexual natures. From a Japanese perspective, "civilized" people distinguish linguistically between the sexes, and women naturally use submissive feminine forms because of their lower status.

Clavell has fun with Japanese attempts to make sense of Western religious schisms, and he contrasts Catholic and Protestant beliefs with the Japanese belief in spirits and in inner harmony, but not in gods or heaven or life after death. The Japanese have no concept of original sin; Western culture depends on this belief. Tyrer's defense of England, his command of world geography, and his pride in Western technological achievement (453–55) leave his Japanese audience dumbfounded and disbelieving, for they have a hard enough time coping with less earthshaking discoveries. Japanese visitors aboard an English vessel are surprised that the *gai-jin* world has a calendar totally different from the Japanese and Chinese lunar calendar, which they have considered the only way to count time "since the beginning of time" (1009). This single difference is enough to make one character conclude that "gai-jin were like monsters in the shape of men who had come from the stars, their ideas and attitudes the wrong side of yin and yang."

In depicting Japanese sexual practices ("pillowing"), the courtesans or "willow ladies" of the "floating world," and the "pleasure houses" or brothels of Yokohama, Clavell sides with the Japanese. He plays Asian openness about sex off against Victorian primness and hypocrisy. His contrasts between the straight-laced European prudery and reverence for premarital virginity and the Japanese matter-of-fact acceptance of sexuality as a natural prerequisite for health provide a very clear comment on cultural differences, and, in this area, what Clavell sees as Eastern superiority.

However, as Asian authority James Fallows points out in his essay

"The Japanese are Different from You and Me" (Fallows 1986: 35–41)
some differences between the cultures are just differences, others are different and better or worse, but still others are different and just wrong.
Fallows praises the Japanese sense of duty and consideration, of tight-
knit organization and community order. He finds Japanese attitudes toward pornography, because of very different attitudes toward sex,
disturbing by Western standards, but simply a trivial cultural phenom-
enon because no harm results. However, he finds Japanese racial exclusion, their obsession with racial purity, not simply clannish, insular, and
parochial, but threatening because it translates into behavior that, judged
by universal standards, is wrong. Clavell agrees. He makes Asian indifference to the plight of masses of people understandable, but he finds
the Japanese treatment of individuals cruel, brutal, and wrong. He voices
this criticism directly through his Japanese fisherman turned translator,
Misamoto, whose positive experiences with a democracy have transformed his view of his country. His life on the line, a matter of complete
indifference to the master he is forced to serve, he muses silently on how
the *gai-jin* family he lived with treated each other and him, for even
though he was a servant, they respected him as a man, and life was
better than he ever dreamed possible. He was most impressed by his
observation that most Western men could walk tall and carry a knife or
gun, were equal under the law, and did not have to worry about being
killed at the whim of some daimyo or samurai. He also appreciated their
impatience to solve a problem and to hurry on to solve the next one—
"if necessary by fist or gun or cannonade"—instead of waiting for solutions to emerge by themselves or simply enduring what had been endured for centuries (154). Clavell voices this criticism throughout the
book, as we see in action the realities of which Misamoto complains.

Although it is a small part of the novel, Clavell powerfully captures
the mutual hatred of Chinese and Japanese. His Japanese brag that they
are not "mealymouthed, cowardly Chinese to be bled to death or fright-
ened to death by these carrion [Europeans]" (38). They look to a future
when they will conquer the Koreans and thereby create a doorway to
the conquest of China. His Chinese marvel that the white barbarians are
so blind to Japanese treachery and cannot feel the "thousand hidden,
hostile eyes" that surround them (134).

A Warning about Japanese Attitudes

Gai-Jin's main focus is on nineteenth-century Japanese reactions to foreigners and on attempts by foreigners to meddle in the Japans. Ironically, *Gai-Jin* ends with two Japanese embracing the world of the foreigners in order to make Japan more their own. Even more ironically, the two are members of a revolutionary, fanatically xenophobic group committed to driving foreigners out of Japan. Hiraga is the leader of the Choshu *shishi*, xenophobic rebels from north of Tokyo. He and Akimoto are close friends of the samurai who attacked the Europeans at the beginning of the novel. What these two rebellious *shishi* do—leave Japan in order to make it more their own—may sound contradictory to Westerners. However, this is in complete accord with Japanese psychology. As has frequently been observed, modern Japanese who want to study in the West may give as a reason "to learn to appreciate Japanese values more fully"; others, more privately, admit, "to learn how to successfully counter Western encroachments on the Japanese way of life." Clavell captures the seeds of such conservative attitudes in Lord Toranaga Yoshi's secret national policy for handling foreigners: "... as policy we must flatter them to sleep, keep them off balance, using their foolish attitudes against them—and employ our superior abilities to cocoon them" (286).

Clavell's underlying message is a warning that he has repeated throughout his writing career, a warning he made firmly in *King Rat*, confirmed in *Shogun*, and repeats in *Gai-Jin*: as an insular island people, homogenous racially and culturally, convinced of the superiority of their culture, and lacking polite forms for outsiders, the Japanese cannot be trusted to deal honestly with foreigners. The nationalistic pride and xenophobia that dominated their past could dominate their future, Clavell warns, and unless Westerners are very careful, he fears that the Japanese belief in their racial superiority could lead them to repeat past atrocities. Clavell's portrait of seventeenth-century Japan in *Shogun* and of nineteenth-century Japan in *Gai-Jin* both end with foreigners being, in effect, kicked out of Japan. The main action of *Gai-Jin* ends with the Westerners in control, but the Afterword reminds readers of the imbalance of shogunate power that historically led to the eventual ousting of Westerners. The thrust of Clavell's canon is that the Japanese atrocities of World War II were predictable, given the nation's history and values, and that such atrocities could recur if Westerners, seeing only a Western perspective, misinterpret Japanese intentions.

The Asian Nature of Russians

A minor theme warns against Russian involvement in Japan, not simply to forge trade agreements with the Japanese, but to wrench from them their northern islands. Clavell warns that, despite its superficial Western overlay, Russia shares an Eastern perception of life, and Clavell's Russians have "Asian eyes." They are xenophobic, imperialistic, and frighteningly ambitious, driven by a need for territory and expansion. Early on in *Gai-Jin*, the French and the Russians make secret agreements for dividing up Japan and agree, "When a vacuum exists, it is our diplomatic duty to fill it . . ." (129). Aggressive Russian expansion lies behind the scenes in *Gai-Jin*.

The Absurdity of Isolationism

An important Clavell theme is that the Industrial Revolution and the technological advances for which it paved the way made and continue to make it self-defeating for any nation to shut out the world, as, for instance, the Iranians in *Whirlwind* try to do. In *Gai-Jin*, the major thrust of Japanese diplomacy is to find the best way to close that country's doors to Westerners. To demonstrate the absurdity of that attempt, Clavell provides a rounded view of the world of 1862, the international stage and key international events. His argument is that discoveries and advances result from the spirit of an age and are tightly bound to education and curiosity. Readers learn that in the 1860s, the serial works of Charles Dickens are in great demand around the globe, as are the poems of Alfred Lord Tennyson; Darwin's *On the Origin of Species* and Marx and Engels's newly translated pamphlet *The Communist Manifesto* are stirring controversy. Clavell keeps readers abreast of Civil War activities in progress—of Bull Run, Fredericksburg, Shiloh, the pillaging by Quantrill's Raiders and the Northern Jayhawkers, and so on. Readers find out about Tsar Alexander II's expansionist ambitions, the massive, state-enforced migration of Siberian tribes into Russia's Alaskan territories, and the Taiping and Manchurian Rebellions in China. There are reminiscences of Indian and Anglo-Indian relationships, of the Sepoy Mutiny and its bloody suppression, and of the British Raj. Characters wax enthusiastic about Burton's books on the discovery of Lake Tanganyika, a pilgrimage to Medina and Mecca, and life among the Mormons of Salt Lake City.

Clavell's point is a valid one. Even in the 1860s, isolationism was an absurdity because steamships and railways had made the world smaller and far-away events eventually had repercussions at home. Not only transportation, but journalism and publishing changed the world irreversibly. The nineteenth century was the beginning of internationalism.

Clavell's image of nineteenth-century Japan is of a nation trapped in a time bubble, medieval at a time when the West was developing a modern view of the world as interlocked through causal chains. An extreme version of this view has it that a butterfly fluttering its wings in a Brazilian rain forest will eventually stimulate a hurricane in the Gulf of Mexico. The case of Japan argues in the opposite direction, that pockets of the world can remain uninfluenced by cultural currents sweeping the globe.

The Nature of Time

Finally, by linking past, present, and future, Clavell demonstrates an Asian view of time. His Europeans press for immediate action; his Japanese delay and thereby gain time to arm their forces, plot strategy, and acquire cannons and ships to resist the West. Toranaga Yoshi summarizes the difference, arguing that *gai-jin* do not understand, consider, or think about time as the Japanese do, for they believe time is finite, whereas the Japanese do not. He asserts that their version of time controls Westerners because it makes them worry about minutes, hours, days, and maybe months, instead of years, generations, and even centuries. This is why exact appointments are so sacrosanct to Westerners, but not to the Japanese, thinks Yoshi. Consequently, Yoshi concludes that time is a "cudgel" with which the Japanese can beat the West. By depicting the links that tie generation to generation and past events to future confrontations, Clavell argues that Westerners need to cultivate a long-term Eastern outlook, rather than concentrating on the short-term. The fact that Clavell's Asian saga breaks the chronological sequence (for example, *Gai-Jin* depicts acts that occurred several generations before *Noble House*) strengthens the theme of the Asian view of time, because foreknowledge prepares readers to take a longer view of history and events than they might otherwise do.

To illustrate his point about time, Clavell interlocks events in his Asian saga. Thus, *Gai-Jin* brings together threads from *Tai-Pan*, *Noble House*, *King Rat*, and *Shogun* and fills in details missing elsewhere. One thread intertwines the fates of the dynastic businesses of the Cooper-Tillmans, Struans, and Brocks and, through Edward Gornt, fills in relationships not fully explored in *Tai-Pan*. The underhanded double-dealing of the Brocks in their competition with the Struans is a continuing theme. The Brocks and the Struans have been at odds since *Tai-Pan*. The Brocks have taken advantage of Culum Struan's weakness and the break in power when Culum died (as they unsuccessfully tried to do when Dirk Struan died at the close of *Tai-Pan*). In *Tai-Pan*, the Brocks tried to steal the sugar market away from the Noble House; in *Gai-Jin*, they try again. The maneuverings of Edward Gornt, Jamie McFay, and Malcolm Struan to counter these plans are like the quasi-illegal but daring acts engaged in by the founder of the Noble House. They establish a pattern that is repeated with variations in the Noble House of the 1960s.

More threads from past Clavell novels occur in the Japanese plot line of *Gai-Jin*. In a minor subplot, a self-sacrificing mother chooses life as a courtesan working for a syphilis-infected Frenchman, André Poncin, in order to finance and assure her son's future as a samurai. That son is a direct descendant of Anjin-san (Blackthorne), the Englishman who built ships for Lord Toranaga. In the main Japanese plot, the ruling shogunate of 1860 is the one founded by Lord Toranaga of *Shogun* fame two and one-half centuries earlier. In 1603, Lord Toranaga had brought all of Japan under one rule and had established a division of power that would last for centuries: it was a military dictatorship in which the shogun was charged with temporal matters and the emperor with spiritual authority. This division of power is under attack in *Gai-Jin*, but the concept of an emperor as spiritual leader and a military governor as temporal leader remained in force in the Japan of 1945, in the period of *King Rat*. *Gai-Jin* reaffirms the merciless, at times sadistic, treatment of the English in *Shogun*, and of World War II Allied soldiers in *King Rat*. All three novels emphasize the Japanese sense of superiority, their distrust of anything outside their own experience, and their high-handed and cruel dealings with subordinates and inferiors. All three books depict Japanese punishments as effective deterrents but barbaric by Western standards. The references to the *kamikaze* wind that destroyed the armadas of the Mongol conqueror Kubla Khan in the thirteenth century pave the way for the Japanese faith in *kamikaze* warriors and in their superior sense of honor in the twentieth-century *King Rat*. A subtheme is that a national Japanese character does indeed exist and that the future behavior of a people and of a nation can be predicted on the basis of past behavior.

Clavell's theme about time includes the idea that present action determines future action and that past choices create future problems or op-portunities. At the end of *Gai-Jin*, the heroine is only eighteen years old; the main surviving European male is in his twenties; the older woman in the story, Tess Struan, is in her prime at thirty-seven. The Sanjuro rebel Hiraga, a quick learner, and his friend Akimoto are on a Struan ship, destined to be introduced to the West and its business codes; the House of Toranaga, strengthened by the disasters at Yokohama, seems once again in a strong position; and Japan seems almost ready to enter the modern world—though in its own way and, from the Japanese point of view, preferably with minimum Western involvement in Japan. Clearly, the events of 1862 mark a beginning, not an end. This ability to learn from the past and to see in the present the threads of the future is a lesson Clavell wants readers to acquire through reading his book; the proof of his success is the tendency of most readers to try to anticipate what will happen next and how events will play out long after Clavell's book ends.

As Poncin teaches Tyrer about the Japanese, and Tyrer and Hiraga teach each other, so Clavell teaches readers lessons about history and culture, about the virtues and dangers of multicultural interaction, about learning to see with the eyes of the Other and, in doing so, being able to anticipate events long-term.

GENRE CONVENTIONS

Gai-Jin contains a mix of genres and stories. There is the disaster story sequence, which recounts how the Yokohama fire begins in the red light district, spreads, and is finally fought. It records the widely differing human responses to disaster as the fire burns out of control, and presents the aftermath: the discovery of the dead, the cleaning up, the rebuilding. As usual in Clavell's works, there are also medical stories, in this case three: Malcolm Struan's sword injury and the inability of the medical science of his day to cure him; Angelique Richaud's unwanted pregnancy and the lack of safe, private means of ending it; and the Frenchman André Poncin's incurable "pox," a venereal disease for which there was no effective treatment. Poncin's story is particularly horrible, for his dis-ease affects not only his body but his mind, and he knowingly passes it on to a sexual partner.

There are several romance stories. One concerns Angelique Richaud and her doomed love affair with Malcolm Struan, which is followed by

her courtship by Edward Gornt, and complicated by the obsession of the
Japanese samurai, Ori, and Angelique's own confused physical responses
to him. Another concerns the love of Maureen Ross for Jamie McFay, a
love that gives her the courage to sail from England to Hong Kong to
Japan to confirm their commitment to each other, and then to face up to
his support of a Japanese courtesan, Nemi. Although she is a courtesan
and a spy, Koiko, who is the highest possible rank of geisha, loves and
respects Lord Toranaga Yoshi; their story is the most mature and the
most tragic, because their love is not based only on physical attraction
but on a meeting of minds, a sharing of cultural enthusiasms (like *haiku*,
a compact poetic form), and an intuitive understanding of values. When
Yoshi understands that Koiko brought his would-be assassin, Sumomo,
into his chambers, he suspects betrayal, and her sacrificing her life to
prevent his death does not make the memory of her and of his loss any
less bitter. Their complex relationship is in direct contrast to the physical
obsessions of Phillip Tyrer for the courtesan Raiko, of André Poncin for
the courtesan Fujiko, and of Ori for Angelique.

Gai-Jin's contrasting studies of behavior, values, and lifestyles make it
a novel of manners that explores how people behave in groups and why.
It is also a continuation of the dynasty saga begun in *Tai-Pan*, and its
depictions of Edward Gornt, Angelique Richaud, and Jamie McFay fit
the Horatio Alger type of financial fantasies that are a part of every
Clavell novel.

However, *Gai-Jin* is also an historical romance or historical fiction, a
swashbuckling history of bygone days. It chronicles an historical period
of Western expansion and exploration, depicts a significant period of
European contact with Japan, and praises the power, competence, and
daring of the British Royal Navy and of the British Merchant Navy. It
makes history come alive by taking readers into the drawing rooms and
bedrooms of historical personalities and by creating fictitious characters
who voice the attitudes of the day and carry out the actions that underlie
the historical record. For example, Clavell provides Sir William Aylesbury, British Minister to the Japans, with a crisis of values. The French
legation spy, André Poncin, has arranged for his secret papers about
Angelique's rape and the ensuing cover-up to be sent to Sir William in
case of his death. Shocked and disbelieving, Sir William classifies Angelique as a victim of libel and André as a dangerous undercover agent
suffering from syphilis-induced mental aberrations, and burns the in-
criminating documents. Angelique's genuine grief and helplessness leave
him content with his decision. In other words, Clavell has taken a real

historical figure, the British Minister to Japan, and given him an important role in his fictitious story of the fortunes of Angelique.

Though predominantly historical fiction, *Gai-Jin* incorporates the varied patterns of a number of genres to create a rounded, complex vision of societies, cultures, and individuals in moments of confrontation, crisis, change, and challenge. Rather than a delicate and detailed portrait, *Gai-Jin* is a salon-sized mural, mythic in proportions, whose slashes of color communicate a sense of vast energies in conflict, of masses and types rather than individuals. This is its strength but also its weakness.

ALTERNATIVE READING: FEMINIST PERSPECTIVES

Boyd Tonkin, a reviewer for the *New Statesman Society*, smugly attacks Clavell as "a monument to the pure gender apartheid that operates in mass-market fiction" and asserts that probably less than one per cent of his audience is female (Tonkin 1993). In fact, however, *Gai-Jin*, while accurately depicting the piteous plight of both Asian and European women in the nineteenth century, creates great sympathy for their situation and explores the creative and competent ways in which women overcome the limitations and restrictions placed on them and find the means to assert their will. Through Angelique Richaud, Maureen Ross, Alexandra Tillman, Tess Struan, Lady Hosaki, Koiko, Princess Yazu, and the women of the "willow world"—the courtesans Fujiko, Nemi, and Hinodey, and the *mama-sans*, Meikin and Raiko—Clavell not only provides a sense of female culture in opposition to male culture, both Asian and European, but also depicts women overcoming and empowering themselves to a much greater degree than one might expect. For a discussion of feminist criticism applicable to *Gai-Jin*, see Chapter 7.

Angelique's complaint is typical. She has no way to make her way in the world except by using men. She must use her beauty, artistry, intelligence, and sexuality to capture a rich, powerful husband before he finds out about her limited fortunes and before age makes her no longer desirable. She must be flirtatious enough to win hearts but not so flirtatious that she loses her good reputation. If she loves the man she wins, so much the better, but love has little to do with this game of survival. When, through no fault of her own, she loses her virginity to a Japanese intruder, she knows that, by the standards of her age, she has lost her bargaining power for marriage. Her secret abortion, her hasty marriage, and her calculated manipulation of Edward Gornt may seem reprehensible by modern standards, but they are clearly compelled by her need to survive. When André Poncin, who has encouraged her in her pursuit of Malcolm Struan and has manipulated her for personal advantage, is shocked that a Catholic would risk eternal damnation by choosing abortion, she silently damns men for her plight. She thinks grimly of how she has agonized over that "with lakes of tears" but keeps her eyes innocent, hating him, hating her need to trust him, and realizing that she should hate all men. She blames men for all the problems women face—the fathers, husbands, brothers, sons, and priests who control and limit women's lives. Most of all she blames the priests whom she calls "the worst of all men" for, though a few may be saints, many are, she says, notorious fornicators, deviates, and liars, who use the church for their own private purposes. Men control her world, she asserts, and ruin it for women: "I hate them all. . . . Damn you that I have to put my life in thrall to you" (341).

Later, when Maureen Ross complains about coming halfway around the world, at great inconvenience and cost, only to find the man she has waited for faithfully now content with a Japanese mistress, she and Angelique share a moment of shock, revulsion, fury, and contempt before laughing at the absurdity of their plight. "A woman's lot is no' a happy one," says Maureen, as she contemplates a bleak future of childbearing that will speed her aging so that whoever she marries will think her and women like her old, and she complains, "we will be old, our hair will be grey and teeth fall out and whoever he is he will turn away" (1228). While she has more economic stability than Angelique and therefore more choices, if she is to have a life of her own and to make her way in the world, she must stay with McFay and through him create a future for herself, despite her disappointment in him.

The experiences of Gornt's mother, Alexandra Tillman, reflect the causal chain Angelique fears: pregnancy out of wedlock, disgrace, and poverty. Alexandra's seducer, Morgan Brock, refused to marry her without a ten-thousand-pound-a-year dowry, and the birth of her illegitimate son (Edward) turned her family against her. Later, her brother's untimely death ended his secret support, and Alexandra's life fell into greater disarray. Marriage to a Virginia planter helped hide the shame of her son's illegitimacy, but when her funds ran out, he treated her and her son with scorn. Disillusionment hastened her end.

That the plight of these three women is not unique is clear from the situation of Tess Struan. Her struggles result from her marriage to a weak incompetent. Though she is clearly as capable as any man at wielding power, it is a male world, and business and tradition demand that a male Struan take power. It does not matter that he is a foolish, immature, inexperienced youth, unsure of his own strengths, and certainly unaware of his limitations and weaknesses. What matters is that he is the male heir: that maleness entitles him to assume the reins of commercial power.

The situation of the Japanese women of the story is much the same, though they have even fewer choices. The women of the "willow world" exist for the pleasure of men: their bodies are used by men, and their livelihood is dependent on pleasing and submitting. Geishas are praised for their beauty, artistry, culture, and delicacy, but are nonetheless servants of men. Even their language emphasizes that servitude. Clavell makes it clear that these women have not chosen this form of prostitution because they enjoy it but because they have no choice. They have been sold into training by families in need of money or have sold themselves to assist or benefit sons or brothers who need the advancement or training money can bring. Only through the careful use of secrets can these women have any power. In the privacy of the bedchamber, they are privy to secrets of state that, in the right hands, could possibly change the world. Money lending also allowed such women to accrue power. But such power could be struck down at any moment by an angry male with only minor authority.

We see other Japanese women taking some control of their lives through their power over men. The sixteen-year-old Princess Yazu, step-sister to the Emperor, uses her sexuality to manipulate the sex-driven young shogun she has been led to marry, and through him she achieves power. The sixteen-year-old fiancée of Hiraga, the leader of the Choshu *shishi*, earns respect for her samurai training and samurai skills, and nearly pulls off an important assassination. However, she has gone outside the traditional bounds of society in her training, in her engagement, and in her rebellion. The fact that no man would expect a woman to have samurai skills is one reason a few select young women were trained to be members of the rebel band. However, Clavell had historical precedent for her samurai training. According to Jan Morris, during the Kamakura period (1185–1333), a period of civil war and intense military activity, several wives of great generals received training and followed their husbands into battle (Worswick, 1979: 42).

Other Japanese women in the novel have taken control of their destinies within the limits of their social position. Lady Hosaki, the wife of Lord Toranaga Yoshi, has won her husband's respect and affection, has borne him children of whom he is proud, and plots with him as an equal to maintain their position and anticipate their needs. Yet his main consort, his love person, is not this loyal wife, but instead a high ranking geisha named Koiko, who has been carefully and strategically maneuvered into this position by forces sympathetic to the *shishi*. She has been trained as a consort for men of power and is highly educated and intelligent. She understands the arts and literature, can appreciate and criticize poetry, and creates poetry of her own. She is renowned for the artistic quality of her calligraphy, the stark beauty of her poems, and her shrewd understanding of art and politics. She understands the subtleties of Zen, and she gives Yoshi good advice that helps him plot his course in order to counter the dangerous games of his opponents. However, at the same time, she works behind the scenes to achieve secret goals. Despite her deep affection for the man on whom she spies, she plays a treacherous game as both lover and spy, a game that costs her her life.

In his depiction of women, Clavell calls attention to the cultural differences that make for different attitudes toward sex, propriety, and success, but he also looks beyond the differences to explore the sexism that restricts women of both worlds. He finds more in common than varying appearance and cultural differences might lead one to believe, including shared limitations and restraints, and male-imposed bondage that takes courage and strength of will to finesse.

CONCLUSION

Clavell's final novel ends with a sense of beginning and a potential for sequels that could have gone in a number of directions—if only Clavell had lived to write them. While *Gai-Jin* can stand alone, it whets the appetite for more, especially for a sequel that would replace the strong male rivals of Clavell's past works with two strong female rivals, as ambitious, versatile, manipulative, and driven as Clavell's male characters, and, because of the constraints of their age, far more interesting in their achievements. However, in a way, this sense of incompleteness, of there being more to be told, is part of the Clavell message: all endings are beginnings, and each of his novels marks an important turning point in East-West relations and prepares readers for conflicts and intrigues to follow. Life, history, and the interactions of diverse cultures are ongoing, and with the end of one important leader, political party, or relationship, another begins. In the end is a beginning that results from all that has come before. *Gai-Jin* argues that the insular nature of the Japanese, their appreciation of and belief in traditional patterns and traditional cycles, guarantees the predictable unpredictability of their responses, or, as Poncin warns Tyrer, Japan has only Japanese solutions (489).

Glossary: A Guide to the International Vocabulary in James Clavell's Novels

CHINESE (MAINLY CANTONESE, BUT SOME MANDARIN)

amah: a household servant

ayeeee yah: an expression of pleasure, anger, disgust, happiness, or help-lessness, depending on intonation and emphasis

baat: eight

bat jam gai: white chicken meat (also sexual slang)

bo-pi: an illegal taxi

chan ts'ao, chu ken: when pulling weeds, make sure you get rid of the roots

chong-sam: a closely fitted, Chinese-style dress with mandarin collar and slit sides

dew neh loh mon: a Chinese curse

dim sum: small, delicate rice-dough pastries filled with shrimp, fried pork, chicken, vegetables, or fish and either steamed or fried

doh jeh: thank you very much

Note: Clavell's use of foreign words in his novels reflect the phonetic spellings, and errors are intentionally introduced. This glossary lists words as they are used in Clavell's novels.

faat: expanding prosperity

Fai Pal: The Express: (a newspaper)

fang pi: an obscene curse

fan-quai: devil barbarian

feng shui/fung sui: an ancient Chinese design system for the correct positioning of a house for the Heaven-Earth-Air currents—not on a dragon's neck—in order to assure good luck

gan sun: a life-long nanny who takes a vow of celibacy and wears a long queue down her back

h'eung yau: "fragrant grease" or kickback, payoff, squeeze

heya/heyaheyaheya: Hong Kong version of the English "Hey!"

ho ho: "Good!", the stock reply to "How are you?" (Cantonese)

hong: business house or company

hua shih: slippery stone

Hung Mun Tong: a secret society committed to the overthrow of the Manchus

joss: luck, fate, god and devil combined

Kai Tak: Hong Kong's airport

Kau-lung: "nine dragons"; the name of the area across the harbor from Hong Kong, pronounced "Kowloon" by Westerners

kowtow: kneeling with forehead touching the floor eight times as obeisance to a superior

lang syin gou fei: wolf's heart; dog's lungs "men without conscience"; a derogatory Mandarin phrase for someone who is really bad and has done something abominable; used to describe Japanese businessmen in Clavell's books

lao-tsi-sing: the Ancient One Hundred Names, the Chinese name for themselves

loi-pan: great head or head leader (of a household or dynasty)

ma foi!: a curse

ma-foo: stable hands

mai dan: "the check, please," or "fried eggs," depending on intonation

moh ching moh meng: no money, no life

mui jai: a daughter given to a creditor forever, in settlement for debts that could not be paid otherwise *neh hoh mah?* *(Ni hao ma?)*: How are you? (Mandarin)

pan tun tse: porcelain clay, "little white blocks," for making bone china

pao pu chu huo: "paper cannot wrap up a fire," meaning a secret cannot be kept forever

qua: bad pronunciation of the Chinese word for "Mr."

quai loh: negative word for whites/Europeans

see yau gai: soya chicken (sexual slang)

sei yap: one of the main dialects of Guandong Province, spoken by many Hong Kong Cantonese

shey-shey: thank you (Mandarin)

Sing Pao: The Times (a newspaper)

tai-fung: the supreme winds, typhoon

tai-pan: colloquial for a man in charge of a whorehouse or a public toilet, misunderstood by Europeans (including Clavell initially) and taken to mean "supreme leader"

tai-tai: supreme of the supreme, head wife

t'ien hsia wu ya i pan hei: "all crows under heaven are black," meaning people belonging to the same group will stick together to destroy the outsider

tong: secret society; brotherhood

t'o t'ai: "without body"; rare blue porcelain, so thin that the outer and inner glazes seem to touch

tsaw an: good morning (Mandarin)

t'ung t'ien yu ming: listen to heaven and follow fate

tun ni: brick mud

Um ho. Cha z'er, doh jeh: No thank you. Please do it later. (American trying to speak Cantonese)

wheyyy?: what? who???; also used when answering the telephone

yan: Europeans who have become natives of Hong Kong

Pidgin

boom-boom: guns

chillo: child

cow: woman

cow chillo: young woman

FRENCH

à bientot: see you later

adieu: goodbye ("in God's hands!")

à la tour, vite, immédiatement: to the tower, right now

allons-y: let's go

alors, mes amis: well, my friends

amatriciana: recipe

au revoir: goodbye ("until we meet again")

bien sur: sure, definitely

bon appétit: eat well; have a good appetite

bonne chance: good luck

ca marche?: how's it going? is it going okay?

c'est bon?: is that good? is it okay?

c'est fini: it's over, it's finished

cheri: dear (masculine)

chérie: dear (feminine)

diplomatique: diplomatic

espéce de con: a curse

et toi?: and you?

fait accompli: something that is an accomplished fact or deed, that can be taken for granted as done

garconnière: a separate apartment for the boys of the family or for a mistress

hors de combat: out of combat, no longer in the battle

Je parle un peu, mais je parle anglais mieux, et M'sieur aussi: I speak a little French, but I speak English better and so does my associate.

le bon Dieu: the good Lord

les cretins: the idiots; the cretins

les gars: guys

merde: shit (a curse)

mon brave: my good fellow; my good man

mon cher ami: my dear friend

mon Dieu: My God!

mon viex: buddy (a familiar greeting)

n'est-ce pas?: Isn't that right/true?

oui: yes

pas probleme: no problem

quel homme: what a man (could be negative)

quelle horreur: how terrible

Tu en parles mon cul, ma téte est malade!: Speak to my backside, my head is sick.

stupides: stupid or crazy ones

voila!: here it is! (like abracadabra)

vous parlez français, madame?: do you speak French, M'am?

GERMAN

Heimat ist immer Heimat: Your homeland is always your homeland!

hein?: dead?

meine kinder: my children

Mein Gott!: My God!

reissen mit scheissen!: traveling with stinking people!

Scheisse!: a curse

verrückt: infamous, wicked

Wie geht's?: How are you?

ITALIAN

allora: at that time

amico: friend

amore: love

buon giorno: good day; hello

che sara, sara: what will be will be

porco misero: miserable pig

scusa: excuse, apology

si, amico: yes, friend

Si, e sei pazzo: Yes, and you are crazy!

stronzo: dung; turd

JAPANESE

Ah so desu ka?: Is that so?

ai-jin: lover person; courtesan

anata wa . . . -san: your name is . . .

anatawa suimin ima: you sleep now

Anata wa yoku nemutta ka?: Did you sleep well?

anjin: engineer, pilot, navigator (a Clavell-invented mix of English and Japanese)

arigato: thanks (*arignato*—mistaken form)

arigato gozaimashita: thank you very much

ashigaru: fifth-level samurai rank, above rural samurai and foot soldiers

baka: "fool," an expression of frustration with someone

Bakufu: board of officials; advisors to the shogun

bansai (*banzai*): an expression of happiness, as when charging an enemy or sharing a group experience

bimi desu: delicious

bonze: prophet (from *bonzu*: a monk)

bushido: originally a feudal samurai code of behavior; later courage expressed through a fanatical disregard for life

cha-no-michi: tea ceremony

cha-no-yu: the hot water of the tea ceremony

daimyos: middle-level lords in the feudal hierarchy

dete: come out/go out

do itashimahité: you're welcome; think nothing of it

Doko no kuni no monoda?: What is your nationality?

domo arigato gozaimashita: thank you very much (extremely polite)

Domo. Genki desu! Anatawa?: Hi! I'm fine. How about you?

Donoyoni?: How?

Doshité?: Why?

Doshité shindanoda?: Why did he die?

dozo: please

Dozo, ga matsu: "Please . . . ." (meant to be an incomprehensible attempt at Japanese by a nonspeaker)

eta: untouchables (butchers and tanners); the lowest people in the social order

gai-jin: foreigner

gei-sha: geisha, a woman specially trained in the art of beauty, entertainment, and social graces

genki desu: I'm fine

giri: obligation

gomen kudosai: Hello. Is anybody home? (polite form)

gomen nasai: I am so sorry.

goshi: fourth- or middle-level samurai rank

Goshujinsama, gokibun wa ikaga desu ka?: My master, how do you feel? (polite form)

gozaimasu: a polite form with no English equivalent and no real meaning in and of itself

gyoi: yes, sir (polite)

hai: yes

haiku (haikai; hokku): a compact poem that is dominated by clever word play and striking images

harigato: dildos

hatarake: get to work

hatamoto: a top-level samurai, higher in the medieval hierarchy than *roju*

Hi ga kurete kara ni itashimasu: We (I) will do it (eat) after sunset

himitsu-kawa: secret skin (a sexual device)

hiparu: pull

hiragana: a phonetic system for writing Japanese

hirazamurai: third-level samurai rank

hiro-gumbi: weary armaments (the name of a plant used to increase sexual strength)

hitachi (watashi-*tachi*): we (incomplete form)

hombun: duty

honto: truth

hotchatore: quick march

Hotté oké!: Leave it, or Leave them!

ichiban: number one; top or best

ii: good

ikaga desu ka?: How do you feel?

ikimasho: let's go

ikimasho ka?: Shall we go?

Ikinasai: Go! (A gentle command, like a mother to her child: "Go to school!")

ima: now

Ima hara hette wa oranu: I'm not hungry now

Isogi! (*Isoge*): Hurry up!

ita: 1) There was/were hurt! or 2) Things made of wood. (incomprehensible Japanese of a learner)

iyé: no

kami: spirit; household god (but also paper, hair or, if *kami-san*, wife)

kamikaze: divine wind of retribution; suicide mission

kampai: Cheers! (a toast)

Kare wa watashi no ichi yujin desu: He is one of my friends

karite iru: I'm borrowing . . . (involves a debt of obligation in Clavell's novels)

karma: fate, destiny, luck

keirei: salute

kiji: pheasant

kimono: a robe-like garment, some very dressy and very expensive used by men and women; the common garment of the seventeenth and nineteenth centuries

kinjiru/kin jiru!: it is forbidden

kiyoskette (kiotsukete): Take care! Have a safe journey!

koi: a carp (a sign of good luck); love

koku: Japanese money of the nineteenth century

konbanwa: good evening

konnichi wa: hello

konomi-shinju: pleasure pearls

Kore wa watashi no tomodachi desu, Tyrer-san: This is my friend, Mr. Tyrer. (pidgin Japanese)

Kotaba shirimasen (kotoba o shirimasen): I don't know the words (incomplete Japanese)

Kowa jozuni shabereru yoni natta na: (Our) child are [*sic*] beginning to speak Japanese very well.

Kyaku wa sazo kufuku de oro: The guests may be very hungry.

majutsu desu: It's magic

masen: a negative verb ending

masu: a positive verb ending

Ma-suware odoroita honto ni mata aete ureshi: Come on, sit down! I am surprised, but I'm really happy to see you again.

matsu: wait (be patient)

Matte kurasai: Wait for me, please.

mikado: chief priest/head official according to nineteenth-century European translators, but really "Emperor of Japan"

musko: son

musuko-san: honorable son or my son, but also "willow world" slang for the male sexual member

musume: daughter, but also "willow world" slang for the female sexual part

Namae ka?: My name? (Are you asking my name?) This name? (Someone asks about someone's name or the word for an object: What is this called? What's its name?)

namu: name

Namu Amida Butsu: In the Name of the Buddha Amida (words of prayer like "Amen")

Nan desu ka?: What is it? What did you say?

nane mo / nani-mo: nothing important

nan(i): what?

Nanigoto da?: What's going on?

Nan ja?: What is it?

Nan no yoda?: What do you need from me? What do you want from me?

ney: hey (a form used only by women or homosexuals)

Nihon go ga hanase-masen: I don't speak Japanese.

Nihongo wa jotzu desu (*Anata wa Nihongo ga jotzu desu*): You speak Japanese very well.

ninja: mercenary assassins, artists in stealth

Nippon: the Japanese name for Japan

ohayo: good morning

Oh, ko!: Ah-ha!

Okagasama de genki desu. Anata wa?: Very well, thank you. And you?

Okashira, sukoshi no aida watakushi wa ikitai no desu: Headmaster, I want to go for a little while, or I want to live for a little while (depending on the context)

omoi dasu: remember

o-negai: favor

Onushi ittai doko kara kitanoda?: Where do you come from?

roju: a member of the medieval hierarchy lower than *hatamoto*

ronin: wave men (men who are as free as waves); masterless or outcast samurai

sabazuki (*sakazuki*): a cup for holding sake

sake: rice wine

samurai: medieval warriors, sword-carrying soldiers

-san, -sama: polite forms added to names to show respect, like "mister" or "lord"

sanken-kotai (*sankin-kotai*): law of alternate residence requiring all daimyos to maintain a suitable residence within the shogun's castle walls, one without defenses, to reside there two of every three years, and to leave a family member there as hostage when the family was not in residence

sansei: third-generation Japanese-American

sayonara: goodbye until we meet again

sei-jin-no-hi: coming of age day (twentieth birthday)

seppuku: traditional suicide by slitting the belly down and across with a sword, which is often followed by beheading by a second person

Shigata (shikata) ga nai!: Nothing you (or I) can do about it! There is nothing to be done!

shikaru-beki: proper, punishable (homonym)

shinda desu: he is dead

Shinpai suruna (Shinpai suru monojanai, neh?): You don't need to worry about that, do you?

shishi: persons of courage; xenophobic rebels; a wild boar (homonym)

shoko: officer

Shokuji wa madaka?: When's dinner (breakfast/lunch)?

shoya: the appointed or hereditary leader of a village or group of villages, charged with magisterial power and responsible for tax assessment, tax collection, and protection of peasants and farmers against unfair practices of samurai overlords

shunga-e: pornography (of a highly graphic and obscene type from a Western point of view)

shunji (shujin): prisoner

shuriken: a star-shaped, five-pronged steel assassin's weapon popular in martial arts

Soji shimasu: I will do it, I clean it.

So ka?: Really?

Sonata wa oyogitamo ka?: Do you swim?

sonno-joi: a *shishi* slogan meaning "Revere the sovereign and expel the barbarians" (interpreted by opponents of the shogunate to mean "Honor the Emperor" rather than the shogun)

Sorewa honto desu ka?: Is it true?

soya (shoyu): a brown, tangy sauce (made from soy beans)

Sumimasen: Excuse me; I'm sorry.

sushi: raw fish artfully prepared for eating

suwaru: sit down

tabi: shoe-socks

tai-fun: a great wind; typhoon

taihenyoi: very good

tairo: first minister

tako: sliced octopus tentacle or just octopus

takonama: a little alcove of honor (for displaying important things)

Tare toru desu ka?: Who took it?

tatami: reed mat

tayu: the highest possible rank of geisha

teki: enemy

tomo: friend

tsuma: wife or wives

tsuyaki (*tsuyaku*): to interpret; interpreter

Tsuyaku ga imasu ka?: Is there any interpreter? Do you have an interpreter?

Ugoku na!: Halt! Stop!

Ukeru anatawa desu: I accept you

ukiyo-e: erotic pictures from the "willow world" (also called the "floating world") of pleasure houses (brothels)

unagi: grilled eel

wa: inner harmony; am, is, are (homonym)

wakarimasen: I (don't) understand. (depending on tone)

Wakarimasu ka?: Do you understand?

Wakatta?: Do you understand?

wako: corsairs; pirates

wasabi: green mustard

watakushi: I; my

Watakushi no funega asoko ni arimasu: My ship is there.

Watakushi no yuya wa hakaisarete imasen ostukai ni narimasen-ka?: My bath wasn't damaged. Would you care to use it?

watashi: I am

Watashi honshii hon, Ing'erish Nihongo, dozo: I want book, English and Japanese, please (pidgin Japanese spoken by a Frenchman who knows little Japanese showing off to an Englishman who knows less)

Watashi no kashitsu desu: It was my fault.

Watashi oyogu ima: I'm going for a swim; I'm swimming now (depending on the context)

Watashi tabetai desu: I want to eat.

Watashi [wa] samurai desu: I am samurai (spoken by a woman) (Clavell leaves out a necessary *wa*)

Watashi wa yoku nemutta: I slept very well.

Yabu-ko wa kiden no goshus-seki or *kon-ya wa hitsuyo to senu to oserareru*: Lord Yabu does not require to see you tonight.

yakitori: baked chicken

Yin ksiao shih ta: We lose much because of a small thing.

Yoi. Motte kuru: Good, fetch him.

Yokoso oide kudasareta: Welcome to my house.

yujin: friend

yukimasu: I/you/he/she/it/we/they go/will go/could have gone

Yukkuri sei!: Slow down!

zaibatsu: close-knit family complex of rich businesses

Western Words Entering Japanese in 1862

kompeni (*kampani*): company

sheru: share (not used today)

stoku: stock

stoku markit: stock market

MALAYAN

bik: sir or ma'am (to show respect)

changi: clinging vine; also the name of a Japanese prison camp *katchung idju* (*katjang idjo*): a Malaysian green bean dish

mahlu (*malu*): ashamed

mahlu senderis (*malu sendiri*): a Malay obscenity: "be ashamed yourself"

nanti-lah: later

puki: female genitals

puki mahlu (*malu*): shamed sexuality; a Malay obscenity

sakit: sick

sakit marah (or *medjan*): dysentery

Salamat (short form of *assalam alaikum*): Peace be with you; good day

tabe: greetings; hello

trima kassih (*terima kasih*): thanks

tuan: sir (a term of respect)

PERSIAN
(Iranian and Arabic root words)

agha: excellency; a polite form of address for males

Allah-u Akbarr (*Allah-o Akbar*): Praise Allah! Praise God!

amir: emir; commander

ayatollah: an Arabic root word meaning "Reflection of God," used for the greatest mullah, a top Moslem religious leader like Khomeini

azadeh: "born free"; a woman's name

baleh: yes, all right

bazaari: pertaining to the bazaar; a local leader from the bazaar

Be bahk shid: Please excuse me.

Be bahk shid man zaban-e shoma ra khoob nami danam: Please excuse me, but I don't speak your language.

Be bahk shid nana dhan konan: Sorry, I don't understand.

bokrah: tomorrow

caliph: a successor

chador: a long, shroudlike robe, covering a woman from head to foot

Cheh karbareh?: What's happening? What's going on? What do you want?

faqih: jurist; expert in Islamic jurisprudence

farmandeh: a commander of the people

Farsi: the Persian or Iranian language

feddayeen: "those who are prepared to sacrifice themselves": Moslem revolutionaries

galabia: a long-flowing Arabian robe

halvah: a Turkish sweet

hashshashin: "they who take hashish"; a name used for assassins who smoked hashish before engaging in zealous conflict

hijab: conservative Moslem clothing requirements for women

houris: the beautiful, alluring female spirits of Paradise

Iman: "the whirlwind of God"; a charismatic, semidivine, infallible Shi'ite leader; an intermediary between the human and the divine

Inglissi me danid, Agha?: Do you speak English, sir?

Insha' Allah: In God's hands

Islam: from Arabic, meaning "submission to the Will of God"; another name for the Moslem religion

Ism Allah ala' zam: Arabic for "the Greatest Name of God," Moslems believe God has 2,999 names plus this hidden name, the greatest name.

jihad: holy war

joub: ditches for trash and sewage

kalandar: a village chief

Kash'kai: one of the nomadic tribes spread across the Zagros

khoda hae-fez/haefez: good-bye

komiteh: a small group of young Moslem fundamentalists who make and enforce the laws; revolutionary committee

loftan: please

Loftan befarma' id shoma ki hastid?: May I ask who you are?

Loftan, gozar nameh: Please, I need our passports. (pidgin Farsi)

Mahdi! (*Imam-e 'asr*): the legendary twelfth Imam who Shi'ites believe is just hidden from human sight and will reappear some day to rule a perfected world

mamoonan/mamnoon am: thank you

Man zaban-e shoma ra khoob nami danam, Agha: Sorry, I don't speak your
    language, Excellency.

Mecca: the holy city toward which all Moslems turn to pray

minaret: a tower from which Moslems are called to prayer

Mojahedin-e Khalq: Fighters for the People; a party of Islamic radicals
    vehemently opposed to the Shah's regime and to the present re-
    gime.

mosque: from Arabic, a "meeting place" or Moslem religious center

Mota assef an, man zaban-e shoma ra khoob nami danam: Sorry, I don't speak
    your language.

muezzin: Islamic religious men who call the faithful to prayer

mujhadin-al-khala: Moslem leftists who believe in Islam and Marx

mullah: "leader"; the man who leads prayers in a mosque

Nah, ajaleh daram: No, I'm in a hurry.

nezami: military

pasadan: ordinary people

pashas: rich rulers

pishkesh: a bribe; an ancient Iranian custom of a gift given in advance for
    a favor that might be granted (like the Chinese *heung yau*); a gift
    for a king

purdah: conservative Moslem clothing requirements for women

qadi: judge

rubaiyat: a hymn praising wine, women, and song, like the famous *Rubaiyat of Omar Khayyam*

sajadey: a small square of lovely tapestry depicting a bowl of sacred sand
    from Cabella, a Moslem holy place

Salaam: Peace be with you

Salaam Ali cum: The peace of God be with you.

SAVAK: the abbreviation for the Shah of Iran's secret police force

SAVAMA: the abbreviation for the new Islamic secret police force

Shab be khayr: Good night

Shah: the king or royal head of government; the Pahlavis

Shah mat: Kill the king (the term used for checkmate in chess)

Shi'a: member of the Shi'ite community

Shi'ite: a Moslem sect that believes religious leadership should have remained with the Prophet Mohammed's family; they celebrate the martyrdom of the last of Mohammed's descendants with processions, whips, and hooks to mortify themselves

Sunni: a Moslem sect that believes a religious leader should be chosen by consensus

taquiyah: "concealment"; the Moslem right for a believer to protect himself by lying about Islam if he considers his life threatened

tudeh: an anti-Khomeini revolutionary faction connected with the Russians

vajeb: obligatory by Sacred Law

Zagros: an Iranian mountain range extending north to south and between Isfahan and Kowiss

zinaat: enticing female parts

zolm: oppression, tyranny

PORTUGUESE

E vero, e solamente vero: It is the truth and only the truth.

Me cago en la leche, che cabron!: I shit on the milk, you cuckold!

Monha casa é vossa casa: My house is yours.

Nao del Trato: Of no concern (nothing of interest)

por favor: please

por nada: "for nothing," used for "you're welcome"

Que va?: What's going on?

salud: health

RUSSIAN

dåcha: country home

doragåya (daragåya): "my dear" (used to address females only)

golubushka: "my dear" (a very intimate form of address used for females only) *matyer*: "mother"; used as a swear word

matyeryebyets (*matyerbozhä*): "mother of God," an expression said by an older person to express surprise or distress

prosit: a toast "to life"

tovårich (*tovarishch*): comrade

vîblyadoks/ublyudok (*vybliadok*): a nasty curse word equivalent to "son of a whore"

yeb tvoyu mat: turdhead

yezdvas: scum

zdråstvuytve (*zdråstvuytye*): a typical greeting meaning "How do you do?"

SPANISH

cojones: balls; male sexual part; a curse

madre de dios: mother of God

SWEDISH

forbannades shitdjaviar: an obscenity

Bibliography

WORKS BY JAMES CLAVELL

Novels

Gai-Jin: A Novel of Japan. New York: Delacorte Press, 1993; Dell, 1994.
King Rat. New York: William Morrow, 1962; Dell, 1980; Delacorte, 1983.
Noble House: A Novel of Contemporary Hong Kong. New York: Delacorte Press, 1981; Dell, 1982.
Shogun: A Novel of Japan: New York: Atheneum Publishers, 1975; Dell, 1976.
Tai-Pan: A Novel of Hong Kong. New York: Atheneum Publishers, 1966; Dell, 1967; Delacorte, 1983.
Whirlwind. New York: William Morrow, 1986; Avon, 1987.

Other Literary Works

The Children's Story but Not for Children. New York: Delacorte, 1981.
Countdown at Armageddon (a play). First produced in Vancouver, British Columbia, by Vancouver Playhouse Theatre, November 1966.
Foreword to Sun Tzu's *The Art of War*. Ed. James Clavell. New York: Delacorte, 1983.
Foreword to *The Making of James Clavell's "Shogun."* New York: Dell, 1980.
"A Place of a Thousand Pleasures." *Travel & Leisure*, April 1992: 55.

Thrump-O-Moto (a children's book). Illustrated by George Sharpe. New York: Delacorte, 1986. [Reprinted as *The Little Samurai*. London: Hodder, 1993.]

Screenplays

"Five Gates to Hell," Twentieth Century-Fox, 1959. (Also produced and directed by James Clavell)

"The Fly," Twentieth Century-Fox, 1958.

"The Great Escape," United Artists, 1963.

"The Last Valley," ABC Pictures, 1969. (Also produced and directed by James Clavell)

"Noble House," Dino de Laurentis Entertainment Group, 1988.

"The Satan Bug," United Artists, 1965.

"Shogun" (film), NBC and Paramount, 1981.

"Shogun" (miniseries), Shogun Productions, 1980.

"633 Squadron," United Artists, 1964.

"To Sir with Love," Columbia, 1967. (Also produced and directed by James Clavell)

"Walk Like a Dragon," Paramount, 1960.

"Watusi," Metro-Goldwyn-Mayer, 1959.

"Where's Jack?," Paramount, 1968.

WORKS ABOUT JAMES CLAVELL

Buckley, William, Jr. "James Clavell, RIP." *National Review*, 10 October 1994: 23.

Contemporary Authors, New Revision Series. Vol. 26. Detroit: Gale Research, 1989: 89–94.

Current Biography. Bronx, NY: H. W. Wilson, 1981: 82–86.

Donahue, Deirdre. "Clavell Gave Readers a Gateway to Asia." *USA Today*, 8 September 1994: D1–2.

Facts on File 54 (15 September 1994): 672.

Grimes, William. "James Clavell, Best-Selling Storyteller of Far Eastern Epics, is Dead at 69." *New York Times*, 8 September 1994: 19.

International Who's Who. London: Europa Publications, 1994.

"James Clavell." *Boston Globe*, 8 September 1994: 37.

"James Clavell." *Variety*, 12 September 1994: 67.

"James Clavell Dies." *Washington Post*, 8 September 1994: D1–4.

"Obituaries: James Clavell." *Current Biography*, November 1994: 58.

"Obituary." *Time*, 19 September 1994: 27.

Oliver, Myrna. "James Clavell." *Los Angeles Times*, 8 September 1994: A1–22.

" 'Shogun' Author Dies After Stroke." Associated Press, London, 8 September 1994.

Thompson, Howard. "Five Gates to Hell," *New York Times*. 10 December 1959: 6.

"Who's Who in America, 1980–1981. Chicago: Macmillan, 1981.

"World-wide: Died: James Clavell." *Wall Street Journal*, 8 September 1994: A3–1.

INTERVIEWS WITH JAMES CLAVELL

Dong, Stella. "James Clavell." *Publishers Weekly*. 24 October 1986: 54–55.

Gorney, Cynthia. "Interview." *Washington Post*, 4 February 1979: 1.

McDowell, Edwin. "Behind the Best Sellers." *New York Times Book Review*, 17 May 1981: 42.

Nolan, Cathy. "Talking with . . . James Clavell: the Rising Sun Never Sets on His Empire." *People Weekly*, 10 May 1993: 27.

Winsten, Archer. "Novelist James Clavell." *New York Post*, 17 May 1971: 21.

REVIEWS AND CRITICISM

King Rat

Bruun, R. R. "King Rat." *Christian Science Monitor*, 9 August 1962: 7.

Hicks, Granville. "Powerful POW in Singapore." *Saturday Review*, 11 August 1962: 21.

Kirkus Reviews, 1 June 1962: 482.

Levin, Martin. "Reader's Report." *New York Times Book Review*, 12 August 1962: 24.

Mills, Bart. "Interview with James Clavell." *Manchester Guardian*, 4 October 1975: 8.

New Yorker, 8 September 1962: 152.

New York Herald Tribune, 5 August 1962: 6.

Noderer, E. R. *"King Rat."* *Chicago Sunday Tribune*, 5 August 1962: 72.

Synder, Ellen J. *"King Rat."* *Magill's Survey of Cinema*, 1966: 911–913.

Windreich, Leland. *"King Rat."* *Library Journal*, 1 September 1966: 2913.

Tai-Pan

"Bigger Than Life." *Time*, 17 June 1966: 108.

Collins, Anne. "Seeking Fortune in Taipan Alley." *Maclean's*, 11 May 1981: 61–62.

Hill, W. B. "*Tai-Pan.*" *America*, 26 November 1966: 708.

Prescott, Orvill. "The Founding of Hong Kong in Brilliant Technicolor." *New York Times*, 4 May 1966: 45.

Rogers, W. G. "Complete with Scrutable Orientals." *New York Times Book Review*, 22 May 1966: 38–39.

Rotondaro, Fred. "*Tai-Pan.*" *Best Sellers*, 15 July 1966: 147.

Vince, T. L. "*Tai-Pan.*" *Library Journal*, 1 May 1966: 2358.

Shogun

Enright, D. J. "*Shogun.*" *New York Review of Books*, 18 September 1975: 44.

Evans, John W. "*Shogun.*" In *Magill's Survey of Contemporary Literature*. Ed. Frank N. Magill. Pasadena: Salem Press.

Hayward, Henry S. "Epic Yarn from Author of '*Shogun.*' " *Christian Science Monitor*, 24 June 1981: 17.

Henry, William A. III. "Sailing through the Storms." *Time*, 26 November 1990: 104.

New Yorker, 28 July 1975: 80.

Pollin, Burton R. "Poe in Clavell's *Shogun: A Novel of Japan.*" *Poe Studies*, June 1983: 1, 13.

Rotondaro, Fred. "*Shogun.*" *Best Sellers*, September 1975: 157.

Schott, Webster. "*Shogun.*" *New York Times Book Review*, 22 June 1975: 5.

"Shows Out of Town—Shogun: The Musical." *Variety*, 10 September 1990: 63.

Simon, John. "Land of Sunrise, Land of Shadows." *New York*, 16 November 1990: 83–85.

Smith, Henry. *Learning from Shogun*. Tokyo: Japanese Society; Santa Barbara: University of California Press, 1980.

Storry, Richard David. "Theater." *New York*, 10 September 1990: 38–39.

Yamamoto, Mitsu. "*Shogun.*" *Library Journal*, July 1975: 1344.

Noble House

Hayward, H. S. "Epic Yarn from Author of '*Shogun.*' " *Christian Science Monitor*, 24 June 1981: 17.

Larson, Christopher. "Hong Kong Homework." *Travel & Leisure*, January 1988: 127–28.

Lehmann-Haupt, Christopher. "*Noble House.*" *Books of the Times*, July 1981: 316–17.

Merrill, Don. "James Clavell's *Noble House.*" *TV Guide*, 20 February 1988: 40.

Pendleton, Dennis. "*Noble House.*" *Library Journal*, 15 April 1981: 902.

Schott, Webster. "Lots of Plot in Hong Kong." *New York Times Book Review*, 3 May 1981: 13, 42.

Selvitella, Barbara. "*Noble House.*" *Southern Library Journal*, October 1981: 160.

Stuewe, Paul. "*Noble House.*" *Quill & Quire*, July 1981: 47.

Time, 6 July 1981: 75.

Whirlwind

Amantia, A.M.B. "*Whirlwind.*" *Library Journal*, 1 November 1986: 109.

Andrews, Peter. "*Whirlwind.*" *New York Times Book Review*, 7 December 1986: 28.

Davis, Dick. "*Whirlwind.*" *Times Literary Supplement* (London), 5 December 1986: 1368.

Edwards, Thomas R. "Gulp!" *New York Review of Books*, 18 December 1986: 58.

Frank, Jerome P. "Lighter-Weight Paper for Mass Market "*Whirlwind*" Saves Avon Some Heavy Cost." *Publishers Weekly*, 16 October 1987: 59–63.

McCormack, Thomas. "What's Five Million Dollars?" *Publishers Weekly*, 7 March 1986: 94.

Nathan, Paul. "The Year in Rights." *Publishers Weekly*, 9 January 1987: 42.

Steinberg, Sybil. "Fiction: *Whirlwind.*" *Publishers Weekly*, 12 September 1986: 84.

Thrump-O-Moto

Kirkus Reviews, 15 August 1986: 1243.

Listener, 13 November 1986: 28.

Roback, Diane. "Children's Books—Picture Books: 'Thrump-O-Moto.' " *Publishers Weekly*, 22 August 1986: 92.

School Library Journal, November 1986: 87.

Times Literary Supplement (London), 26 December 1986: 1458.

Wall Street Journal, 7 October 1986: 30.

Gai-Jin

Bernikow, Louise. "*Gai-Jin.*" *Cosmopolitan*, May 1993: 22.

Hellmuth, Ann. " '*Gai-Jin*': A Mesmerizing Asian Saga." *Boston Globe*, 8 May 1993: 24.

Kirkpatrick, Melanie. "*Gai-Jin.*" *People Weekly*, 10 May 1993: 27.

Lehmann-Haupt, Christopher. "The Sixth Episode in James Clavell's Asian Saga." *New York Times*, 24 May 1993: C1–16.

Notehelfer, F. G. "The Wild West of the Far East, *Gai-Jin*: A Novel of Japan."
      New York Times Book Review, 18 April 1993: 131.
Pousner, Michael. "Clavell's War for Soul of Japan." *Atlanta Journal and Atlanta
      Constitution*, 18 July 1993: N3–8.
Publishers Weekly, 22 March 1993: 69.
Scherer, Ron. "Drama and Intrigue in Emerging Japan." *Christian Science Monitor*,
      12 May 1993: 13.
Scott, Jay. "*Gai-Jin*." *Chatelaine*, June 1933: 10.
Tanabe, Kunio Francis. "Barbarians at the Gate." *Washington Post*, 25 April 1993:
      2.
Tonkin, Boyd. "*Gai-Jin*." *New Statesman Society*, 7 May 1993: 41.
West Coast Review of Books, Spring 1993: 21.

OTHER SECONDARY SOURCES

General Readings

Brownmiller, Susan. "Sisterhood is Powerful." *New York Times Magazine*, 15
      March 1970: 134.
Burne, Glenn S. *Richard F. Burton*. Boston: Twayne Publishers, 1985.
Fallows, James. "Asia: Nobody Wants a Melting Pot." *U.S. News & World Report*,
      22 June 1987: 39.
———. "So You'll Be Moving to Asia." *Fortune*, 120 (Fall 1989): 91–98.
Farwell, Byron. *Burton: A Biography of Sir Richard Francis Burton*. New York: Holt,
      Rinehart and Winston, 1963.
Hall, Richard. *Lovers on the Nile*. New York: Random House, 1980.
Kluznick, J. C., N. Speed, C. VanValkenburg, and R. Magraw. "Forty-Year Fol-
      low-Up of United States Prisoners of War." *American Journal of Psychiatry*,
      143 (1986): 1443–1449.
Love, John F. *McDonald's: Behind the Arches*. New York: Bantam, 1986.
Rice, Edward. *Captain Sir Richard Francis Burton*. New York: Charles Scribner's
      Sons, 1990.
Scrignar, C. B. *Post-Traumatic Stress Disorder*. New Orleans: Bruno Press, 1988.
Warinner, Emily V. *Voyager to Destiny*. Indianapolis: Bobbs-Merrill, 1956.
Witkiewicz, Stanislaw. *Insatiability*. Urbana: University of Illinois Press, 1977.

King Rat

Bettelheim, Bruno. "Individual and Group Behavior in Extreme Situations," *Jour-
      nal of Abnormal Social Psychology*, October 1943: 417–52.

Daws, Gavan. *Prisoners of the Japanese: POWs of World War II in the Pacific*. New York: William Morrow, 1994.

Fallows, James. "The Japanese are Different from You and Me," *Atlantic Monthly*, September 1986: 35–41.

Goozner, Merrill. "Japan's Atrocities Toward POWs Detailed." *The Times-Picayune*, 7 May 1995: A34.

Storry, Richard. *A History of Modern Japan*. Baltimore: Penguin Books, 1960.

Yamaguchi, Mari. "Japanese Games Attempt to Reverse History of War." *The Times-Picayune*, 25 June 1994.

Tai-Pan

Chan, Wai Kwan. *The Making of Hong Kong Society*. Oxford: Clarendon Press, 1991.

Cohen, Paul A. *Discovering History in China*. New York: Cambridge University Press, 1984.

Collis, Maurice. *Foreign Mud*. New York: Knopf, 1947.

Crisswell, Colin N. *The Taipans: Hong Kong's Merchant Princes*. Hong Kong: Oxford University Press, 1981.

Fox, Grace. *British Admirals and Chinese Pirates, 1832–69*. London: Kegan Paul, Trench, Trubner, 1940.

Hao, Yen-p'ing. *The Comprador in Nineteenth-Century China: Bridge between East and West*. Cambridge: Harvard University Press, 1970.

Hsiang-lin, Lo. *Hong Kong and Western Cultures*. Honolulu: East West Center Press, 1964.

Jaschok, Maria. *Concubines and Bondservants: The Social History of a Chinese Custom*. London: Zed Books, 1988.

Mill, John Stuart. *On the Subjection of Women*. London, 1869.

Morgan, W. P. *Triad Societies in Hong Kong*. Hong Kong: Government Press, 1960.

Pryor, E. F. "The Great Plague of Hong Kong." *Journal of Hong Kong British Asian Studies* 15 (1975): 61–70.

Rowe, David Nelson. *Modern China: A Brief History*. Princeton: Van Nostrand, 1959.

Smith, Carl T. "The Chinese Settlement of British Hong Kong." *Chung Chi Journal*, May 1970: 28–32.

———. "English-Educated Chinese Elites in Nineteenth-Century Hong Kong." In *Hong Kong, the Interactions of Traditions and Life in the Towns*, 65–86. Hong Kong: Hong Kong Branch of the Royal Asiatic Society, 1975.

Teng, Ssu-yü, and John K. Fairbank. *China's Response to the West: A Documentary Survey, 1839–1923*. Cambridge: Harvard University Press, 1954.

Shogun

Akutagawa, Ryunosuke. *Rashomon and Other Stories*. Trans. Takashhi Kojima. Tokyo and Rutland, Vermont: Charles E. Tuttle Co., 1952.

Bangert, William V., S.J. *A Bibliographical Essay on the History of the Society of Jesus*. St. Louis: Institute of Jesuit Sources, 1976.

Boxer, Charles R. *The Christian Century in Japan, 1549–1650*. Berkeley: University of California Press, 1951.

Caddell, Cecilia Mary. *Japan and Paraguay*. New York: Sadlier and Co., 1857.

Cooper, Michael, S.J. *Rodrigues the Interpreter*. New York and Tokyo: Weatherhill, 1974.

———, ed. *The Southern Barbarians: The First Europeans in Japan*. Palo Alto: Kodansha International, 1971.

———, ed. *They Came to Japan: An Anthology of European Reports on Japan, 1543– 1640*. Berkeley: University of California Press, 1965.

Elison, George, and Bardwell L. Smith, eds. *Warlords, Artists, and Commoners: Japan in the Sixteenth Century*. Honolulu: University of Hawaii Press, 1981.

Endo, Shusaku. *The Samurai*. Trans. Van C. Gessel. New York: Adventura, Vintage Books, 1984.

———. *Silence*. Trans. William Johnston. New York: Taplinger, 1976.

Laures, Johannes, S.J. *The Catholic Church in Japan: A Short History*. Rutland, Vermont: Charles E. Tuttle, 1954.

Moran, J. F. *The Japanese and the Jesuits: Allessandro Valignano in Sixteenth-Century Japan*. New York: Routledge, 1993.

Perrin, Noel. *Giving Up the Gun: Japan's Reversion to the Sword, 1543–1858*. Boston: David R. Godine, 1979.

Plattner, Felix Alfred. *Jesuits Go East*. Trans. Lody Sudley and Oscar Blobel. Westminster, Maryland: Newman Press, 1952.

Ritchie, Donald, ed. *Rashomon: A Film by Akiro Kurosawa*. New York: Grove Press, 1969.

Rogers, Philip G. *The First Englishman in Japan: The Story of Will Adams*. London: Harvill Press, 1956.

Ross, Andrew C. *A Vision Betrayed: The Jesuits in Japan and China, 1542–1742*. Maryknoll, New York: Orbis, 1994.

Rudofsky, Bernard. *The Kimono Mind*. Garden City, New York: Doubleday, 1965.

Sadler, A. L. *The Maker of Modern Japan: The Life of Tokugawa Ieyasu*. London: Allen and Unwin, 1937.

Sansom, George. *A History of Japan, 1615–1867*. Stanford: Stanford University Press, 1963.

———. *The Western World and Japan*. New York: Knopf, 1950.

Schurhammer, G. *Francis Xavier: His Life, His Times*. Translated by M. J. Costelloe, S.J. Rome: Jesuit Historical Institute, 1982.

Shimmura, Izuru. *Western Influences on Japanese History and Culture in Earlier Periods (1540–1860).* Tokyo: Society for International Cultural Relations (Kokusai Bunka Shinkokai), 1936.

Van Zandt, Howard F. *Pioneer American Merchants in Japan.* Tokyo: Lotus Press, 1980.

Von Siebod, Dr. Philip Franz. *Manners and Customs of the Japanese.* 1841. Reprint, Rutland, Vermont: Charles E. Tuttle, 1981.

Walworth, Arthur. *Black Ships Off Japan.* New York: Alfred Knopf, 1946.

Webb, Herschel. *The Japanese Imperial Institution in the Tokugawa Period.* New York: Columbia University Press, 1968.

Noble House

Cremer, R. D., ed. *Macau: City of Commerce and Culture.* Hong Kong: UEA Press: 1987.

Khokhlov, A. N. "Hong Kong." In *Great Soviet Encyclopaedia.* Vol. 25. New York: Macmillan, 1980.

King, Frank H. *The History of the Hong Kong and Shanghai Banking Corporation.* 3 vols. Cambridge: Cambridge University Press, 1988–1900.

Lane, Kevin P. *Sovereignty and the Status Quo: The Historical Roots of China's Hong Kong Policy.* San Francisco: Westview Press, 1990.

Okuley, B., and F. King-Poole. *Gambler's Guide to Macao.* Hong Kong: South China Morning Post, 1979.

Perlmen, S. K., and M.K.C. Chan. *The Chinese Game of Mahjong.* Hong Kong: Book Marketing Ltd., 1984.

Salzman, Mark. *Iron and Silk.* New York: Random House, 1986.

Tsai, Jung-fang. *Hong Kong in Chinese History.* New York: Columbia University Press, 1993.

Twitchett, Denis, and John K. Fairbank. *The Cambridge History of China.* Vol. 11. New York: Cambridge University Press, 1980.

Whirlwind

Arjomand, Said Amir. *The Turban for the Crown: The Islamic Revolution in Iran.* New York: Oxford University Press, 1988.

Hall, Edward T. "Proxemics in the Arab World." In *The Hidden Dimension.* Garden City, New York: Doubleday, 1966.

Millett, Kate. "Arriving in Tehran." In *Going to Iran.* New York: Georges Borchardt, 1982.

Sadat, Jehan. *Woman of Egypt.* New York: Simon and Schuster, 1987.

Scullion, Rosemarie. "Michel Foucault the Orientalist: On Revolutionary Iran and the 'Spirit of Islam.' " *South Central Review*, 12 (Summer 1995): 16–40.

Gai-Jin

Blumberg, Rhoda. *Commodore Perry in the Land of the Shogun*. New York: Lathrop, Lee & Shepard Books, 1985.

Bush, Noel F. *The Horizon Concise History of Japan*. New York: American Heritage Publishing Co., 1972.

Dilts, Marion May. *The Pageant of Japanese History*. New York: Longmans, Green and Co., 1961.

Hall, John Whitney. *Japan from Prehistory to Modern Times*. New York: Delacorte Press, 1970.

Kaneko, Hirakazu. *Manjiro: The Man Who Discovered America*. Boston: Houghton Mifflin, 1956.

Preble, George Henry. *The Opening of Japan: A Diary of Discovery in the Far East, 1853–1856*. Norman: University of Oklahoma Press, 1962.

Reischauer, Edwin, and Albert Craig. *Japan: Tradition and Transformation*. Boston: Houghton Mifflin, 1978.

Tsunoda, Ryusaku, W. Theodore De Bary, and Donald Keene. *Sources of Japanese Tradition*. New York: Columbia University Press, 1958.

Worswick, Clark, ed. *Japan: Photographs, 1854–1904*. New York: Knopf, 1979.

Index

About the Author

GINA MACDONALD is Visiting Assistant Professor of English at Loyola University in New Orleans, Louisiana. She has published well over one hundred articles in periodicals and books on popular fiction, detective fiction, and popular culture. She is also co-author of a text for bilingual writing students. She has a special interest in Russian culture, contrastive rhetorics, and world literature.